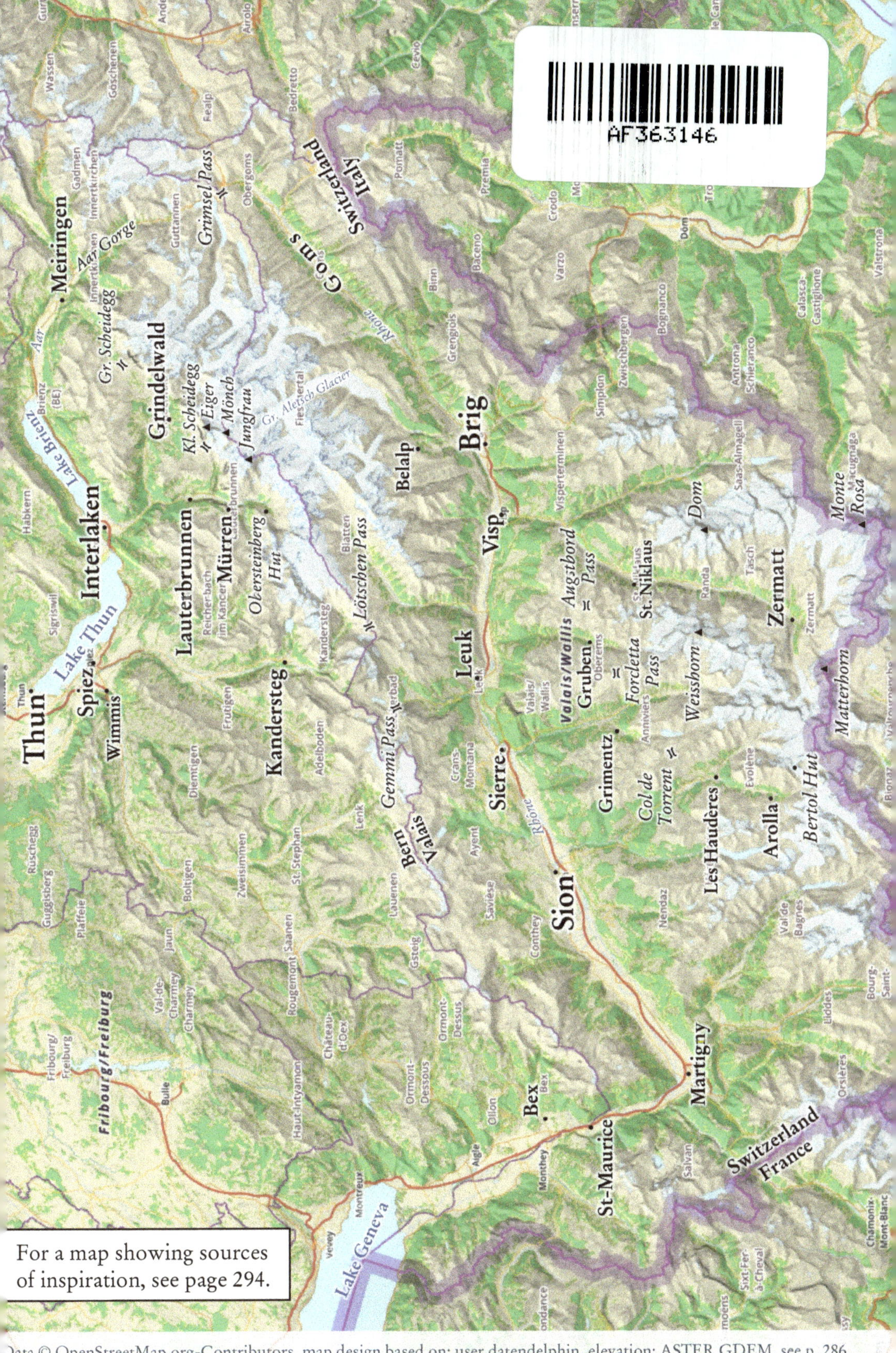

For a map showing sources of inspiration, see page 294.

Data © OpenStreetMap.org-Contributors, map design based on: user datendelphin, elevation: ASTER GDEM, see p. 286.

SWITZERLAND IN
TOLKIEN'S MIDDLE-EARTH

In the footsteps of his adventurous summer journey in 1911

M. S. MONSCH

To Camilla and my parents,
with love.

First edition
© 2021 Martin S. Monsch
Eglistrasse 30, 8004 Zurich, Switzerland
Contact: martin@msmonsch.com

With special thanks to John Howe for his thoughtful foreword and Jennifer Paxman for allowing me to quote from Colin Brookes-Smith's memoir.

Editor: Kathie Weaver, Jericho Writers (final changes and decisions by the author, for example, regarding the capitalization of fantasy people's names)
Cover design: Elisa Pinizzotto
Cover image: aquatint by Mathias Gabriel Lori (Gabriel Lory the Younger), *Vue de Sion prise du cote du levant* (View of Sion from the east), 1811, digitized by the Swiss National Library, GS-GUGE-125-62, detail, extended upwards by Elisa Pinizzotto.

Printed by: Lightning Source LLC, 1246 Heil Quaker Blvd, La Vergne, TN, 37086-3515 – U.S.A. (or a subsidary, see last page)

ISBN 978-3-907323-02-1

Follow Martin on the web: msmonsch.com

Table of Contents

Part 3: Back to Lake Thun: The Finale of *The Hobbit*....197

The Wilderland of the Imagination

John Howe[1]

I would like to begin this foreword with two seemingly contradictory thoughts.

Firstly, I cannot agree with everything in this book. Conversely, I immensely enjoyed reading it and am honoured to have been asked to contribute this foreword; it truly is a book long overdue.

When nineteen-year-old J. R. R. Tolkien undertook his walking tour of the Alps in the fine summer holidays of 1911, he travelled in a very different Switzerland than today. Dr. Monsch takes us back, in Tolkien's company, to a Switzerland that has long since disappeared. It is worth reconsidering "Tolkien's Switzerland," for if the silhouettes of the mountains have themselves remained largely unscathed, power lines, ski lifts, panoramic restaurants and hydroelectric dams have left their imprint. The Alps Tolkien experienced were a less domesticated and accessible world, infinitely closer to the novels he was to write decades after his trip.

The very wildness of the landscape must have grandly impressed young Tolkien. Through the filter of his memories, we are no longer strictly dealing with topography, but with archetypes. We are less attempting to identify observable features than dealing with inspirations, which, in themselves, invite extrapolation and distortion of scale. Dr. Monsch is not necessarily proposing that *every* parallel he draws is true, but that all are worthwhile weighing and considering.

What a grand shame Tolkien kept no diary of his Alpine escapade! Additionally, he was not leading the expedition, so his memories, when he came to write of it, are vivid but disjointed and delocalized. This is another key to

---

[1] Note of the book author: As most readers will know, John Howe is a Canadian illustrator and conceptual designer who is probably best known for his illustrations of Middle-earth and his role as concept artist for Peter Jackson's film adaptions of *The Lord of the Rings* and *The Hobbit*. But he has also worked on many other exciting projects, and with all of them, he has made millions of people around the world travel, dream, and forget their troubles. On top of that—as you will see in this text— he is also a philosopher, who happens to live in Neuchâtel, Switzerland. Thank you, John! I am delighted and honored that you were willing and found the time to write this profound and beautifully composed foreword.

reading Dr. Monsch's book. Because Tolkien (not unlike Bilbo) wrote about his journey far later in life, the spatial relationship linking experiences, outside of ascent and descent, was blurred by time. (In a letter written to Michael Tolkien in 1967 or 68, Tolkien directly equates Bilbo's adventure to his own.) The series of impressions that remained from a relatively modest portion of the map had by that time expanded to fill a world. Therefore, if upon the author's maps, Middle-earth transposed on the Valais seems an impossible fit, it is necessary to ignore the relative exiguity of the topography and imagine instead a series of loosely conjoined vignettes, excerpts or flashes from a larger narrative.

The Lord of the Rings and *The Hobbit* deal in archetypes, in the symbolism of landscape and in the essence of our relationship to nature. The landscapes of Middle-earth are directly inherited from Romanticism, drawing intimate and essential parallels between each *contrée* and its lords or denizens. Tolkien claimed to be allergic to allegory, but each land in Middle-earth is the topographical metaphor of the spirit of the peoples that dwell therein. Evaluating the validity of an inspirational landscape is as much down to feeling and impression as it is to feature and contour. How can we hope, a century later, to capture the spirit of the landscape through which Tolkien walked, factoring in the *dépaysement* of an Englishman abroad for the first time[2], the strenuous marching and the vigour and enthusiasm of his nineteen summers? He says as much himself: the vividness of his experience remained undiminished by time. Perhaps his memories of Switzerland were even enhanced by the passage of time, purified and refined to their essential elements. To judge the validity of Dr. Monsch's proposals, we must abandon a periods-and-commas approach, ignore scale, and adjust our views to a remembered but far-ago world.

Some Alpine landmarks are cited by Tolkien as inspiration, the most explicit being the Silberhorn, a side peak of the Jungfrau. "I left the view of *Jungfrau* with deep regret: eternal snow, etched as it seemed against eternal sunshine, and the *Silberhorn* sharp against dark blue: the *Silvertine (Celebdil)* of my dreams."[3] It is a reminder—and a bit of a word of warning—that inspiration does not always follow logic; it was not the obvious and famous mountain trio of Jungfrau, Eiger and Mönch that inspired Tolkien, but rather a side peak of one of these. (Context is all-important here: Tolkien's comment tells us as much about the light—fleeting and dramatic—as it does about the

---

2   Although he was born in South Africa, Tolkien had lived in England since the age of three.

3   Letter to Michael Tolkien, 1967 or 1968 (*Letters of Tolkien*, no. 306).

mountain.) Nearly a century before, Byron had remarked on the same peak: "On one side our view comprized the Yungfrau with all her glaciers—then the Dent d'Argent—shining like truth—then the little Giant (the Kleiner Eigher) & the great Giant (the Grosser Eigher) and last not least—the Wetterhorn." The Dent d'Argent is, of course, the Silberhorn. Dreams and poetic truth are essential features of the alpine landscape. When considering inspirations, we must often venture beyond simple topographical considerations.

The valley of Lauterbrunnen is a clear candidate for Rivendell. The forest fires of August 1911 might have cast a pall over the country during the time he was present in the Valais. The encroaching and disquieting darkness of the smoke is surely evocative of the tangible Darkness spreading from Mordor as Sauron's power waxes. If the mountain vista identified as a source for Mordor, above the village of Ferpecle, is rather tamer today, with easy access by paved road, the wilderness of stone below the glacier, devoid of any vegetation, does evoke Mordor, not as a precise topographical anchor point or a literal transposition, but as the incarnation of an atmosphere of mineral desolation that, if applied to an entire landscape, could very well represent the dead and desolate land of Sauron.[4] In other words, Tolkien did not directly lift sections of landscape from the Swiss Alps and sprinkle them across his far vaster Middle-earth, but took back with him a series of vivid and sublime impressions that may well have resurfaced naturally as he wrote.

Equally, the search for Tolkien's sources of inspiration, focusing on those aspects of landscape mirrored in Middle-earth, help us see more clearly the evocative power of the landscape itself. In this sense, Tolkien is a guide who takes us back in time, to better consider the changes the intervening century has wrought.

Today, we have left Romanticism so far behind that Tolkien's Switzerland is akin to a foreign country. This exploration incites us not so much to check and compare salient features, (although there is a certain satisfaction in trying them on for size, and assuredly this thorough text will be greeted with much nodding and shaking of heads) but to *experience* the landscape, to erase the pylons and lifts and imagine the Alps as seen in 1911 by a vibrant nineteen-year-old with a vivid imagination and a penchant for storytelling.

Above all, this book is an invitation to consider the narrative qualities of the landscape, its storytelling power to evoke and inspire. Pinpointing a

---

4   Inspiration may be indirect: Tolkien passed through Switzerland when the Swiss Lake Dwellers enjoyed immense popularity and may have contributed to the imagining of Lake Town. (The piquant fact that the whole notion was based on enthusiastic national rivalry and wishful thinking nonetheless is all the more ironic: historical error begetting enduring fiction.)

source of inspiration is not as simple as following a watercourse upstream to its fountainhead. Inspiration may go underground, change direction and flow, branch as well as receive tributaries. Inspiration is syncretic, a source may not be exclusive, but a conjoining of impressions. Additionally, fantasy is hardly subject to practical considerations.

On a personal note, I have been wandering, pencils and paintbrushes in hand, for more than four decades in Middle-earth. I know how incidental and serendipitous inspiration can be, and what deep-seated convictions it may reveal. I know the Canadian Rockies as well as the Alps, but they do not work for me as a visual source for Tolkien. The Alps are far more to my liking. I certainly agree there is no real or logically defendable reason for this, it is simply based on the hard-to-define notion of what is "right." (On the other hand, only Patagonia will do for the mountains of the Second Age, and only New Zealand for the shores of Numenór and Beleriand.) Inspiration can be infinite and intimate. The sweep and the grandeur of the Alps can combine harmoniously with the more personal and secretive landscapes of the Jura, the former providing scope and scale, the latter credibility of detail necessary for the willing suspension of disbelief so crucial to fantasy. Where on earth *is* Middle-earth? As much a landscape of the mind as it is identifiable on a map, it is everywhere that story and narration are present in the landscape.

This book is above all else an invitation to step into Tolkien's hiking shoes, shoulder his pack, and step back a century into a world which is as far from today as Middle-earth is from our world; a guidebook of impressions, a walking tour of the nature of imagination and the imagination of nature.

Departure

I am [...] delighted that you have made the acquaintance of Switzerland, and of the very part that I once knew best and which had the deepest effect on me. The hobbit's (Bilbo's) journey from Rivendell to the other side of the Misty Mountains, including the glissade down the slithering stones into the pine woods, is based on my adventures in 1911: the *annus mirabilis* of sunshine in which there was virtually no rain between April and the end of October, except on the eve and morning of George V's coronation. (Adfuit Omen [that was an omen]!)[5] (J. R. R. Tolkien)

With these words, J. R. R. Tolkien began a letter to his son Michael in 1967. In it, he told him in great detail about the trip to Switzerland he had undertaken as a nineteen-year-old in the summer of 1911 before beginning his studies at Oxford. When reading the letter, it is easy to forget that Tolkien's Swiss journey took place fifty-six years earlier and that he was now seventy-five years old—yes, Bilbo was getting on in years, but this adventure was deeply engraved in his memory. While his memories were no longer clear in sequence, Tolkien said, the journey had left many vivid pictures "as clear as yesterday (that is as clear as an old man's remoter memories become)."

In this letter and another one from 1961,[6] Tolkien mentioned specific places and events that had served as sources of inspiration for his novels. Thus, he himself linked places in Middle-earth with concrete locations in Switzerland. He also mentioned that the size of his travel party corresponded roughly to that in *The Hobbit*, and he even described one member of the group as "one of the hobbits." But there is a limited amount of information we can draw from Tolkien's letters, and so he left us a riddle: Was this journey merely a vague source of inspiration for Bilbo's crossing of the Misty Mountains, or did Tolkien, over large parts, autobiographically describe his own journey through Switzerland in both *The Hobbit* and *The Lord of the Rings*?

The first step to solving this riddle is to reconstruct Tolkien's exact journey. For this, apart from Tolkien's own account, Tolkien's travel companion at the time, Colin Brookes-Smith, also gave us some information in his un-

---

[5] Carpenter and Tolkien (1981), no. 306, from now on referred to as *Letters of Tolkien*.

[6] *Letters of Tolkien*, no. 232.

published memoirs.[7] The trip probably began at the end of July and lasted at least until the end of August, but perhaps into September. Tolkien's last day of school was July 26 and he must have left soon after that—maybe head over heels like Bilbo in *The Hobbit*.[8] For two dates of his journey are known: On Saturday, August 5, Tolkien signed the guestbook in the Obersteinberg mountain inn in the rearmost Lauterbrunnen Valley, and on Friday, August 25, he put his name in the guestbook of the Bertol Hut near Arolla.[9] But these dates were neither the beginning nor the end of the journey. Assuming that the group traveled on weekends, they probably spent at least the time between July 29 or 30 and September 2 or 3 in Switzerland, but a later return is also conceivable.[10]

Regarding the route, I believe that Tolkien chose the way shown in Figure 1.[11] The first part of the journey to the Aletsch Glacier and the detour to Zermatt are based on his own remarks; the second part to Sion are based on those of Colin Brookes-Smith; the reasoning for a possible third part back to Lake Thun, I will discuss later. Surprisingly, there is little overlap between the travel accounts of Tolkien and Brookes-Smith. But Tolkien mentioned that his memories of the trip through the Valais were less clear, and his presence at the Obersteinberg mountain inn and the Bertol Hut near Arolla is now documented. However, whether Tolkien was indeed in Zermatt is not entirely certain since the route depicted by Brookes-Smith does not lead to Zermatt and Tolkien's recollections of it may refer to Arolla.

Looking at this route, one thing seems clear: at least five weeks were necessary to complete the journey. The length their hike from Interlaken to Sion alone was over 150 miles (250 kilometers), and according to Tolkien, the group covered this distance mainly on foot and with heavy packs.[12] The additional trips the group undertook from the various places where they stayed longer, such as Belalp and Arolla, are not yet included in this calculation. And if they returned to Lake Thun at the end of the trip, as I suspect, there were many more miles they yet had to cover. Regardless, it was a forced march.

---

[7]   Brookes-Smith (1982); see, for example, Morton and Hayes (2008), 69 ff.; Frías Sánchez (2009); Garth (2020), 83 ff., 89 f., 102 f.

[8]   In addition, Christopher Wiseman thanked Tolkien in a letter of August 17, 1911, for postcards he had sent to him, see Scull and Hammond (2017a), 32, 34.

[9]   See Lewis and Currie (2019), 48 und 166 f.

[10]   The group hardly returned to England the very next day after the ascent to the Bertol Hut; but the way to Switzerland may have taken a little longer, for according to Brookes-Smith (1982), 1, it included a boat trip on the Rhine.

[11]   Similar Frías Sánchez (2009), 3 f.

[12]   *Letters of Tolkien*, nos. 232, 306.

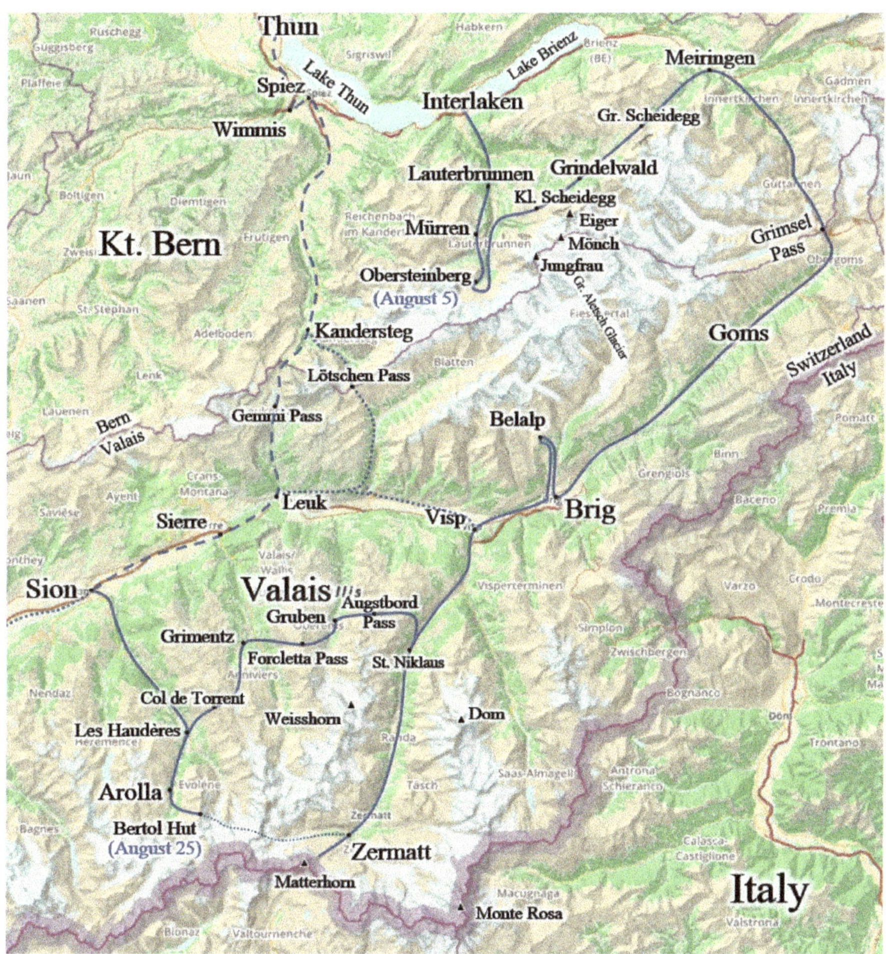

1 Tolkien's (presumed) route through Switzerland; the solid line is based on Tolkien's and Colin Brookes-Smith's comments. Map data: © OpenStreetMap.org-Contributors, see p. 286, no. 1.

Equipped with this map, I myself set out on a journey in Tolkien's footsteps through the Bernese Oberland and the Valais in search of his sources of inspiration. It was a journey through some of the most spectacular parts of the Alps, and it also became quite a treasure hunt—for Tolkien's treasures of inspiration. Not unlike Bilbo, Tolkien seems to have found something precious in these mountains, something that was to take hold of him for the rest of his life. And it appears to have taken hold of me, too. So please be warned: not everyone can resist the visual temptations of the wonderful landscape.

In addition to the landscape, I was on the lookout for local tales, legends, and literary works by other famous travelers. Since Tolkien was a language professor specializing in mythology, I suspected that he might have been inspired not only by the geography but also by the stories connected with the landscape. And this treasure trove soon proved to be also more fruitful than I had expected—or even hoped for.

These links to Switzerland should not give the impression that Middle-earth is based entirely on that country: Tolkien was inspired by a wealth of sources, including his native England, Germanic-Norse and Celtic legends, the history of the decline of the Roman Empire, and the novels of William Morris and George MacDonald, to name but a few. Nevertheless, during my research I became convinced that the influence of the Swiss journey was immense, not only for the geography of Middle-earth and the plot in *The Hobbit* but also for the plot in its sequel, *The Lord of the Rings*.[13]

I increasingly came to believe that *The Hobbit* is autobiographically based on the first and third part of Tolkien's journey, while *The Lord of the Rings* was strongly inspired by the first and second part. This allows me to follow both Tolkien's path through Switzerland and plot topics of his novels at the same time. But more and more, and perhaps unintentionally at first, this book also became a journey through space and time, a journey in which the Alpine landscape, with its history and stories, brings to life a mysterious and multi-faceted world: a world that helped shape Middle-earth.

---

[13]   Tolkien himself called *The Lord of the Rings* a sequel in *Letters of Tolkien*, no. 33.

Part 1: In the Bernese Oberland
Rivendell and the Misty Mountains

2 The Jungfrau and the Lauterbrunnen Valley.

Rivendell

I.   The Path to Lauterbrunnen

> We went on foot carrying great packs practically all the way from Interlaken, mainly by mountain paths, to Lauterbrunnen and so to Mürren and eventually to the head of the Lauterbrunnenthal in a wilderness of morains. We slept rough — the men-folk — often in hayloft or cowbyre, since we were walking by map and avoided roads and never booked, and after a meagre breakfast fed ourselves in the open: cooking utensils and quantities of [methylated alcohol].[14] (J. R. R. Tolkien)

Thus, Tolkien and his companions first hiked from their starting point in the town of Interlaken to the Lauterbrunnen Valley. And in his letter to his son Michael, Tolkien gives us a vivid picture of how they traveled, a picture that recalls the hikes in *The Hobbit* and *The Lord of the Rings*. What perhaps stands out is Tolkien's comment that they avoided roads, for so do Frodo and his companions in *The Lord of the Rings*. Avoiding roads was maybe a somewhat irrational behavior for the young Tolkien, so he might have sought an explanation for it in his imagination. In *The Lord of the Rings*, at any rate, there is a creative rationale why Frodo and his companions avoid roads: the searching Black Riders (Nazgûl).

Tolkien did not mention whether the group had horses, mules, or even, like in *The Hobbit*, ponies with them, yet this is probable. According to an English guidebook from the time of Tolkien's journey, "mountain ponies" could be rented in Interlaken for eleven francs a day — a rather proud price for that time.[15] However, Colin Brookes-Smith's memoirs suggest that they had mules, for he remembered a particularly reluctant member of the species.[16]

The village of Lauterbrunnen can be reached from Interlaken directly following the Lütschine stream, but Tolkien's group did not necessarily choose this easy route. Similar to Bilbo in *The Hobbit*, Tolkien's path may have led from the right side of the valley (left on the map), from the hamlet Isenfluh,

---

14   *Letters of Tolkien*, no. 306.

15   Murray (1904), 82.

16   Brookes-Smith (1982), 2.

3 Tolkien's approximate route into the Lauterbrunnen Valley and then to Grindelwald and Meiringen; the mountain giants forced him to turn around. For the way from Interlaken to Lauterbrunnen, different paths are conceivable; afterwards, the route is clearer. The map is based on: Bergfex OSM, © OpenStreetMap.org-Contributors, CC-BY-SA, see p. 286, no. 2.

into the Lauterbrunnen Valley: at least this is suggested by one of Tolkien's drawings, the topographic situation, and the fact that the group later left the valley via the left side. However, it is also conceivable that Tolkien and his companions first climbed up to the mountain ridge viewpoint of Schynige Platte and then steeply descended to the hamlet of Zweilütschinen and—after crossing the Lütschine stream—reached Lauterbrunnen.[17] This would explain why in both *The Lord of the Rings* and *The Hobbit*, the traveling party has to cross the river Bruinen on their way to the Hidden Valley of the Elves.

---

[17]   See also Murray (1904), 81 ff.

20

II.   Lauterbrunnen as Rivendell

In Lauterbrunnen, we find ourselves for the first time on our journey quite clearly at a place that inspired a location in Middle-earth: Rivendell, the Hidden Valley of the Elves. This connection, however, rests only to a limited extent on Tolkien's own remarks. Although he did state in his letter of 1967 that Bilbo's journey from Rivendell to the other side of the Misty Mountains was based on his hiking adventure in Switzerland, Tolkien did not explicitly reveal his source of inspiration for Rivendell. And yet, it is considered certain[18] that it was the Lauterbrunnen Valley: the deep valley of seventy-two waterfalls, which shows itself in its greatest splendor after a heavy rain when the sky clears up, the waterfalls tumble over the rock faces on all sides, and the *Jungfrau* (mountain; meaning "virgin" or "maiden") glistens high above the valley in her eternal white. When I visited the Lauterbrunnen Valley for the first time, I was deeply impressed—and this as a Swiss! How must it have been for Tolkien, who probably was seeing real mountains for the first time in his life.

4 The Lauterbrunnen Valley with Staubbach Falls (right) as a source of inspiration for Rivendell, the rugged Hidden Valley of the Elves.

---

18   E.g., Scull and Hammond (2017b), 1278, with reference to Marie Barnfield (1996), "The Lyfe ant the Auncestrye."

Tolkien's drawings of Rivendell are a first clue to his source of inspiration: the rock faces on both sides, the flat valley with the stream in between, and the high mountains in the background—all these elements strongly recall the Lauterbrunnen Valley.[19] The name Rivendell and Tolkien's written accounts confirm this first impression. In *The Lord of the Rings*, he likely described a scene from the Lauterbrunnen Valley autobiographically with the following words:

> [Sam] found his friends sitting in a porch on the side of the house looking east. Shadows had fallen in the valley below, but there was still a light on the faces of the mountains far above. The air was warm. The sound of running and falling water was loud, and the evening was filled with a faint scent of trees and flowers, as if summer still lingered in Elronds gardens.[20]

Elsewhere, Tolkien mentioned oaks and beeches, which also fit Lauterbrunnen.[21] The village itself is situated at an altitude of just about 2,600 feet (800 meters), which means that many trees are deciduous, and summer evenings can be quite warm.

Ultimately, however, it is the name of the stream flowing through the valley that leaves little room for doubt. In the Common Speech of Middle-earth, for which Tolkien used English in his novels, it is Loudwater, a natural—but probably wrong—translation of Lauterbrunnen. The Elvish name makes the

5 The view back, the Lauterbrunnen Valley from Stechelberg.

---

[19] See Hammond and Scull (1995), 115, 117, from now on referred to as *Artist & Illustrator*.

[20] *The Fellowship of the Ring*, Book 2, chap. I.

[21] *The Hobbit*, chap. III; *The Fellowship of the Ring*, Book 2, chaps. I and II.

6 The Obersteinberg mountain inn, where Tolkien signed the guest book on August 5, 1911.

influence even more evident as it is Bruinen. However, the stream should actually rather be called Clearwater or Clearspring, for the word part *lauter* in Lauterbrunnen is said to come from the Old High German word *hlūttar, lūtar* meaning "bright," "clear," or "pure."[22] My apologies to the language professor, but I take the liberty of making this heretical remark—Clearwater would perhaps fit even better to the Hidden Valley of the Elves.

By the way, Tolkien wanted to develop an unrecorded Germanic language first, before he came across Finnish, which then, along with Welsh, had significant influence on the Elvien languages; and the Elvish word *Bruinen* may still be a relic of this Germanic language as it is related to the Germanic *Brunnen* (meaning "well," "spring," or perhaps "water").[23]

From Lauterbrunnen, Tolkien hiked to the village of Mürren and then to the head of the Lauterbrunnen Valley, where he signed the guestbook in the

---

[22] See "Lauterbrunnen," ortsnamen.ch, https://search.ortsnamen.ch/de/record/802000 584 with further references.

[23] See *Letters of Tolkien*, no. 163 and his unpublished letter to David Masson of December 12, 1955, in which he stated: "Quenya still retains the traces of the impact upon me of Finnish. Sindarin was deliberately composed to resemble (with a difference) Welsh;" for Tolkien's fascination with Gothic see also *Letters of Tolkien*, nos. 43, 257, and 272.

Obersteinberg mountain inn,[24] a most beautiful place, which is—fortunately—still only accessible by a longer hike. But you are rewarded with a most stunning view of the surrounding mountain landscape and the Schmadribach Falls (Figure 6). It is the valley's last homely house (which is how Tolkien also called Rivendell).

It has already been suggested, the entrance to the Beatus Caves near Interlaken may have served as a source of inspiration for Peter Jackson's film visualization of Rivendell.[25] There, in a spectacular location above Lake Thun, the water shoots out of a rock face, and at this very spot there is a relatively old building that evokes memories of Elrond's house in the films (see Figure 88, page 220). However, the Beatus Caves hardly inspired Tolkien's Rivendell; Tolkien's sketches do not indicate any such inspiration.

III. Inspirations from Goethe

When Bilbo reaches Rivendell, he hears elves singing. Tolkien is not the first famous writer to bring mystical chants to the Lauterbrunnen Valley: in the poem "Gesang der Geister über den Wassern" ("Song of the Spirits Over the Waters"), no one less than Johann Wolfgang von Goethe preceded him.

In this poem, Goethe compares humankind's soul to the majestic Staubbach Falls, which often waft in the wind like a veil. He concludes with the words, "Soul of man, how like thou art to water! Fate of man, how like thou art to the wind!"[26] It might thus not be a coincidence that humankind's fate is decided at this very place in *The Lord of the Rings*. In the Council of Elrond, Frodo offers to carry the Ring over the Misty Mountains to Mordor and throw the Ring into the fires of Mount Doom. The freedom of humankind and Middle-earth's other people is at stake.

An influence by Goethe's "Song of the Spirits Over the Waters" may be speculative, but it has already been pointed out that the path to Rivendell recalls Goethe's poem "Erlkönig" ("Erlking"), one of his most famous poems.[27] The name of the poem should actually better be called *Elfkönig* in German or *Elfking* in English—this time, it was Goethe who translated his Danish source *Ellerkonge* wrong.

------

[24]   Lewis and Currie (2019), 48.

[25]   Lewis and Currie (2019), 24.

[26]   Goethe (1779).

[27]   Snyder (2013), 132 f.

7 The Jungfrau and the Lauterbrunnen Valley with Staubbach Falls (right).

Excerpts of this poem from Edgar Alfred Bowring's (not literal) translation:

> Who rides there so late through the night dark and drear?
> The father it is, with his infant so dear;
> He holdeth the boy tightly clasp'd in his arm,
> He holdeth him safely, he keepeth him warm.
>
> My son, wherefore seek'st thou thy face thus to hide? –
> Look, father, the Erl-King is close by our side!
> Dost see not the Erl-King, with crown and with train? –
> My son, 'tis the mist rising over the plain. –
>
> […]
>
> My father, my father, he seizes me fast,
> For sorely the Erl-King has hurt me at last. –
>
> The father now gallops, with terror half wild,
> He grasps in his arms the poor shuddering child;
> He reaches his courtyard with toil and with dread, –
> The child in his arms finds he motionless, dead.

Like the son in the "Erlking," Frodo is wounded by a Nazgûl on his way to Rivendell, and like the son, only Frodo can see the shape of his attacker, thanks to the Ring. Furthermore, Frodo gets to Rivendell on Glorfindel's horse, so he rides at least part of the way to his salvation. But unlike in the "Erlking," Frodo survives, or so it seems, and the Elvenking does not hurt Frodo but heals him.

Although it is conceivable that Tolkien was inspired not by Goethe but by the primary source (the myth behind the poem), he almost certainly knew Goethe's famous work, as Tolkien spoke German, loved poetry, was highly educated, and owned Goethe's Faust, among many other German language books.[28] Furthermore, the continuation of the story in *The Lord of the Rings*, after Frodo's recovery (or perhaps death)—as will be shown later—recalls Schiller's "Berglied," Dante's *Divine Comedy* and Byron's *Manfred*, which makes it seem more likely that Goethe influenced the part before Rivendell.[29] The path from Rivendell to the other side of the Misty Mountains thus seems to lead, poetically staged, from Goethe via Schiller and Dante to Byron, and apart from Goethe's "Erlking" and Dante's *Divine Comedy*, all the relevant works of these authors show a connection to Switzerland.

The Misty Mountains

I. The Jungfrau, the Silberhorn, and the Rottalhorn as the Mountains of Moria

> We must then have gone eastward over the two Scheidegge to Grindelwald, with Eiger and Mönch on our right, and eventually reached Meiringen. I left the view of *Jungfrau* with deep regret: eternal snow, etched as it seemed against eternal sunshine, and the *Silberhorn* sharp against dark blue: the *Silvertine* (*Celebdil*) of my dreams.[30] (J. R. R. Tolkien)

Thus, Tolkien and his companions went onward from the Lauterbrunnen Valley over the Kleine Scheidegg pass to the village of Grindelwald and then over the Grosse Scheidegg pass to the village of Meiringen, and Tolkien's words testify to an extraordinarily emotional first encounter with the mountain world. Further on in the same letter, he added how memorable this whole

---

28   Cilli (2019), no. 785.

29   Cf. below, pp. 45 ff.

30   *Letters of Tolkien*, no. 306.

8 Eiger, Mönch (in the clouds), and Jungfrau—the Misty Mountains.

experience had been for him after a poor boy's childhood. At the beginning of the twentieth century, Tolkien did not have access to today's media, and he hardly traveled; so this hike must have been an extreme visual experience for him. But even today, photos and movies can scarcely convey the same impressions, the same feeling—you simply have to go there and witness it yourself.

Tolkien's descriptions also make it clear that the mountains in the Bernese Oberland inspired the Misty Mountains. He hinted at this already at the beginning of the letter by stating that Bilbo's journey from Rivendell to the other side of the Misty Mountains was based on his adventures in 1911. And the passage quoted here shows that even Tolkien's Silvertine, one of the Mountains of Moria, had a concrete source of inspiration in Switzerland.

The *Silberhorn* (Silverhorn), a rather inconspicuous secondary peak of the Jungfrau at first sight, is thus a source of inspiration for the Silvertine. If Tolkien had not given us this information, we would never have guessed. On closer inspection, however, the Silberhorn does indeed show a formidable form, and Lord Byron already had remarked that it shines like the truth.[31]

This link between the Silberhorn and the Silvertine illustrates for the first time that the Swiss journey inspired Tolkien not only for *The Hobbit* but

---

[31]   Byron (1816), diary entry from September 23.

9 The Silberhorn, Tolkien's Silvertine.

also for *The Lord of the Rings*. For while the Mountains of Moria are of practically no importance in *The Hobbit*, they provide an essential scenery in the plot of *The Lord of the Rings*. And the mountain peak of the Silvertine plays an especially crucial role in it, as it is on this peak that Gandalf defeats the Balrog and becomes Gandalf the White. Perhaps inspired by Byron, Gandalf shows his true destiny here.

Given this inspiration for the Silvertine, the question arises whether the sources of inspiration for the other Mountains of Moria—*Caradhras (Redhorn)* and *Fanuidhol (Cloudyhead)*—can also be identified. The three mountains Eiger, Mönch, and Jungfrau, famous as they are, have already been suggested as possible candidates for the three Mountains of Moria.[32] However, the glorious trio does not seem to fit very well, especially since Tolkien

10 The Silberhorn, the Jungfrau, and the Rottalhorn from behind, possibly inspirations for the Mountains of Moria.

---

[32]   For example Frías Sánchez (2009), 10 f.

11 The view back from above Trachsellauenen in the direction of Lauterbrunnen.

did not mention the Jungfrau, but instead named one of its side peaks as a source of inspiration for the Silvertine. There are some mountains with the name *Rothorn* (Redhorn) in the Bernese Oberland and the Valais, but the *Rottalhorn* (Redvalleyhorn), a second side peak of the Jungfrau, is probably the best candidate for the role of Caradhras.[33] Tolkien's route also speaks for this, for the Jungfrau with its two side peaks looms for quite a while to the left side of his route from Mürren to the Obersteinberg mountain inn.

The hypothesis of an inspiration by the Rottalhorn is supported by the legend of "The Lords of the Red Valley" ("Rotentaler Herren"). According to that legend, a golden city once stood in the Rottal Valley, which is today filled with glacial ice and debris.[34] I discuss this in more detail later. For now, it is worth noting that there are mines near the Rottalhorn and further down near the hamlet of Trachsellauenen, and some remains of these mining operations and the red ore are still visible today. After Tolkien turned back at the head of the Lauterbrunnen Valley—like the Companions in *The Lord of the Rings*—he must have passed by there and seen this. Reports show that some

---

[33]   Cf. Rampton (2019); Scull and Hammond (2017b), 1278 with reference to Marie Barnfield (1996), "The Lyfe ant the Auncestrye;" in front, there is also a mountain called Roti Flue, which is another possible source of inspiration.

[34]   See below, pp. 42 ff.

of the tunnels are still accessible—but they are hidden and I could not find them when I explored the area. The gate of Moria remained closed to me.

Apart from the Rottalhorn, two other Redhorns deserve mention. One of them is located right next to Lake Oeschinen, just one valley further to the west, not far from the north entrance of the Lötschberg Tunnel. This would fit Caradhras since there is also a gloomy lake at the mines' entrance there.[35] Another Redhorn, the *Brienzer Rothorn,* is located at Lake Brienz, where, according to legend, there were once rich gold caves. However, these—like the Mines of Moria—were only accessible to those who knew the spell, and there came a time when no one remembered the words.[36] Although this is a common myth (the story of Ali Baba, e.g., contains a similar element), the legend is worth mentioning. For aside from the similar episode in *The Lord of the Rings* at the entrance to the Mines of Moria, there is also a similar episode in *The Hobbit,* when Bilbo and the dwarves try to get into the Lonely

12 Lake Oeschinen with the Blüemlisalp mountains (the Rothorn in the mist)—not far from the Lötschberg Tunnel perhaps a source of inspiration for the West-gate of Moria with the Watcher in the Water.

---

35   Also Lewis and Currie (2019), **223**; while there is no evidence that Tolkien was there, he could have been inspired by postcards; see below, p. 41, or he could have passed by there on his way back.

36   Streich (1978), 76.

Mountain. And this mountain, just like the Brienzer Rothorn, happens to be situated at a long lake, or better, the Long Lake.

II.   The Mines of Moria

1.   The Lötschberg Tunnel

If Tolkien was inspired for the Mountains of Moria in Switzerland, the question arises whether the same is true for the Mines of Moria. Sources of inspiration for the Mines of Moria were almost certainly the Norse underworld of Hel, Dante's Hell (Inferno) from his *Divine Comedy*, and George MacDonald's mines and goblins in his Curdie stories; but Swiss sources of inspiration should also be considered.

The disused mining tunnels in Trachsellauenen are one possible source of inspiration, but there are others. As various authors have already pointed out, a compelling one is the Lötschberg Tunnel.[37] This tunnel is over nine miles long (14,621 meters) and pierces the very mountains that inspired Tolkien for the Misty Mountains, and it also leads to precisely the area where I suspect sources of inspiration for Rohan. Moreover, the tunnel was under construction when Tolkien traveled through Switzerland, and the terror of Moria becomes tangible when you consider that the building of the tunnel claimed sixty-four lives, along with 4,596 injured.[38]

Two particularly severe accidents occurred in 1908, just three years before Tolkien's trip. On February 29, an avalanche hit a workers' building in the hamlet of Goppenstein and claimed twelve lives. An even worse accident happened on July 24 of the same year, when water and sedimentary rock collapsed during the drilling work and, within just ten minutes, filled the tunnel over a length of about a mile. Twenty-five Italian miners found their graves in the rubble.[39] As a result, the problem zone was tunneled around, which can still be seen on maps today that show the tunnel route (see Figure 78, page 205).

The breakthrough was achieved on March 31, 1911. This means that at the time of Tolkien's trip to Switzerland, an alternative route to the mountain passes theoretically already existed in the form of the tunnel. Still, it would

---

37   See for example Frías Sánchez (2009), 13; Gottet (2017).

38   "14,612 Kilometer Tunnel in viereinhalb Jahren," *Baublatt*, last modified April 11, 2011, www.baublatt.ch/baubranche/14612-kilometer-tunnel-in-viereinhalb-jahren-10849.

39   "Scheiteltunnel," Goppenstein, https://goppenstein.info/eisenbahnprojekte/scheiteltunnel.

13 The real Dwarves of Moria? Excavations in the Lötschberg Tunnel in 1910. Photo: ETH Library Zurich, Image Archive | Photographer: Wehrli, Leo | Dia_247-00975 | CC BY-SA 4.0.

only have been possible to cross the tunnel on foot, as the tracks were only laid in 1912 and 1913.[40] So did Tolkien and his companions perhaps cross the nine-mile tunnel on foot? Certainly not on the way from the Bernese Oberland to the Valais, for they hiked over the Grimsel Pass.[41]

2.　The Jungfrau Railway

In 1911, there was a second large tunnel under construction in the region, the Jungfrau Railway. Of the 6.6 miles between the Kleine Scheidegg and the Jungfraujoch, a mountain saddle near the top of the Jungfrau, more than four are underground. Since this railway leads directly through the Mountains of Moria up to the Jungfrau, it should not be left out as a possible source of inspiration for the Mines of Moria. At least it seems very likely that it inspired Tolkien for the Endless Stair leading up to the Celebdil, especially since it was

---

[40]　Ibid.

[41]　Below, pp. 199 ff.

32

initially planned that the railroad would lead all the way to the summit of the Jungfrau.[42]

3.   The Aar Gorge

Besides the tunnels and the mines in Trachsellauenen, there is another good candidate for a Swiss source of inspiration for the Mines of Moria, the Aar Gorge (Aareschlucht).[43] Tolkien's path probably led through this gorge when he hiked from Meiringen to the Grimsel Pass, for it was the most interesting and most direct path for this section—but not necessarily the easiest one. Even today, the path through the narrow and dark gorge is impressive, but as historical pictures show, it was once even more spectacular. Most notably, a thin bridge had to be crossed at the end of the narrowest passages. The Tol-

14 The old path through the Aar Gorge with the bridge "Trockene Lamm" (right). Left image: ETH Library Zurich, Image Archive | Photographer: Lichtenberger, C. | Ans_09604 | Public Domain Mark; right image: ETH Library Zurich, Image Archive | Photographer: Unknown | Fel_004671-RE | Public Domain Mark.

---

[42]   Convincing Lewis and Currie (2019), 66.

[43]   Lewis and Currie (2019), 90 f.

15 The Aar Gorge, where it slowly opens.

kien researchers Lewis and Currie (2019) convincingly suggested that it could be a source of inspiration for the Bridge of Khazad-dûm.[44]

The plot in *The Lord of the Rings* supports their hypothesis. While Tolkien turned around at the end of the Lauterbrunnen Valley and crossed over the Kleine and Grosse Scheidegg passes to the Aar Gorge, the companions in *The Lord of the Rings* reach Moria similarly after failing to cross the Misty Mountains. Further supported is this link by the fact that Tolkien's companion Colin Brookes-Smith was reminded of the Swiss journey in particular by the chapter "The Ring Goes South" in *The Lord of the Rings*.[45] The distance would also fit since Moria is about fifteen miles away as the crow flies from the foot of Caradhras and about twenty miles as the wolf runs, according to Gandalf. This corresponds approximately to the distance between the hamlet of Stechelberg (which lies below the Jungfrau) and the Aar Gorge, and incidentally also approximately to that between Stechelberg and the north portal of the Lötschberg Tunnel.

It has also already been suggested that the Aar Gorge may have inspired Tolkien for the Argonath Gorge, through which the companions pass at the end of the second book.[46] This is certainly conceivable, but apart from the form, further evidence would have to be added to substantiate the hypothesis. Besides, as will be discussed later, there is probably a more obvious source of inspiration (but, of course, they do not need to exclude each other).[47]

---

[44]   Ibid.

[45]   Cf. Morton and Hayes (2008), 72 f.

[46]   Lewis and Currie (2019), 86.

[47]   See 133 ff.

4.   The Schöllenen Gorge and the Gotthard Tunnel

Finally, two other possible Swiss sources of inspiration for the Mines of Moria should be mentioned: the Schöllenen Gorge and the Gotthard Tunnel. As far as we know, Tolkien did not visit these places himself, but they inspired famous writers and artists of the Classical and Romantic periods.[48] From the thirteenth century onward, the path through the Schöllenen Gorge was one of the main routes to cross the Alps; beforehand, the gorge was impassible. The first path was suspended with chains; a blacksmith is said to have had the idea. Later, in 1595, a massive stone bridge over the Reuss River was built, the first so-called Devil's Bridge (*Teufelsbrücke*). According to legend, the help of the devil was enlisted for the construction. And in 1708, the *Urner Loch* (Hole of Uri), a tunnel seventy yards (sixty-four meters) in length, was dug to supplement the bridge. These were pioneering achievements in Alpine transit.

Another such pioneering achievement was the Gotthard Tunnel commissioned in 1882. Over nine miles (fifteen kilometers) in length, it was the longest tunnel in the world at the time. But its construction caused even more deaths than the digging of the Lötschberg Tunnel: 199 workers died in the construction work, four in the suppression of a strike, and many more are said to have died from murder, infections, hookworms, and diseases. The terror of Moria is tangible here. The dead even caught the attention of the Swiss government, and Hans Hold, a member of the *Ständerat*, the Swiss Senate, was sent to the scene to inspect the situation. It only recently became known that, in addition to the official report, he submitted a secret one due to remorse. In it, he reported on the shocking misery, lawlessness, and exploitation of the workers, but the government did nothing.[49] For Alfred Escher, the entrepreneur, politician, and great initiator of the construction, a monument was erected on the Bahnhofplatz in Zurich.

The Lötschberg Tunnel was probably a more important source of inspiration for the Mines of Moria than the Gotthard Tunnel, but the history of the Gotthard Tunnel once again illustrates the horrors of tunnel construction at that time. Human lives were almost deliberately sacrificed to—what was called—progress, while safety measures were only taken slowly. And this dark side of industrialization and mechanization had a strong influence on

---

[48]   See 45 ff.

[49]   See H. Zumstein, "Ein Geheimbericht entlarvte die Ausbeutung am Gotthard," last modified December 9, 2016, www.srf.ch/kultur/gotthard/ein-geheimbericht-entlarv te-die-ausbeutung-am-gotthard with links to the sources.

the dark side of Middle-earth, for Tolkien experienced this whole process in his youth. During his first years in England, he lived in a pre-mechanical idyllic village, which he later described as a great influence on his work. From this point of view, the Orcs, in a way, embody the tunnel workers, whom the industrialists of that time used like inhuman, consumable tools.

In the Devil's Bridge, I see a probable source of inspiration for the Bridge of Khazad-dûm within Moria. As you probably remember, the angelic Gandalf is pulled down into the abyss from the bridge into something like hell by a demonic Balrog. An inspiration by the Devil's Bridge, therefore, does seem quite conceivable, not only from its appearance and transit function but also from its name. And the bridge fascinated poets and painters of the Classical and Romantic periods alike.

III. Possible Inspiration in Legend, Art, and Poetry

1.   Tolkien's Comments

Let us turn to nicer things: Tolkien's Switzerland related inspirations in legends, art, and poetry. It is well-known and well-researched that Tolkien drew much of his inspiration from legends, myths, and fairy tales. This is not surprising. As a professor of Anglo-Saxon (Old English) and later of English language and literature at the renowned University of Oxford, he was one of the greatest experts in this field. As for the origin of his sources of inspiration for *The Hobbit*, Tolkien himself once stated that he derived the story "from (previously digested) epic, mythology, and fairy-story—not, however, Victorian in authorship, as a rule to which George MacDonald [was] the chief exception."[50] Much has been written about the Germanic-Norse, Celtic, and Finnish legends that inspired Tolkien, but few have directed the view through the crystal ball, the Palantír so to speak, towards Switzerland. Stories in general and myths in particular are inextricably linked to the world in which they are set—would it thus not be natural if Tolkien was inspired by Switzerland in this respect too?

Well, Tolkien left hardly any direct evidence of such inspiration. He did associate Gandalf with both a mountain spirit and Switzerland in a note,[51] and according to Colin Brookes-Smith he told a joke about Hannibal's crossing

---

[50]   *Letters of Tolkien*, no. 25.
[51]   Below, pp. 53 ff.

of the Alps while still in Switzerland.[52] But this is all I could find, and therefore I looked for indirect evidence, such as similarities, which cannot be explained other than by inspiration. Looking around in the Swiss world of legends bears a certain danger, for often these tales are local variations of Germanic legends. So although Tolkien was by no means inspired only by primary sources—but also, for example, by George MacDonald and William Morris—caution is advised before jumping to hasty conclusions.

My search in Switzerland quickly proved to be more fruitful than expected. In particular, the book *Bernese Oberland in legend and history (Berner Oberland in Sage und Geschichte)* by Hermann Hartmann, published in 1910, aroused my interest, for a glance into the book is enough to make you feel transported to Middle-earth. Apart from that, Heinrich Zschokke's novella "The Shepherd of Lake Heli" ("Der Hirt von Helisee") and the legend of "The Lords of the Red Valley" ("Rotentaler Herren") are of particular interest for the plot around Rivendell and the Dwarf-realm of Moria. And of the prominent international artists with a connection to Switzerland, the painters Emil Nolde and William Turner and the writers Friedrich Schiller and Lord Byron deserve special attention.

2.   Heinrich Zschokke: Dwarves and Elves in Moria

"The Shepherd of Lake Heli" by Heinrich Zschokke is a beautiful novella set first in the *Schwarzenburgerland* (lit. Black Castle Land), a cozy Bernese region in the foothills of the Alps, and then in the Jungfrau region. In the novella, Zschokke claims to have recorded an existing legend. What follows is a summary (spoiler alert), but I do recommend the whole story.[53] Look for my website as I am planning to put an English translation of the entire novella and other material there (msmonsch.com).

2.1   *The Legend of "The Shepherd of Lake Heli"*

The legend tells of a young shepherd named Erni, who once searched for hidden treasures and thereby found, in an underground vault, a marble statue resting on a black stone with an enigmatic inscription. The statue depicted a delicate female figure of immense grace. Fascinated by this female figure's beauty almost to the point of worship, Erni believed that he was holding the statue of a saint in his hands. Fearing that she would be taken away from him, he hid the marble statue but carried the black stone to a priest to find out his

---

52   Below, pp. 166 ff.
53   Zschokke (1836), 216 ff.

saint's name. But the priest read the word Helva in the inscription, shook his head, claimed it was no saint, and kept the stone.

From then on, Erni loved his statue as if it were alive and looked at living girls indifferently as if they were made of stone—even though he had reached the "dangerous age of twenty-five." One day, while he was sitting in the bushes in front of a torn rock face, a little man with a snow-white beard appeared before Erni, revealing himself as Mungg, a brother of Helva. He offered Erni the most beautiful maiden of the mountains for the statue, but Erni refused; so the little man disappeared again. A short time later, another little man appeared, who introduced himself as Eiger and also a brother of Helva. For the statue, he offered Erni diamonds, rubies, and sapphires, more exquisite than any king's treasure. But once again, Erni resolutely refused and embraced the marble statue with even greater ardor.

Then Erni heard a soft voice, and when he looked up, he saw a multitude of beautiful maidens the size of five-year-old children but of completed stature; Zschokke identified these maidens as elves. The most beautiful of them was Helva the Alpine queen, and she urged Erni to smash the statue and love her instead. Erni accepted this offer, but he asked Helva how he could love her as a being of a higher kind. She replied that he must never love her like a human maiden; but then she added comfortingly that she did love him, and she leaned towards him and kissed him.

Helva asked Erni to follow her, and so he and the maidens did. Soon, the wet, cold mountain cleft widened into shining crystal caves, from where corridors stretched out in all directions. The high walls and vaults were filled with magnificent veins of silver, gold, platinum, copper, and tin. And above all, Helva and the maidens were no longer small but almost as tall as Erni. They continued to walk under high temple vaults of granite until they reached an endless abyss that stretched both downward and upward. There, Helva said that they were standing in the earth's hollow interior, and she pressed Erni to her chest and threw herself with him into the emptiness. After they unexpectedly found solid ground again, porticoes rose before them, and after some time, they reached a place where wide crystal roads ran out to the right and left. At this intersection, Helva explained to Erni that the left path led to Mungg's apartment, the one on the right to Eiger's palace, and that in the middle was her room, where he would be accommodated. And she added that their eternal houses rose above the lands of men up to the clouds and the sky, that their roofs were built of eternal ice, and that she was the daughter of Jol, Jol the eternal light.

At this point in the story, the protagonists are below the mountain trio of Eiger, Mönch, and Jungfrau. Inside these mountains, Erni gained a sixth sense through the breath of the Alpine queen; and this sixth sense allowed him to perceive everything that was happening wherever he put himself with his thoughts. Eiger and Mungg showed Erni many astonishing things inside the mountain, from the enormous lakes of the underworld to the gables of the glaciers, and Helva asked him how he liked it. If only he could live with her forever, Erni replied. But Helva told him that, as an imperfect creature, he was subject to much faster transformations than she was as a being of a higher order: his year was her day. And so Erni sighed, if only she were mortal or he like her. She kissed him tenderly, and Erni loved Helva more humanly every day.

The two were always together except for one hour every day when Helva went away to take a bath; Erni was not allowed to follow her there. For five days, he managed not to think about the bathing grotto. However, on the sixth day, he went there in his mind, for he was no longer master of his thoughts and his wild longings. As if in a dream, he found himself going to the grotto in his thoughts and saw a fire-colored curtain at its entrance but not what was going on behind it. He realized that his sixth sense did not allow him to observe the life of the elves. So, on the seventh day, he crept after Helva in person, moved the curtain to the side, and looked into the sanctuary. There, Helva was sitting in the bath, with her back to him. Instead of water, there was only a pink cloud, in which the maiden was half immersed, and for the first time, Erni saw one of her feet, for she stretched it out of the cloud. But this foot was not like an ordinary foot; it was strangely spread apart like a fan and had webbed skin and shiny feathers.

When the elves saw Erni, they screamed and sprayed the rosy cloud towards him. It hit his eyes like piercing sparks. He staggered back, and he heard a thundering and raving as if the vast universe were collapsing over his head. He fell, but luckily two arms caught him, and a rough male voice asked him where he had been wandering about for seven years to show up now more miserable than a beggar in these rotten and decaying clothes. When asked by Erni, who could not see, the man explained that he was the brother of Erni's mother, who had died of grief and heartache six years ago. Erni cried bitterly and let himself be led into the village. The girls no longer recognized Erni, for he now resembled a gaunt ghost, and when he told them about the extraordinary things he had encountered, they did not believe him. And so Erni isolated himself, kept sighing Helva's name, spurned food and drink, and died on the third day with the sigh "Helva!"

2.2   *Indications of an Influence on Tolkien*

Dwarf kings with palaces and porticoes within the very mountains that Tolkien himself associated with the Mountains of Moria are in itself a strong indication that the "The Legend of the Shepherd od Lake Heli" or a related legend directly or indirectly inspired him. And there are other similar physical features: the high gallery walls and vaults, which are, like in Moria or the Lonely Mountain, traversed by magnificent veins of silver, gold, and other minerals, and an infinite abyss into which Helva draws Erni just like the Balrog does with Gandalf. Also, Erni's path to the lakes of the underworld and to the gables of the glaciers is quite similar to the route that Gandalf and the Balrog take during their battle. This legend may thus have influenced Moria and the events therein.

Human-sized elves, or better Elves, in the region of Rivendell could also indicate that Tolkien was inspired by this legend. Zschokke, a native of northern Germany, brought the Elves to the Bernese Oberland a good hundred years before Tolkien. To be more precise, he purports to identify the local legendary figures as Elves. And not only that, the story of the mortal Erni and the she-elf Helva is somewhat reminiscent of the love between the mortal Aragorn and the she-elf Arwen (or the love between Beren and Lúthien). Aragorn and Arwen had met each other in Rivendell when Aragorn was a good twenty years old and thus stood, in the words of Arwen's father Elrond, "like a yearling shoot beside a young birch of many summers."[54] About thirty years later, Arwen was faced with the decision of whether to choose Aragorn and a mortal life—and unlike Helva she did. Apart from Arwen, Helva, as Daughter of Light, also recalls Galadriel, the Elf-queen of Lothlórien and guardian of the Light. A light, the Phial, Galadriel gives to Frodo in *The Lord of the Rings* to use in dark places.[55] Although it is conceivable that Zschokke and Tolkien used the same sources of inspiration, such as the "Virginal Poem" of the saga complex around the legendary hero of Dietrich von Bern,[56] the parallels are nevertheless remarkable.

Furthermore, Erni's story shows some remarkable parallels with the tale of the Ring-bearer Sméagol, better known as Gollum. Erni, just like Sméagol, finds a treasure with an enigmatic inscription that takes possession of him, and in his obsession, like Sméagol, he enters the interior of the Misty Moun-

---

[54]   Appendix A (v) of *The Lord of the Rings*.

[55]   See also below, pp. 58 ff.

[56]   See below, pp. 68 ff.

tains, where he hardly ages[57], but increasingly takes on a ghostly appearance. And he also reaches an underground lake within these mountains. Unlike Erni, Gollum, however, stays there for a while and—as you might remember—loses his precious treasure there to the thievish hobbit Bilbo. Although the way in which Bilbo meets Gollum is somewhat reminiscent of the meeting of Dante and Virgil in Dante's *Inferno,* there are good reasons to believe that Tolkien was inspired by Zschokke also for Gollum.[58]

Finally, there are also parallels between Erni and Frodo. Within the mountains, Erni acquires a sixth sense that allows him to perceive everything wherever he puts his thoughts, and after days of self-control, Erni succumbs to the temptation to follow Helva to the bath. In his thoughts, he finds himself on the way to the grotto entrance, but it is closed by a fire-colored curtain. And later, when he goes there himself, he is discovered. After hearing a thundering and raving, as if the vast universe were collapsing, he wakes up outside the Misty Mountains. As Ring-bearer, Frodo is drawn to Sauron in a similar way, and at least partially, he can also see places outside his field of sight. Sitting on the hill Amon Hen after fleeing from Boromir, the Ring is taking possession of him, and thereby, he has visions of all sorts of distant events. But everywhere he looks, he sees the signs of war. From Minas Tirith, his gaze, similar to Erni's, is involuntarily drawn to Mount Doom and Sauron, and he is also tracked down. But Frodo succeeds in tearing the Ring from his finger, and while he wakes up again as Erni does, he does so yet in time before being caught.

Was Tolkien inspired by Zschokke's "The Shepherd of Lake Heli"? Since it is unknown whether Tolkien knew the story, caution is advised, for it is also possible that the authors had the same sources of inspiration. For example, when Tolkien was in Switzerland, there were postcards showing the Eiger and the Mönch with dwarf faces.[59] Tolkien, who is said to have taken some postcards from Switzerland with him to England,[60] may have thus gained indirect knowledge of the dwarf kingdom in Moria. Nevertheless, the abundance of parallels between Zschokke's "The Shepherd of Lake Heli" and the events in *The Lord of the Rings* reaches a degree where a non-influence by Zschokke becomes rather improbable. Moreover, the libraries of the Univer-

---

[57]   However, this is a common element in Elven lands, see Shippey (2003), 68.

[58]   See also below, pp. 61 ff.

[59]   I could see such postcards when I visited the Beatus Caves.

[60]   Carpenter (1977), 59 at least indicated this; however, Tolkien could not have taken the poscard mentioned by Carpenter with him, for it did not exist at that time; see 53 f.

sity of Oxford do have some of Zschokke's works. Perhaps, future research can clarify the question of whether Tolkien knew the story and remove last doubts about an influence by Zschokke.

3.   The Lords of the Red Valley as Rulers over Moria

"The Lords of the Red Valley" is another legend set in the same area. According to this legend, there was once a golden city below the Jungfrau in the Rottal (Red Valley), a valley now filled with glacial ice and debris, and a spectacular mountain pass led from there to the Valais.[61] The city's inhabitants lived under the arbitrary rule of cruel masters; no one was safe. But when one of these lords, the most vicious, once persecuted a young shepherdess girl, the wrath of the sky arose. A black goat appeared, which had never been seen before, and it hurled the persecutor over the steep rock face down into an abyss. The icy mountains started trembling, and the rolling rocks and ice transformed the once flourishing and fertile valley into a glacial wasteland. It is said that those who brought the wrath of the sky upon the valley were condemned to eternal penance and still mourn their fate throughout the land; when they come close, drums beating and unholy spirits howling in horrible ways can be heard, and the curse still affects the descendants of the family.

Elsewhere, it is reported that the evil spirits of the departed were banished long ago into the rock and ice chasms in closed vessels at the entrance to the wild Red Valley.[62] And these spirits of the mountains are said to often show up on the icy ridges, even today, sneeringly challenging each other and throwing large chunks of snow at each other like boys' snowballs, and if one is hit, avalanches and falling rock debris are the result.[63] Often, they go hunting for creatures, especially for humans. Above all, they are said to hate the miners and crystal diggers, who ransack the interior of their possessions, the mountains, for precious metals and rob their homes, the crystal caves, of their most beautiful ornaments. And therefore, the spirits let them suffer a slow death under the most horrible tortures, sometimes clamped in narrow crevices, sometimes in shafts and caves whose entrance the spirits then bury. But men penetrate deeper and deeper into their realm as if they were the lords of the mountains, which angers the spirits irreconcilably.[64]

---

[61]   See Hartmann (1910), 37 f.; Kohlrusch (1854), 35 f.; Wyss (1817), 420; Gotthelf (1941).

[62]   Hartmann (1910), 38.

[63]   Kohlrusch (1854), 31.

[64]   Kohlrusch (1854), 33.

As you can see, dark stories are told in these deep mountain valleys, and some parallels with Tolkien's work seem quite remarkable. The miners are reminiscent of the Dwarves under Durin, ancient king of Moria; they both penetrate too far into the mountain and thereby draw the wrath of the mountain spirits upon themselves, in Tolkien's case in the form of the Balrog Durin's Bane. And the outcast lords of the Red Valley are reminiscent of Thorin Oakenshield's dwarves in *The Hobbit*, who also roam the land driven from their realm. Besides, the stone giants who Bilbo and the dwarves encounter when crossing the Misty Mountains throw stones at each other, quite similar to the mountain spirits in the second record of the legend. And the pass next to the Rottalhorn mentioned in the tale recalls the Redhorn Pass, which the companions try to cross in *The Lord of the Rings* before passing through Moria.

Quite some parallels, I would say, and it does seem probable that this legend inspired Tolkien; for apart from the similarities, the Rottalhorn (Redvalleyhorn) is the best candidate for the mountain Caradhras (Redhorn) — given that Tolkien identified another side peak of the Jungfrau as his source of inspiration for the Celebdil (Silvertine). And this Caradhras is precisely the one of the Mountains of Moria in which the Dwarves awaken the Balrog. Furthermore, Tolkien himself was near the Rottal valley when he hiked to the Obersteinberg mountain inn, and even Murray's famous handbook for

16=10 The Rottal Valley (right) with the Silberhorn, the Jungfrau, and the Rottalhorn.

travelers of 1904 mentioned that evil spirits supposedly haunted the Rottal Valley.[65] Perhaps, a Swiss guide or the hut keeper in Obersteinberg told further details, or Tolkien procured these himself.

The element of mining too deep alone would certainly not be sufficient evidence. It is an element frequently found in stories, and it also shows up, for example, in George MacDonald's *The Princess and the Goblin*.[66] However, the miners in George MacDonald's tale open the way to the goblins, not to evil mountain spirits; and even though this additional element is probably also not unique, it is significant evidence together with the location of the tale.

4.   Emil Nolde: Orcs in the Dwarf Kingdom

In the previous paragraphs, we have learned about a dwarf kingdom and evil mountain spirits in Moria, of a once golden city, and of its outcast inhabitants, but we have not yet met any orcs or goblins. A possible influence in this respect could be the work of Hans Emil Hansen, better known as Emil Nolde. Nolde painted postcards depicting Eiger, Mönch, and Jungfrau as mountain spirits with sometimes orkish faces, and these postcards aroused enormous interest among the public. He is said to have had 100,000 such postcards printed in 1897, which were sold out within only ten days.[67] And we can infer from Carpenter's biography of Tolkien that Swiss postcards seem to have played a role in the creation of Middle-earth.[68]

Nolde also visually captured the construction of the Jungfrau Railway visually, both the beginning and the end. The pictures—which, unfortunately, I am not allowed to show here—imply, as the legend of the Lords of the Red Valley suggests, that the mountain spirits were not exactly enthusiastic about the human diggers. Maybe superstitious voices or even pastors at the time warned against digging too deep to not awaken the evil of the underworld. And it also likely hat the postcards reminded Tolkien of George MacDonald's Curdie stories and thereby triggered a link that was crucial for the creation of *The Hobbit*.

---

[65]   Murray (1904), 225.

[66]   See below, pp. 80 ff.

[67]   See for example "Ausstellung: Emil Noldes Berggesichter," Culture Valais http:// agenda.culturevalais.ch/de/event/show/5838.

[68]   Carpenter (1977), 59, see above, p. 41.

By the way, the Eiger probably owes its orkish appearance to its name, for it is often interpreted as Ogre or Giant. However, the etymological origin of the name is unknown, and there are other, more probable hypotheses.[69]

5.   Schiller's "Song of the Mountain" and William Turner's *The Devil's Bridge*

If we look at literary works, there are some remarkable parallels with Friedrich Schiller's and Lord Byron's writings, apart from Dante's *Inferno*. Schiller was a famous representative of Weimar Classicism and a pen pal of Goethe. Although a German, he essentially created the Swiss national hero William Tell. And this Tell, more precisely his crossbow shot at the tyrant Gessler, has already been compared to Bard's killing of Smaug in *The Hobbit*.[70] However, Schiller's "Berglied" ("Song of the Mountain") bears even more striking similarities to Tolkien's work, for it reads as follows (literal translation):

> At the abyss, the dizzying path runs,
> it leads between life and death,
> the giants block the lonely path
> and threaten you with eternal ruin.
> And if thou wilt not awake the sleeping lioness[71],
> walk quietly through the Street of Terrors.
>
> A bridge hovers high above the edge
> bent over the terrible depths,
> it was not built by human hands,
> none would have dared it,
> the river roars beneath it late and early,
> spits up forever and never breaks it.
>
> In black, a gruesome gate opens,
> though thinkest thyself in the realm of shadows,
> but then a laughing terrain appears,
> where autumn and spring meet,

---

[69]   See for example "Eiger, Mönch und Jungfrau," Jungfrau Region, https://stories.jung frauregion.swiss/de/dreigestirn.

[70]   Lewis and Currie (2019), 254.

[71]   Poetic for *avalanche*.

> from life's toil and eternal anguish,
> I wish to flee to this blissful valley.
>
> Four streams roar down into the field,
> their spring, it is hidden forever,
> they flow to all four roads of the world,
> to evening, north, noon, and morning,
> and as the mother has born them rushing,
> they flee away and remain lost forever.
>
> Two prongs protrude into the blue of the air,
> high above the realm of man,
> on them are dancing, veiled with golden scent,
> the clouds, the heavenly daughters.
> They perform the lonely round dance up there,
> where no witness, no earthly one, sees them.
>
> The queen sits high and clear
> on an imperishable throne,
> her forehead she wonderfully encircles
> with a diamond crown,
> On it the sun shoots the arrows of light,
> They only gild her and do not warm her.

A number of the elements of this poem can be found again in Tolkien's novels. The protagonists are similarly forced by (stone) giants and snowfall to choose the Street of Terrors, the Goblins' realm in *The Hobbit* and Moria in *The Lord of the Rings*. When Gandalf mentions the Mines of Moria as a possibility, the name alone makes his companions shudder, and when they step into the mines, all dark premonitions come true.[72] The "gruesome gate" and the "realm of shadows" in the "Berglied" also fit in. Moreover, within this realm of shadows, the Companions of the Ring cross the Bridge of Khazad-Dûm, which spans an abyss of unknown depth. Gandalf is famously pulled down into it by the Balrog, and just as in the "Berglied," this bridge was not built by human hands—but by dwarven hands, I assume.[73] While I cannot say for sure, it seems likely that Tolkien knew Schiller's "Berglied," as he was a very well-read poetry enthusiast and owned at least one of Schiller's works, *The History of the Thirty Years' War*.[74] And the parallels are considerable.

---

72   *The Fellowship of the Ring*, Book 2, chap. IV.
73   *The Fellowship of the Ring*, Book 2, chap. V.
74   Cilli (2019), no. 2018.

17 *The Devil's Bridge* by Joseph Mallord William Turner (1803-4), Photo: Wikimedia Commons User Andrewrabbott, slightly edited, CC-BY-SA 4.0.

In the "Berglied," Schiller described the path through the Schöllenen Gorge with its Devil's Bridge and the Hole of Uri.[75] And this is also one of the reasons why I suspect that this part of Switzerland may have had some influence on Moria, too, although Tolkien himself did not visit the region as far as we know. But the queen in the last paragraph is probably the Jungfrau, so at least at that point, there is again a direct link to Tolkien's Mountains of Moria.

Perhaps an even more obvious source of inspiration for the link between the Devil's Bridge and the Bridge of Khazad-dûm can be found in the work of William Turner, the famous English "Painter of Light," for he immortalized the bridge in several paintings. Two of them are kept in the Ashmolean Museum in Oxford, close to where Tolkien lived and worked. *The Devil's Bridge*, which you see on the previous page, seems to be the perfect choice to illustrate *The Lord of the Rings*.

6.   Lord Byron's *Manfred*

Whereas an inspiration by Schiller and Turner is somewhat speculative, it seems quite certain that Lord Byron's dramatic poem *Manfred* influenced Tolkien. This should come as no surprise, for *Manfred* is one of the most well-known works of one of the leading figures of English Romanticism, a piece that was musically interpreted by Schumann, Tchaikovsky, and even Nietsche. In other words, as a professor of English Language and Literature, Tolkien certainly knew it.

In the first scene of the first act, Manfred summons seven spirits. Of them, he asks for only one thing: he wants to forget. But the spirits cannot fulfill this wish; the only possibility would be death, they explain to him. Although it remains unclear at that point exactly what Manfred wants to forget, at the end of the first scene, one of the spirits takes the shape of a beautiful young woman whom Manfred seems to know. But when he wants to hold her, she disappears, and he falls unconscious. At the beginning of the second scene, Manfred wakes up on the top of the Jungfrau. An eagle flies by, and Manfred wants to throw himself from the summit to his death, but he is held back by a chamois hunter, who appears at just that moment.

This second scene is reminiscent of the episode in *The Lord of the Rings* in which Gandalf comes to rest on the top of the Silvertine after fighting the Balrog.[76] As mentioned above, Tolkien named the Silberhorn, a side peak of

---

75   For example Grün (1844), 592 f.
76   *The Two Towers*, Book 3, chap. V.

the Jungfrau and, according to Byron, the Summit of Truth, as the source of inspiration for the Silvertine:[77] Manfred and Gandalf thus wake up on the same mountain after they both lose consciousness. Both are between life and death at this point: while Manfred wants to throw himself off the summit, Gandalf is sent back to earth naked after walking on roads he does not want to name.[78] And both Manfred and Gandalf are magicians, both fight demons, and both are picked up from the summit. But while the eagle just flies by in Byron's *Manfred*, Gandalf is picked up by it.

Also noteworthy is the subsequent scene of Byron's poem. For there, Manfred meets the Witch of the Alps, a character who is reminiscent of Galadriel; and Galadriel happens to be the very person to whom the eagle brings Gandalf in *The Lord of the Rings*. But I will come back to this later when I talk about Galadriel.[79]

Manfred is considered an autobiographical work.[80] Byron wrote it shortly after his scandalous separation from his wife and the spreading of rumors about an incestuous affair with his half-sister. Disgraced in England, he went to Switzerland, where he traveled around and dealt with his feelings in nature and by writing *Manfred*. He was never to return to England again. After his stay in Switzerland, he traveled on to Italy, where he once again made powerful enemies due to a love affair with the young and unfortunately married Countess Teresa Guiccioli—who, on top, like her father, belonged to the Carbonari freedom movement. The two spent a few wonderful years of love together, but finally the Austrian authorities forced her to break off contact with Byron for her father's freedom. She complied, and so a heartbreaking separation ensued, after which Byron left Italy and took command of Greek forces in the War of Independence against the Ottoman Empire. And only one year later, his eventful life came to an end there when he succumbed to the consequences of hypothermia and bloodletting ordered by doctors. The writer Byron, driven from his homeland, thus became a war hero in Greece.

7.   Appraisal

Quite a lot has come together in the previous paragraphs, I would say. What follows is, according to two of my editors, a bit "technical" or "nerdy." So if

---

[77]   Above, pp. 26 ff.

[78]   *The Two Towers*, Book 3, chap. V.

[79]   Below, pp. 48 ff.

[80]   See for example McGann (2002), 29.

you would not consider yourself to be part of the nerd species—or others you—I must strongly advise against reading it; just jump to the next title.

Back to the topic: to better appreciate Tolkien's potential sources of inspiration, a look at plagiarism control might help. To be clear, I do not want to accuse Tolkien of plagiarism; the use of sources of inspiration is entirely legitimate; I am just interested in assessing the probabilities. In plagiarism control, one searches for identical so-called n-grams in different texts: a sequence of identical words. A sequence of eight identical words, for example, is highly improbable unless two authors copy each other or quote a third author literally; but even a sequence of five identical words is rare without a direct quote or a general phrase.

The same applies to topic elements that are the same in two different works. Two matching topics are not exceptional unless, within the topics, several similarities in features independent of each other occur. It also depends on how often or rarely an element appears: it is improbable that a magician in two different works would happen to stand on the same mountain, the Jungfrau, and find himself there between life and death, even though the Jungfrau is a well-known mountain. In contrast, it is not unlikely that dwarfs are greedy miners in two different works since the elements are not independent: mining and greed are just typical characteristics of dwarfs. However, there is likely more to it than that when, for example, the dwarfs live in precisely the same mountain, porticoes criss-cross this mountain, and the protagonists entering the mountain bear close resemblances.

For all the works listed in this chapter, an influence on Tolkien seemed likely to me, but please see for yourself. There is always a certain danger that a third source influenced both Tolkien and the text.

One could go a scientific step further by systematically searching a corpus with a large collection of texts for the matching elements to assess quantitatively how likely or unlikely the occurrence of a particular combination of similar features is. Potentially, one could use so-called *topic models* to identify these topics automatically. From there, the jump to a program that automatically searches for sources of inspiration would not be far. I would call it the "Deconstructor," and works that inspire particularly often "Influencers." *The Lord of the Rings* would undoubtedly be among them.

Characters with a Possible Swiss Connection

Having concentrated on geography and plot in the two previous chapters, I would now like to focus on Middle-earth's more famous inhabitants. Some of them were already mentioned, but only briefly; I was intentionally short in each case. After a few remarks on Hobbits, this chapter will primarily focus on Gandalf, Galadriel, and Gollum; later on, I will turn my attention to Bilbo, Aragorn, and Sauron.

18 Sarehole Mill, Tolkien's Shire. Around here, Tolkien spent his early years in England. Photo: Tanya Dedyukhina, *Sarehole mill Birmingham*, slightly edited, CC-BY 3.0.

I.   English Hobbits in Switzerland

The Hobbits' "home," the Shire, is not based on locations Switzerland but is drawn from rural England; that much seems clear. Tolkien himself confirmed this in his letters, in which he also called himself a hobbit more than once — in all but size.[81] That does, of course, not exclude sources of inspiration elsewhere, but there is no known evidence for a source of inspiration in Switzerland. The only certain connection there is to Switzerland is the fact that Tolkien explicitly referred to hobbits in both letters in which he mentioned his Swiss journey.

In the first of these letters, he noted that their hiking party was about the same size as the one in *The Hobbit*.[82] Tolkien probably identified most closely with Bilbo. He hinted at this when he wrote in the second letter that Bilbo's journey was based on his own adventures in Switzerland. Gandalf, on the other hand, was probably co-inspired by his aunt Jane Neave, who seems to have invited Tolkien to the trip.[83] If Tolkien is Bilbo and Jane Neave is Gandalf, for the rest of the group, this leaves the dwarves. I wonder if he ever told them.

From *The Hobbit*, we can potentially deduce that Jane Neaves' offer came at short notice and Tolkien's acceptance not without hesitation. Jane Neave might have suddenly knocked on Tolkien's door one day and invited him to the Swiss adventure. The trip was not without danger; many English lost their lives in the Swiss Alps in those days, and Tolkien was without any mountain experience. Therefore, it is conceivable that Tolkien negotiated a period of reflection and, like Bilbo, received a letter in which he was informed

19 Perhaps also a source of inspiration, Arthur Rackham's cover of the book *English Fairy Tales*, edited by Flora Annie Webster Steel, 1916.

---

81   See for example *Letters of Tolkien*, nos. 76, 178, 190, and especially 213.

82   *Letters of Tolkien*, no. 232.

83   Cf. Bunting and Currie (2021) with interesting additional information and insights; Morton and Hayes (2008), 69 f.; below, pp. 56 f.

about the conditions and dangers of the trip. This may be speculative, but it does not seem too far-fetched, for the note in *The Hobbit* almost suggests an autobiographical element.

In the second letter, Tolkien noted that one of the hobbits had, at one point, shouted "lunch" and that this hobbit was still alive.[84] By doing so, Tolkien might have given us a hint that his English companions on the trip—or at least a part of them—served as models for the four hobbits and other members of the Fellowship of the Ring; for in *The Hobbit*, there is only one traveling hobbit: Bilbo. Candidates for these four hobbits would be, in addition to Tolkien himself, Hilary Tolkien (Tolkien's younger brother), Tony Robson, and Colin Brookes-Smith, for the latter recalled that the four of them slept together in the same room on the trip.[85] However, the four core members of the tea club (T.C.B.S.) at King Edward's School, as well as Tolkien's four children and historical figures such as Conan Meriadoc and Pepin the Short, also make good candidates for the four hobbits in *The Lord of the Rings*.

II.   Gandalf the Oberland Mountain Spirit

1.   Tolkien's Postcard of Madlener's *Mountain Spirit*

Gandalf is more closely connected to Switzerland than the Hobbits. At least, that is what Humphrey Carpenter suggested in his famous Tolkien biography *J. R. R. Tolkien*. According to him, Tolkien bought some postcards in Switzerland before returning to England, and one of them showed Josef Madlener's painting *Der Berggeist (The Mountain Spirit)*. The painting depicts an older man who sits on a stone in a mountain forest and feeds a goat.[86] According to Carpenter, Tolkien kept the postcard for a long time and much later wrote "Origin of Gandalf" on the envelope in which he preserved it.[87]

Doubts about this story grew in the following years. According to Madlener's daughter, her father did not paint the picture until the 1920s, and the postcard appears to be from a series from 1935.[88] By that time, *The Hob-*

---

[84]   *Letters of Tolkien*, no. 306.

[85]   Cf. Carpenter (1977), 57 f.; Morton and Hayes (2008), 69 f.

[86]   Carpenter (1977), 59.

[87]   Ibid.

[88]   Zimmerman (1983), 22; see "Josef Madlener," Tolkien Gateway, http://tolkiengateway.net/wiki/Josef_Madlener.

bit, which appeared in 1937, was already essentially finished, so it is unlikely that the postcard inspired Tolkien for Gandalf. Since it is known that Tolkien sent a postcard depicting one of Madlener's paintings in 1938[89], it is even probable that he did not acquire the postcard until after he had published *The Hobbit*.

Carpenter justified his remarks by stating that they were based on Tolkien's own notes enclosed with the postcard.[90] These notes are unfortunately lost. But the view is increasingly accepted that it was not the postcard itself but the mythical figure depicted on it, the mountain spirit, that inspired Gandalf.[91] Norako, for example, refers to the figure of Rübezahl, about which there is a story in Andrew Lang's *The Brown Fairy Book*.[92]

An influence by the mythical figure of the mountain spirit seems convincing, and it is also conceivable that the figure of Rübezahl inspired Tolkien. However, this would not explain why Tolkien—as Carpenter suggests—associated Gandalf with Switzerland. Would it then not be more natural to look for Tolkien's mountain spirit in the mythical world of the Swiss Alps?

2.   Mountain Spirit Legends in the Bernese Oberland

The mountain spirit is firmly anchored in the mythical world of the Bernese Oberland. Johann Rudolf Meyer, for example, reported on him in his romantic novella *Der Geist des Gebirges (The Spirit of the Mountains)*, published in 1830. In it, the mountain spirit appears in the form of an older man of tall stature and silver hair that curls around his cheeks.[93] His eyes are young, clear, fiery, and superhuman, and his glances radiate commanding, loving words that animate and bless. They also seem to call to the stars, to shake rocks, and to lure animals. The grasses and flowers stretch out towards him, the waters gush livelier near him, and the animals come to him, such as the eagles, which descend to him from the sky.

Another tale links the mountain spirit with the creation of Eiger, Mönch, and Jungfrau.[94] According to this legend, a family of giants once lived on the *Wengernalp* (Alp of Wengen) above Lauterbrunnen. For a long time, they were sociable and lived on good terms with their fellow humans. However,

---

[89]   Ibid.

[90]   Zimmerman (1983), 22.

[91]   Norako (2014), 168; Rateliff (2015).

[92]   This was pointed out by Norako (2014), 168.

[93]   Meyer (1831), 180.

[94]   See for example Wellig (2017); I am not sure how old this story is.

with increasing age, they grew more stubborn and rude and did not even shy away from evil deeds anymore. One summer day, when a poor old man in shabby clothes came over the Scheidegg and asked the rich giants for a bowl of milk, they refused it to him and asked him to drink water instead. This, it seems, was a felony. And so the old man—who happened to be the mountain spirit—announced: "You are hard, and you shall become even harder!" These words had hardly died away when the giants began to grow, high and ever higher, and they became rock and ice—the father became the Eiger, the sons became the *Weisser Mönch* and *Schwarzer Mönch* (White and Black Monk), and the daughter became the Jungfrau.

Together with Tolkien's note, these stories support the hypothesis that the Bernese Oberland mountain spirit influenced Gandalf. The eagle that sinks to him is one such element, and the second story even reminds us a bit of the episode in *The Hobbit* in which Gandalf delays the conversation with the trolls so that they turn to stone in the morning sun.[95] I would not pay too much attention to this similarity, though; Carpenter's comments on Tolkien's note are certainly the central clue.

By the way, the author of *Der Geist des Gebirges* was the son of the Johann Rudolf Meyer who achieved fame in 1811 as the first to ascend the Jungfrau—exactly one hundred years before Tolkien's journey—which probably inspired important parts of both Byron's *Manfred* and H. C. Andersen's *The Ice-Maiden*.[96] Both Meyers led eventful lives: The father was a silk manufacturer, natural scientist, teacher, revolutionary, and alpinist before he fell out of favor when he was convicted of counterfeiting. The son, on the other hand, was a writer, doctor, resistance fighter, and also a natural scientist, teacher, and alpinist; and he was a Byronian hero who renounced his citizenship to marry the (only one year older) half-sister of his deceased mother.

3.   Odin, Merlin, and Ahasver

However, the mountain spirit was most probably not Tolkien's only source of inspiration. Gandalf has already been compared to Merlin, but Odin, the important god of Germanic-Norse mythology, is perhaps an even better fit.[97] Tolkien's own words support this, for he once described Gandalf in a letter as an "Odinic wanderer."[98] Odin is often depicted as a wanderer with a hat

---

[95]   *The Hobbit*, chap. II.

[96]   Byron's *Manfred* and Andersen's *The Ice-Maiden*.

[97]   See Norako (2014); see also *Letters of Tolkien*, no. 145.

[98]   *Letters of Tolkien*, no. 107.

and stick, for example in the famous painting by Georg von Rosen from 1886 (see Figure 20). And Gandalf's Elvish name *Mithrandir* also contains this image, for the name means "gray pilgrim" or "gray wanderer."[99]

Further ahead, I put forward the hypothesis that Hartmann's collection of legends from the Bernese Oberland might have influenced Tolkien. Some stories in that book also contain an Odinic wanderer, the Wandering Jew Ahasver.[100] Ever since the famous anti-Semitic propaganda movie with the same name, the figure of the Wandering Jew (or Eternal Jew) has had a bitter aftertaste. In Hartmann's work, however, Ahasver is a compassionate, supernatural figure, an Odinic wanderer, who visits the villages in the Bernese Oberland from time to time—a true Gandalf.

20 *Odin, the Wanderer*, Georg von Rosen, 1886.

Even the mountain spirit of the Bernese Oberland ultimately resembles Odin. Both the mountain spirit and the Eternal Jew thus seem to be linked to the old Germanic god. And therefore, it is perhaps irrelevant whether Gandalf was influenced more by one or the other. As Gandalf himself explains, he is known by many names: as Mithrandir among the Elves, as Tharkûn to the Dwarves, as Olórin in his youth in the West, as Incánus in the South, as Gandalf in the North—and to the East, he does not go.[101]

4.   Aunt Jane Neave or a Swiss Mountain Guide

Gandalf's connection to Switzerland may have yet another reason: Tolkien's aunt Jane Neave. It was Jane Neave who took Tolkien to Switzerland and their fellow traveler Colin Brookes-Smith who suspected such a link. Many years later, when Brookes-Smith reached the chapter "The Ring goes South" in *The Lord of the Rings*, he immediately recognized Jane Neave as Gandalf, according to Brookes-Smith's grandson Richard Paxman.[102] Since Brookes-

---

[99]   See "Gandalf/Names," Tolkien Gateway, http://tolkiengateway.net/wiki/Gandalf/Names#cite_note-3.

[100]   The name goes at least back to the *Volksbuch vom Ewigen Juden*, Leiden 1602.

[101]   *The Two Towers*, Book 4, chap. V.

[102]   See Morton and Hayes (2008), 72.

Smith knew Jane Neave very well and traveled with her and Tolkien through Switzerland, this assessment carries weight.

Morton and Hayes describe Jane Neave as "tall, learned, mystically inclined, single-minded and not without a decided sense of humour."[103] And regarding her role on the trip, Colin Brookes-Smith mentioned that "[i]t was Mrs. Neave who efficiently organised the commissariat and [made sure that they] always had good picnic food and tea made on methylated spirit stoves."[104] She thus took the role of an organizer and showed additional character traits that make an influence on Gandalf seem plausible.

Apart from that, it is also conceivable that Swiss mountain guides co-inspired Gandalf (and Gollum) to a certain extent. This is supported by Gandalf's role as guide of the group and the fact that Tolkien's group had only guides with them on parts of their trip. Similarly, Gandalf appears in Tolkien's novels only now and then to help. In addition, the name *Bladorthin*, which Tolkien initially used for Gandalf, could also be an indication.[105]

21 The alp-uncle Gandalf with hobbit Heidi?—illustrations by Jessie Willcox Smith, from the English 1922 edition of Johanna Spyri's *Heidi*.

---

[103]   Ibid.

[104]   Brookes-Smith (1982), 1; Morton and Hayes (2008), 71 f.

[105]   Cf. Norako (2014), 153.

"Bladorthin" or perhaps rather "Bla, bla, bla... dorthin" (German, meaning "Bla, bla, bla... over there") may have been the repeated answer of guides or other locals to the question where to go. Gandalf would thus have evolved out of a family saying. This might be speculative, but Colin Brookes-Smith recalled that the muleteers encouragement of "Allez, allez, Hu" became a family saying, for many years after, when an extra effort was needed in any task.[106] Similar to that, Gandalf's original name Bladortin could be something like a running, or better wandering gag.

The appearance of an older Swiss mountain guide may well have fit Gandalf. At least it seems like that when looking at Jessie Wilcox Smith's pictures of the *Alpöhi* ("Alp-uncle," typically referred to as "grandfather") in the 1922 English edition of the classic novel *Heidi*; and this man is, by the way, also a bit like a mountain spirit.

5.　Conclusion

From Tolkien biographer Humphrey Carpenter's statements we can infer that Tolkien associated Gandalf's "origin" with Switzerland in a note enclosed with a postcard depicting Josef Madleners painting *Der Berggeist* (*The Mountain Spirit*). This unfortunately lost note suggests that the mythical figure of the Bernese Oberland mountain spirit might have been an important source of inspiration for Gandalf, and a look into the Bernese Oberland mythology supports this hypothesis. Apart from that, Odin, Merlin, Tolkien's aunt Jane Neave, angels[107], the old professor and mentor Joseph Wright[108], Virgil in Dante's *Inferno*, and perhaps even Swiss mountain guides may have had a significant influence on Gandalf, too. Maybe only in combination did all these characters create the Gandalf we all love.

III.　Galadriel the Witch of the Alps

The next character I want to turn to is Galadriel, the Elven ruler of Lothlórien. The Elves—and thus probably also their ruler—were, to a certain extent, inspired by the Celtic peoples. Tolkien hinted at this by stating that he wanted to give the Elven language Quenya a British-Welsh character since it fit the Celtic-like legends and stories told by its speakers, and he also deliberately

---

[106]　Brookes-Smith (1982), 2.

[107]　*Letters of Tolkien*, nos. 156, 325.

[108]　*Letters of Tolkien*, no. 250 (cynical words of warning), 272 (influence by his book on the Gothic language), and 308 (good friend and adviser).

composed Sindarin to resemble Welsh.[109] An influence of Celtic legends on Galadriel would not be surprising, and parallels with figures of the Arthurian legends such as the Lady of the Lake and Guinevere have rightly already been pointed out.[110]

Nevertheless—or perhaps because of this—the Elven ruler of Lothlórien also seems to be connected to Switzerland.[111] In Byron's *Manfred*, there is, as already mentioned, a scene in which Manfred conjures up the Witch of the Alps at a waterfall. The German translations speak of the *Alpenfee* (Fairy of the Alps), which may be due to Byron's way of describing her: with "hair of light," and "dazzling eyes of glory,

22 Guinevere, drawn by Arthur Rackham, from Alfred W. Pollard's *The Romance of King Arthur and his Knights of the Round Table*, 1917.

in whose form the charms of earth's least mortals daughters grow."[112] This description is strongly reminiscent of Galadriel, whose name means "maiden crowned with radiant garland"[113] and whose eyes Tolkien describes as "keen as lances in the starlight, and yet profound, the wells of deep memory."[114] Apart from the appearance, the plot also fits: Manfred reaches the Witch of the Alps after the Jungfrau scene, and Gandalf is carried by the eagle Gwaihir to Galadriel from the Silvertine. This is probably the strongest indication that the Witch of the Alps was one source of inspiration for Galadriel.

Apart from the Lady of the Lake, Guinevere, and the Witch of the Alps, other likely sources of inspiration for Galadriel are the figure of Virginal in the poem *Virginal* of the Dietrich epic and perhaps also the already mentioned Elf-queen Helva from Zschokke's novella "The Shepherd of Lake Heli" or, connected to this character, the virtuous Celtic Swiss national per-

---

109   *Letters of Tolkien*, no. 144; unpubl. letter to David Masson of December 12, 1955.
110   See for example Snyder (2013), 137 f.
111   Already Lewis and Currie (2019), 60.
112   Byron, Act II, Scene II.
113   *Letters of Tolkien*, no. 348.
114   *The Fellowship of the Ring*, Book 2, chap. VII.

sonification Helvetia.[115] Looking at it closely, Zschokke even created already a link between the Elves and the Celts:

> Don't you realize, Helva's people, the Helvetians! Helva, and the elves with her, the Nordic Ulfa, mountain spirits! The Celtic alp, white; Alps; Helva! [...] Helva, the Daughter of Light, [...] of the sun god of Celtic antiquity, the bringer of spring, whom the Swiss people in many valleys of the Alps and the Jura still call out to of old custom![116]

On the one hand, this could indicate an influence of Zschokke on Tolkien: Tolkien was not the first to link the Elves with the Celts and the Alpine region. On the other hand, this results in a homogeneous picture despite different potential sources of inspiration. Whether it is the Witch of the Alps, Virginal, Helva, the Lady of the Lake, or Guinevere, these characters can be linked well together. And besides, the fact that Zschokke called Helva a mountain spirit fits well with Gandalf: the two make a beautiful mountain spirit couple.

Also, there might be a connection between Galadriel and Helva's house, the Jungfrau. Schiller's description of that mountain, at least, fits the Elven ruler well. As a queen seated on a throne, he describes her, her forehead wonderfully encircled with a diamond-studded crown, gilded with arrows of light. And Tolkien himself was very fond of this mountain: he left the view of it, he wrote, "with deep regret: eternal snow, etched as it seemed against eternal sunshine, and the *Silberhorn* sharp against dark blue: the *Silvertine (Celebdil)* of [his] dreams."[117]

The Jungfrau, the Alps, the Elves, Helva: I wonder whether Zschokke in the passage above and Tolkien, possibly following him, even etymo-

23 Manfred and the Witch of the Alps, engraving by T. Stocks after F. Meadows entitled *A traveler being entranced by a witch disguised as a beautiful woman in the Alps*, 1849.

---

115   See above, pp. 37 ff., and below, pp. 67 ff., 76.

116   Zschokke (1836), 223 f.

117   *Letters of Tolkien*, no. 306.

logically connected the Alps with the Elves. For in his translation instructions, Tolkien pondered whether *elf* should be translated into German as *Alp*, or even better *Alb*, since the German word *Elf* is—as he believed—borrowed from English and had connotations he wanted to avoid.[118] If *Alps* means "Elves," this would also have consequences for Byron's Witch if the Alps, for she would become an elf: Helva, Virginal, or Galadriel.

IV. Gollum the Shepherd of Lake Heli

Sméagol or Gollum is another important character from Middle-earth with a possible connection to Switzerland. Since Bilbo meets Gollum in the interior of the Misty Mountains, such a connection would not be too surprising.

1.   The Dwarf Andvari in the Nibelung Saga

It should first be noted that Gollum was probably at least co-inspired by the dwarf Andvari (or Alberich) of the Germanic heroic legends about the Nibe-

24 Alberich, a somewhat hairy Gollum stealing the Ring; details of illustrations by Arthur Rackham from Richard Wagner's *The Rhinegold and the Valkyrie*, 1910 (part 1 of the English printed edition of Wagner's opera *Der Ring des Nibelungen*).

---

[118]   Tolkien and Tolkien (1975), 5.

25 Fafner kills his brother Fasolt, similar to Sméagol (and Cain in the Bible), illustration by Arthur Rackham from Richard Wagner's *The Rhinegold and the Valkyrie*, 1910.

lungs.[119] According to a Nordic Edda tradition, the dwarf guarded the Nibelungs' treasure in a dark mountain cave, taking the form of a pike, feeding on fish, and always hiding in a deep pond below a waterfall.[120] But one day, when the dodgy god Loki demanded the treasure from him, Andvari cursed it so that the following bearers of the treasure would only find misfortune with it. Its last owners, the Burgundians Gunnar (Gunther) and Hogni (Hagen), finally sank it—probably near Worms—into the Rhine before the Hunnic invaders killed them.

Although there is no direct connection between the legends about the Nibelungs and Switzerland, there might be an indirect one. According to his fellow traveler Colin Brookes-Smith, Tolkien traveled on his way to Switzerland from Cologne to Frankfurt on a riverboat along the Rhine and Main rivers. Thus, he passed by near the area where the legends about the Nibelungs are set.[121] Moreover, the Roman commander Aëtius settled the Burgundians as *foederati* in the Lake Geneva and Rhône region after their defeat against the Romans and Huns in 435 and 436. This land included the Bernese Oberland and the Valais, through which Tolkien traveled—and who knows, perhaps they took the treasure with them and hid it there in the Misty Mountains. At least, Tolkien seems to suggest this and that it was Andvari.

Tolkien also hinted at an inspiration from the Burgundian migration by giving one of the mountains in the Misty Mountains the name Mount Gun-

---

119 See, e.g., Wendling (2008), who already referred to Arthur Rackham's illustrations as well.

120 See Mackenzie (1912), chap. XXV; cf. Magnusson and Morris (1888), chap. XIV.

121 Cf. Garth (2020), 102 f.; Morton and Hayes (2008), 70.

dabad; the historic Gundobad was a Burgundian king at the time of Theodoric the Great.

By the way, the illustrations shown here were created by Arthur Rackham and published in the English translation of Wagner's *Der Ring der Nibelungen* (*The Ring of the Nibelung*) in 1910 and 1911. That is precisely at the time when Tolkien made his trip to Switzerland. Therefore, it is quite possible that Tolkien overlaid this work, especially the pictures, with his trip to Switzerland—even though he did not like any association with Wagner. Besides, Tolkien mentioned Rackham in two letters. In one of these, a letter from 1957, he said that an American movie-agent had brought him some "astonishingly good pictures," in the style of "Rackham rather than Disney."[122]

2.   "The Shepherd of Lake Heli," George MacDonald, and Lamarck

Parallels between Gollum and the shepherd of Lake Heli in Zschokke's novella of the same name have already been pointed out.[123] In that tale, the shepherd, like Sméagol, comes into possession of a treasure, which in turn takes control of him. This is not so special since we similarly find this in the Nibelung saga as we have just seen. However, it is remarkable that the shepherd, like Gollum, then enters the interior of the very mountains that inspired Tolkien for the Misty Mountains and that he, like Gollum, reaches an underground lake there, hardly ages, but increasingly takes on a ghostly appearance. Therefore, the novella's influence on Tolkien is quite well supported by evidence, especially if the additional parallels are also taken into account. Although both authors may have drawn inspiration from the same sources, a co-influence by "The Shepherd of Lake Heli" still seems likely given the geographical context.

Furthermore, there is probably also a connection to George MacDonald's *The Princess and the Goblin*, a book to which I will return to in the following chapter in the context of the Orcs and Goblins. The transformation of Sméagol into Gollum in the caves' darkness shows parallels with the Lamarckian adaptation of MacDonald's goblins to their environment. Lamarckism is the theory according to which organisms transfer physiological properties that they acquire during their lifetime to their descendants. Thus, living beings physically adapt to their environment during their lifetimes. This idea is found in Gollum's adaptation to life in a cave system, which is favored by

---

[122]   *Letters of Tolkien*, no. 202 (and 235).

[123]   Above, pp. 40 f.

his slow aging. Until the mid-twentieth century, Darwin's theory of mutation and selection was not fully established, and the Lamarckian view remained widespread, even when Tolkien wrote *The Hobbit*.[124] In other words, this transformation was probably not as fantastic then as it seems today but rather quasi-scientific. That being said, there are mechanisms known today that show similarities to the Lamarckian view.[125]

3.   The Legend of the Dwarf King Nuithon

Somewhat unexpectedly, I found another figure with similarities to Gollum in the work of the author Gonzague de Reynold. De Reynold, a controversial anti-democrat, whom Albert Einstein called the "Donkey in Bern,"[126] was a professor, like Tolkien. And, again like Tolkien, he was also a writer and was nominated for the Nobel Prize in Literature six times.[127]

3.1   *The Legend*

In his *Tales and Legends of Heroic Switzerland (Contes et légendes de la Suisse héroïque)* from 1913, de Reynold recounted a legend with the title "The Legend of the Dwarf King Nuithon and the Treasure Hidden in the Sarine." He took inspiration for this story from the Nibelung saga, and probably from Wagner, so parallels with *The Lord of the Rings* should come as no surprise. Yet, the story is worth mentioning with regard to Gollum.

The tale tells of dwarfs who once lived by the river Sarine in what is now the Canton of Fribourg in Switzerland. There, they guarded a treasure lying in the riverbed. From the sky, one could see a luminous ring under the waves and surrounded by pebbles, a ring that gave power and knowledge of all the elements. The more agile dwarfs rode on foxes, and so did their king. It was a time when spirits, monsters, and gods fought for the kingdom of the world; humans were few and far between, and those who existed lived fearfully in caves.

The dwarfs lived in vigilance but in peace until the gods of the north and the south simultaneously learned of this treasure and put out their feelers for it. While Asgard sent a giant raven, Olympus sent a giant eagle, and they both found the treasure lying in the riverbed. The gods of the south sent Orpheus

---

[124]   Slavet (2008), 37 ff.

[125]   See for example Jablonka et al. (1998); Wang et al. (2017).

[126]   Kormos Buchwald et al. (2015), no. 368 (563).

[127]   For de Reynold www.nobelprize.org/nomination/redirector/?redir=archive/show _people.php&id=12271.

immediately, but he was mauled by a giant dog and a huge bull when a string of his beguiling lyre snapped. The gods of the north, in turn, sent their hero Sigurd and were more successful; for Sigurd managed to defeat both the dog and the bull in battle.

Satisfied with his victory, Sigurd proceeded to take possession of the treasure. But then he saw a pitiful figure: a hideous little man with an animal skin around his hips and so hairy that he could have been mistaken for an animal. He was hunchbacked, had long arms and curved legs, and had only one eye, which shone like that of a wolf. Crouching, he searched the ground, sometimes scratching with his hands and feet like a dog, sometimes using a stone from the riverbank as a shovel and pickaxe. In between, he would pause to growl, sigh, and groan, and then he would resume his search.

Suddenly, Sigurd saw that this pathetic figure was holding gold coins in his hands, and so he thought he was just in time and called out to him. Frightened, the little man looked up and put his hands behind his back to hide the gold coins. But Sigurd acted trustworthy, and so this figure asked him for help in his search for the ring—or better, *the Ring*. Before long, the little man suddenly cried out that he had found the Ring, and so Sigurd took off his helmet and sword to reach for the Ring with both hands and pull it out of the water with all his might. But just at that moment, the little man placed a dagger in Sigurd's neck, and the hero fell forward and died immediately.

The little man was the dwarf king Nuithon, who had changed his shape and thus deceived Sigurd. But the dwarfs could not enjoy their victory. They no longer felt safe since they knew that both the gods of the north and the south were aware of the location of the treasure. The gods, for their part, reached out to the good-natured but stupid giant Ogo and promised him all kinds of things so that he would bring them the Ring. Ogo reached Nuithon quickly and suggested that he hide the treasure in the mountains. Although the dwarfs sneered at Ogo, they trusted him and no longer believed the Ring to be safe; so they let him take the Ring and go.

When the dwarfs realized that Ogo had deceived them, they searched for him for a long time, and when they finally found him, Nuithon outsmarted Ogo in a way similar to how he had outsmarted Sigurd. And so, the question of what to do with the treasure arose again. After giving it some thought, Nuithon found the solution: the Ring had to be divided among the dwarfs, for a buried treasure was, after all, a useless one.

3.2   Parallels with Gollum

The episode in the Sarine, in which Nuithon deceitfully kills Sigurd, is somewhat reminiscent of how Sméagol gains possession of the Ring; for Sméagol strangles his friend in the process, and both stories are set on a river. But then again, so is the Nibelung saga, and in Wagner's version of it, there is a similar episode in which Fafner kills his brother Fasolt (Figure 25, page 62). Nevertheless, the ugly, pitiful appearance of Nuithon, sobbing and moaning in the riverbed while he searches for the Ring, does awaken memories of Gollum and the way he behaves while searching for the Ring on his underground island in *The Hobbit*.[128] Also, Nuithon's only eye shines like Gollum's eyes, and he is also just as treacherous. In *The Lord of the Rings*, Aragorn mentions at one point that Gollum's deceitfulness gives him a strength that one would hardly expect,[129] and similarly, Nuithon is capable of killing much stronger opponents.

This is hardly enough for a solid hypothesis, for this dwarf king Nuithon is probably based, just like Gollum, on the figure of the dwarf Alberich or Andvari of the Nibelung saga; and yet, it seemed enough to deserve mention here as it might open up new clues. By the way, the story is set not far from the one of "The Shepherd of Lake Heli."

4.   The Gold Demon

One last potential Swiss source of inspiration for Gollum seems worth mentioning. When I consulted the newspapers of the time when Tolkien was in Switzerland, I discovered that at that very time there was a continuation story called "Dämon Gold" (Demon Gold) in the main local newspaper of the Bernese Oberland, *Oberländer Tagblatt*; and this happened to be a story about being possessed by gold. Each daily edition of the *Oberländer Tagblatt* only had about four pages at that time (including one page of advertising), so the story had a big presence.[130] In other words, every time Tolkien looked into the local newspaper, he must have found the gold demon again: a shadow that accompanied him on his journey.

This gold demon fits, as ultimately do the other stories, with two other already suggested sources of inspiration for Gollum: the Old Norse word *gull*

---

[128]   *The Hobbit*, chap. V.

[129]   *The Fellowship of the Ring*, Book 2, chap. II.

[130]   The issues of the *Berner Oberländer Tagblatt* are available at www.e-newspaperarchives.ch.

or *goll* for "gold" and, somewhat more questionable, the golem of Jewish folklore.[131] All of these sources of inspiration are not mutually exclusive, but perhaps rather add up to a complex overall picture.

5.   Conclusion

Gollum might thus also have a connection to Switzerland. There are striking parallels with "The Shepherd of Lake Heli" and, to a lesser extent, with the dwarf king Nuithon and a continuation story about a gold demon. At the very least, Tolkien traced the Burgundians' resettlement from their realm at the Rhine to their new empire on the edge of the Alps with Gollum's journey from the Anduin to the Misty Mountains. And he seems to imply that someone, probably the dwarf Andvari, took the treasure of the Nibelungs to the new settlement site. And besides, Tolkien followed the Burgundians' migration on his way to Switzerland, so there is also a connection to his trip.

V.   Bilbo, Aragorn, and Sauron as Dietrich von Bern

1.   Dietrich von Bern or Theodoric the Great

Bilbo, Aragorn, and Sauron could not be more different, right? And yet, all three characters seem to have been (co-)inspired by the same person, Theodoric the Great. More precisely, Tolkien appears to have used some elements of the legendary figure of Dietrich von Bern for both Bilbo and Aragorn while he also used aspects of the ecclesiastical representation of the historical Theodoric for Sauron. But this is the same person; according to the prevailing opinion—including Tolkien's[132]—Dietrich von Bern is essentially based on Theodoric the Great.

Although the addition *von Bern* ("of Bern") refers to the Italian city of Verona—which Theodoric conquered in a bloody battle[133]—the legendary figure involuntarily evokes, through his name, associations with the Swiss capital. And only four years before Tolkien's journey, an article was published still stating that the term *Bern* does refer to the Swiss capital, a view that was gladly taken up by the daily press in Switzerland.[134] So it should

---

[131]   Cf. Wendling (2008)

[132]   Bowers (2019), 145.

[133]   Heinzle (1999), 1, 4 f.; Vetter (1908), 2, with further references.

[134]   Vetter (1908), 1.

come as no surprise if Tolkien superimposed his hiking adventure through the Bernese Oberland with the legends around the figure of Dietrich von Bern.

Donald A. MacKenzie summarized the legends about Dietrich von Bern in six chapters at the end of his book *Teutonic Myth and Legend.* The book was published in 1912, so perhaps this summary also served as a first introduction for the young Tolkien. The chapter names are: "Dietrich of Bern;" "The Land of Giants;" "The Wonderful Rose Garden;" "Virginal, Queen of the Mountains;" "Dietrich in Exile;" and "The King's Homecoming." These titles alone evoke memories of *The Lord of the Rings* books, most notably the title of MacKenzie's last chapter, "The King's Homecoming," which almost literally corresponds to the title of the third (physical) book of *The Lord of the Rings*: *The Return of the King.* And the fourth chapter title, "Virginal, Queen of the Mountains," together with the suffix *von Bern,* evoke additional associations with Switzerland.

2.   The Legend of Dietrich von Bern

Dietrich grows up as the son of the King of Bern.[135] At the age of seven, he becomes a pupil of the well-known hero Hildebrand, and after a few years of apprenticeship, he embarks on his first adventure with him: they set out to fight the giants Grim and Hilde, who are ravaging the country. On their way to the giants, they meet the dwarf Alberich[136], who promises them the wondrous and powerful sword, Naglering, if they spare him and eliminate Grim and Hilde. However, Alberich must first steal the sword from the giants' camp, as he had initially forged it for Grim. In the fight that follows, Hildebrand is overpowered and tied up by Hilde, but with Naglering, Dietrich finally succeeds in defeating the giants. After his return to Bern, he is therefore made a knight by his father.

Some time later, Dietrich sets out again, this time to the hunt, and he ventures alone into a deep forest. There, he is surprised by a third giant, Sigenot, who is especially strong and lusts after revenge. In the fight that follows, Dietrich has no chance: he is overpowered, tied up, and then dragged into a snake-filled dragon-cave. In the meantime, Hildebrand had set out to look for Dietrich; and soon, he also meets and fights the giant. But Hildebrand is also overpowered by Sigenot and pulled towards the dragon-cave by his beard. This angers Hildebrand so much that he succeeds in picking up

---

[135]   This summary is based on MacKenzie's version.

[136]   I already mentioned him in the context of the Nibelung saga.

26 Dietrich fights Sigenot; Hans Burgkmair I, *The Battle in the Forest*, ca. 1500, Courtesy National Gallery of Art, Washington, slightly edited.

Naglering on the way; and with that sword, Hildebrand can defeat the giant. Afterward, he frees Dietrich from the dragon-cave, and they return together to Bern, where Dietrich gathers very talented companions due to his newly gained fame—nobody had to know the details. These companions were the dwarfish Heime and the Dane Witege, a skillful archer and expert swordsman, who, with his sword Mimung, even defeats Dietrich in a duel.

Troubled by these defeats, Dietrich decides to set out on an adventure once more. When he reaches the Land of Giants, he defeats two more giants; although with the first one, Ecke, it is only thanks to Dietrich's horse. The second giant joins Dietrich after their fight, and so the two track down a dragon, which they find with the knight Sintram in its mouth. To kill the dragon, Dietrich must pull Sintram's sword from the dragon's throat; for it is only with this miraculous sword that he can pierce the dragon's skin. And he succeeds. But back in Bern, Dietrich's companions Witege and Heime, get into a fight, which prompts Dietrich to send Heime away. However, this is not to Heime's disadvantage, as he makes a successful career as a robber chief and highwayman—similar to Túrin in *The Children of Húrin*.

One day, the Dane Dietleib and his sister Kunhild visit Dietrich, but their mood soon worsens, for Kunhild is kidnapped by the dwarf king Laurin while dancing with her maids on a green meadow. Laurin, who uses a camouflage cloak for the abduction, takes Kunhild to his palace in the mountains as he wants to make her his wife. When Dietrich learns of the kidnapping, he calls for his knights at once and sets off for Laurin's palace. After a short skirmish in the palace's beautiful rose garden, they are received by the dwarf king. But the cunning Laurin uses wine to put his visitors into a sleep and blindness and throws them into a deep dungeon. Luckily, though, Kunhild succeeds in bringing her brother Dietleib a ring that breaks the spell during the night, and so he can free first himself and then his fellow knights. A fight breaks out, in which Laurin is quickly overpowered and captured; but he gets unexpected help, for Kunhild shows signs of Stockholm syndrome and agrees to marry him. And so, thanks to the immortality she gained, they still live happily there in the mountains today.

Back in Bern, Dietrich learns that Virginal, Queen of the Mountains and ruler of Elfland, is in great trouble: the giant Orkise has been ravaging her land and forces her to deliver a beautiful maiden to him at every new moon. Dietrich does not hesitate and sets off with his knights once more. Again, it is Hildebrand who succeeds in defeating the giant while Dietrich takes care of the giant's wild companions. After that, Dietrich and Hildebrand head on to the defeated giant's palace, but when they reach it, more giants oppose them. And a black rider, Orkise's son Janibas, an evil magician, appears. With strange words, he lets the giants rise again each time Dietrich or Hildebrand defeats them. And later on, he summons snakes and nameless reptiles. The black rider does not join the fight directly, and he disappears in the dawn when the battle finally comes to an end. Dietrich and Hildebrand cannot get hold of him, but they succeed in freeing the three maidens from the palace.

After defeating another dragon with a knight in its throat, Dietrich rides ahead foolishly fast on their return to Queen Virginal's palace in Jeraspunt, and thereby, he becomes lost and falls again into the captivity of giants. After his loyal companions free him once again, they finally head together to Jeraspunt. On their way, they learn that Janibas, the evil magician, has surrounded the castle with a large army and is demanding possession all the maidens and the queen's magic crown jewel. The queen's jewel gives her the power to rule over all her subjects — I wonder why the noble ruler needs it. When Dietrich and his knights reach her palace amidst the mountains, the battle is in full swing. In the turmoil, Dietrich finds Janibas, who is casting spells with an iron tablet in his hand. Dietrich finally succeeds in breaking the tablet and slaying the dreaded assistant of evil. At that very moment, a thunder resounds in the middle of the mountains, the glaciers are shattered, and avalanches fall on the evil army of Janibas, burying it—as in Disney's *Mulan*. Soon, there is silence and peace: the terrible conflict has come to an end.

In this silence, Dietrich suddenly sees Queen Virginal, sitting alone and enthroned high in her mountain palace, motionless and beautiful, the jewel of her crown shining brightly. A glittering silver veil is drawn around her body; her maidens cower trembling—trembling?—at her feet. When Dietrich approaches the queen, she calls him a hero and welcomes him with love. She proclaims that she cannot rule Elfland any longer as she desires to leave her home and her kingdom and live with Dietrich among men until the end of her days. There is a splendid marriage feast with the elves and heroes; they celebrate, drink wine, and laugh. Soon, Dietrich and Virginal leave Elfland for Bern, where they live happily for quite some time; and as Dietrich's father dies, Dietrich takes his place as king.

Dietrich's uncle Ermenrich is meanwhile the mighty King of the Southland, and Dietrich sends Witege and the reconciled Heime to his uncle as support in his uncle's wars. But Ermenrich is advised by the evil Sibeche, who poisons the king's mind against his sons and Dietrich. As a result, Ermenrich's three sons die, and the southern king demands tribute from Dietrich. But Dietrich refuses, and so Ermenrich marches with a great army against Bern. Even though Dietrich wins the first battle, he lacks the means to continue the war, and when his noble knights want to bring him the necessary treasures, they are ambushed and taken prisoner, all but the Dane Dietleib.

To make matters worse, Virginal dies, and so Dietrich makes an offer to Ermenrich: Dietrich will depart from his kingdom without battle, provided Ermenrich leaves Dietrich's knights alive. And that is what happens: Dietrich marches off, accompanied only by a few. Among them are his younger brother Diether and the faithful Hildebrand, who even leaves his wife and his son Hadubrand in Bern. They find refuge at the Court of Etzel (Attila), King of the Huns.

For Etzel, Dietrich successfully fights many battles, but he keeps mourning for his lost kingdom—he seems to have gotten over Virginal faster. Helche, the queen of the Huns, takes pity on him and gives him her niece, the gentle Princess Herrad, as his wife. King Etzel also wants to help Dietrich and promises him a large army to win back his kingdom. The next spring, Dietrich—like Daenerys in *A Song of Ice and Fire*—sets out with Hun horsemen, his companions, and King Etzel's sons to reclaim his kingdom. North of the imperial city of Ravenna, Sibeche—the commander of the army of the sick Ermenrich—awaits him at a river crossing. But Dietrich can bypass him and put Sibeche and his army to flight. Only Witege and a few others stay to oppose the attackers. But when Etzel's sons challenge Witege, he kills them both. And when Dietrich's brother Diether attacks Witege thereafter, Witege kills Diether too. As Dietrich hears about what happened, he starts crying and pursues Witege, who is fleeing on Diether's horse. But when Witege tries to cross the river, a mermaid appears and pulls him beneath the waves to her underground cave, and nobody has ever seen him since.

After this victory, Dietrich breaks off the campaign since he cannot count on the Huns without Etzel's sons. Although he fears to return to the land of the Huns, he finally returns and reconciles first with the queen and later with Etzel. But the disaster takes its course there too. The good queen dies only two years later, and with her last words, she warns Etzel against marrying a woman from the Land of the Nibelungs. But King Etzel is not dissuaded, and after his wife's death, he sends envoys to King Gunther to ask whether he might have Kriemhild for his bride. He should have listened to his queen, of course. For back at Etzel's court, there is a wedding full of blood; Dietrich's remaining knights are killed and old Hildebrand is wounded. In the revenge campaign that follows, Dietrich kills King Gunther and his right-hand Hagen while Hildebrand takes care of Kriemhild. After the slaughter finally comes to an end, Hagen's son Aldrian agrees to show Etzel the treasure of the Nibelungs and leads him into a cave under the Rhine where all the treasures are hidden. All's well that ends well? Not quite, at least not for the King of the Huns. For while Etzel is still beaming at the sight of the treasures, Aldrian takes a step back and closes the door to the cave—and Etzel, too, was never seen again.

Sometime later, Dietrich learns that his uncle Ermenrich was murdered and that Sibeche is trying to seize the throne. Therefore, he again raises an army to invade his own kingdom—after thirty-two years in exile. As Dietrich and his army approach his kingdom, Hildebrand's son Hadubrand moves against them—his only son, who he had left in Bern as an infant. Between the ranks of the troops, the father and son meet. Hildebrand tries to convince his son that he is his father, but it is in vain. A long fight ensues, and Hildebrand critically wounds Hadubrand with a stroke of his sword. He sits down next to his dying son, weeping bitter tears, and remains there during the battle. The battle passes him by; he talks to no one, and his face turns deathly white. Later, father and son are both found dead. Hadubrand had died from his wound, Hildebrand from grief.

Dietrich goes on to win the battle, but he is sad as he marches triumphantly into Bern without Hildebrand, his first and last companion of many years. But the people receive him with great jubilation, and he is celebrated as the rightful king—if one believes the tradition. The danger is not yet averted, though, for Sibeche marches against Bern. But Dietrich can crush his army, and during the battle, Sibeche is killed. And so Dietrich becomes king over his lost kingdom, the lands of Ermenrich, and those of the Huns. From exile, he thus becomes the greatest monarch of his time.

For a long time, Dietrich rules, and there is peace over all his vast dominions for Dietrich is as wise as he is powerful. He grows old, very old, and more than a few believe he is still alive today. Because once, when he was hunting a huge stag, a noble and high-stepping black steed appeared without a rider. Dietrich reacted promptly. He jumped into the saddle and urged the black horse on, and it ran faster than the wind. To a dwarf who happened to be around, Dietrich reported that he could neither hold back the evil steed nor dismount from it; and so he disappeared and was never seen again. Yet when the wind blows high, and the world is stricken by tempest, the sound of hooves can be heard in mid-air, and men know then that Dietrich, seated on his black steed, is pursuing the stag of old across the heavens.

3.   Elements of the Saga in Tolkien's Work

Did one or the other element in the Dietrich legend seem familiar to you? Some of them are definitely reminiscent of features in *The Hobbit*, *The Lord of the Rings*, and *The Children of Húrin*. Especially remarkable is the multitude of different characters that the figure of Dietrich seems to have influenced: from Bilbo to Aragorn, to the Nazgûl, and even Sauron.

3.1   Bilbo and His Journey in The Hobbit

Already Dietrich's first adventure, the fight against the two giants Grim and Hilde, is reminiscent of Bilbo's journey in *The Hobbit*. It shows similarities to the episode with the trolls that Bilbo and the dwarves encounter on their way to Rivendell. Not only is Hildebrand—and also Dietrich in the fight against Sigenot—tied up by the giants; Dietrich, like Bilbo, attains a special sword through it. Apart from this first episode, Dietrich, like Bilbo, also makes a trip into a land of Elves in the mountains and once gets imprisoned in a palace-dungeon. Especially Dietrich's capture by the dwarf king Laurin and the following liberation action remind strongly of the capture of the dwarves by the Elvenking in the Woodland Realm in *The Hobbit*. In general, it is noticeable that Dietrich, like the dwarves in *The Hobbit*, is captured several times and fights giants suspiciously often as if he were a halfling. And he experiences a refreshing amount of difficulty defeating his opponents; he is certainly not a superhero—and not a rapist like Siegfried. Moreover, the Dietrich

27 The historical Theodoric looked like a true hobbit. Early medieval coin; photo: Paolo Monti, Servizio fotografico (Roma, 1968), made available by the BEIC Foundation, detail, slightly edited, CC-BY-SA 4.0.

legend is linked to the Nibelung saga with its cursed treasure. The leap from the Dietrich legend to the Nibelung saga thus seems as natural as the leap from *The Hobbit* to *The Lord of the Rings*.

Unlike in *The Hobbit*, Dietrich receives a dwarfish and not an elven sword, and he and his companions are taken prisoner by a dwarf king, not by an elven king. On closer inspection, however, the question arises whether this is true. The dwarf from whom Dietrich receives the sword has the name *Alberich*, and part of this name—*Alb*—points to an elven descent. Tolkien was certainly aware of this. As mentioned earlier, he suggested translating the English word *elf* into German as *Alp* or even better *Alb*, and he also pointed out that the name *Alboin* means "Elf-friend."[137] Moreover, he mentioned once that he does not recall any "Dwarf or Elf" that plays an actual role in any old tale save Andvari (Alberich) in the Norse versions of the Nibelung matter.[138] In other words, Alberich is an elf rather than a dwarf, and the sword Dietrich receives, therefore, an elven sword. Similarly, Tolkien may have reinterpreted the dwarf king Laurin as an elven king.

3.2   *Aragorn*

In the second part of the legend, Dietrich is more reminiscent of Aragorn.[139] Like Aragorn, he is the rightful king in exile and celebrated on his return; and this is reflected in both Mackenzie's chapter title "The King's Homecoming" and Tolkien's book title *The Return of the King*. Also, Dietrich, like Aragorn, meets a she-elf who leaves her realm and renounces her immortality for a life with a mortal man; and Dietrich's companions, the dwarfish Heime and the

---

[137]   Tolkien and Tolkien (1975), 5.

[138]   *Letters of Tolkien*, no. 236.

[139]   Snyder (2013), 199, already mentioned a possible connection between Aragorn and Theodoric.

Dane Witege, show similarities to Aragorn's companions Gimli and Legolas. Last but not least, Aragorn, like Dietrich, becomes unnaturally old.

Apart from the similarities, there are, however, considerable differences between Dietrich and Aragorn. The most important one is that Dietrich fights on the side of the Huns, the people who probably co-inspired Tolkien's Orcs. At this point, the reader might wonder whether Dietrich turned to evil in exile, much like Daenerys in *The Song of Ice and Fire*. Also, Dietrich tries to retake his realm, much like Daenerys, and Aragorn acts as a defender. In this respect, Aragorn may have been more inspired by King Arthur, Alfred the Great, or the German king Otto I.[140] Nevertheless, there are strong indications that the figure of Aragorn was at least co-inspired by Dietrich.

By the way, Tolkien himself connected Aragorn in a letter with the Lombard king Alboin, the Elf-friend mentioned above.[141] The historical Alboin walked with his people southward across the Alps and is considered the father of the medieval Kingdom of the Lombards in Northern Italy. When he arrived there, the Italian peninsula was devastated by the wars between the Ostrogoths and the Byzantine Empire and additionally depopulated by the Justinian plague, so Alboin met with little resistance. A connection between Aragorn and Alboin by no means excludes an influence by the Dietrich legend. On the contrary, it rather strengthens it, for the Dietrich legend refers to several historical rulers. Theodoric the Great was not a contemporary of Attila: parts of the tale, therefore, seem to refer more to Theodoric's uncle Valamir, who, as King of the Ostrogoths, fought on Attila's side in the Battle of the Catalaunian Fields. And it was probably also Valamir who helped to destroy the Burgundian Empire at the river Rhine, the historical core of the Nibelung saga. Tolkien may have connected later parts of the Dietrich legend with Alboin, who in turn was possibly related to Theodoric on his mother's side.[142] Therefore, his invasion into Italy could be regarded as the king's return—or at least sold as such. Moreover, Alboin was killed in Verona, the Lombard Bern, and the same city later became one of the seats of government of the Lombard kings while a conquest of Ravenna repeatedly failed. And this may also be the reason why Dietrich, according to the legend, comes from Bern, today's Verona, and not from Ravenna, Theodoric's seat of government.[143]

---

140   See for example Snyder (2013), 77.

141   *Letters of Tolkien*, no. 257; cf. Tolkien and Tolkien (1975), 5.

142   According to Jarnut (2009), 282, we know nothing of Rodelinda, Alboin's mother, but another wife of Alboin's father was a grandniece of Theodoric.

143   See Wisniewski (1986), 3 f.

3.3 Nazgûl

As if this were not enough, Dietrich also shows characteristics of the Nazgûl, the Ringwraiths. At the end of the legend, Dietrich rides away on a black steed, and on it, he is said to roam the land against his will to this day, spreading fear and terror in stormy nights as if he were a servant of the devil. In Tolkien's legendarium, the Nazgûl were also once great lords of Men before they were corrupted and enslaved by Sauron's will; and like Dietrich, they then roamed the land as black horsemen in search of the Ring. Dietrich's switch to the side of the Huns, and thus the Orcs, also fits well with this connection.[144] For connected to the Nibelung saga, it is Dietrich who, as a servant of the dark lord Attila, leads the Huns against the Burgundians—out of revenge but also to acquire their treasure, the Ring.

Apart from the Dietrich legend, the Nazgûl were, I believe, also inspired by the folklore motif of the Wild Hunt.[145] However, there is probably a connection between the Dietrich legend and the Wild Hunt. At least, this is what Wilhelm Grimm, the younger of the Grimm brothers, believed.[146]

3.4 Sauron

Finally, Dietrich and his main model, the historical Theodoric, also show parallels with Sauron himself. In the legend, Dietrich becomes King of the Huns, the successor of Attila, so to speak, just as Sauron is Melkor's successor in Tolkien's books. And according to ecclesiastical tradition, Theodoric was, as offspring of the devil, plunged into the Liparian volcano by Pope John and Symmachus—since he was responsible for their deaths.[147] In *The Lord of the Rings*, Sauron's power is—as the reader should know—destroyed in a very similar way. And Tolkien hinted at such an inspiration once when he, on a cruise with his wife Edith in 1960, compared the Liparian volcano Stromboli with Mount Doom.[148]

3.5 Saruman, Orcs, Galadriel, Théoden, and Gríma Wormtongue

Other figures of the Dietrich legend show similarities to characters in *The Lord of the Rings*. Panibas, the evil magician, is reminiscent of Saruman or the Witch-king of Angmar. And Dietrich's shattering of the tablet ends the

---

[144] See below, pp. 169 ff.

[145] Below, pp. 90 ff.

[146] Grimm (1867), 41; see also Heinzle (1999), 9.

[147] Pope Gregory I (ca. 590), chap. 30; see Heinzle (1999), 8 f.

[148] Scull and Hammond (2017a), 862.

siege of Jeraspunt, similar to the One Ring's destruction in *The Lord of the Rings*. Furthermore, Panibas' father, Orkise, inevitably reminds us of the Orcs, and the Elf-queen Virginal with her jewel of Galadriel—although the gem has features of the One Ring.

Above all, however, Ermenrich and his evil advisor Sibeche are reminiscent of Théoden and his evil advisor Gríma Wormtongue. Such a connection is not too surprising, for the Riders of Rohan were inspired largely by the Goths.[149] The historical Ermanaric was a king of the Greutungi (pre-Ostrogoths), who ruled over a large empire before the Hun invasion of 375. In the legend, however, Ermenrich was probably co-inspired by Odoacer and the Visigoth king Eurich, a contemporary of Theodoric the Great and son of the Visigoth king Theodoric I, who died in the battle on the Catalaunian Fields and probably also inspired the figure of Théoden.[150] If you feel like your grandmother is beginning to talk about family relations, I can understand that. The bards and scalds of the Middle Ages probably felt the same way, and so different stories were mixed up, especially if the characters involved had similar names or came from the same people.

The Germanic name Gríma, by the way, is considered to be at the origin of the name of the town Grimentz, which Tolkien visited when he was in Switzerland, according to Colin Brookes-Smith's route description.[151] And it is also possible that Tolkien connected the name with the Grimsel Pass.

4. Appraisal

The influence of the Dietrich legend on Tolkien's work can hardly be underestimated. The list of characters with parallels to Dietrich is long, containing some of the most positive figures, such as Bilbo and Aragorn, but also including Sauron, the epitome of evil. Apart from Dietrich's change, the background is probably due to the different historiography perspectives: the Germanic heroic epic contrasts with an ecclesiastical tradition that demonizes Theodoric. Tolkien harmoniously united these different perspectives in one work and, in doing so, did not, for example, recreate a historical Theodoric. No, he adopted both views and let the different historiographies fight against each other, so to speak, with the victory of good, the triumph of the heroic epic.

---

[149] See see below, pp. 108 ff., 169 ff.

[150] More on this below, pp. 169 ff.

[151] See "Grimentz" at www.ortsnamen.ch; Brookes-Smith (1982), 3.

According to Tolkien, he did not want to link allegories to his work.[152] Yet, the large number of characters influenced by the historical Theodoric suggest that his work reflects the inner struggle between good and evil. And this happens to be precisely what Tolkien himself indicated in one of his letters to his son Christopher as he wrote:

> For 'romance' has grown out of 'allegory', and its wars are still derived from the 'inner war' of allegory in which good is on one side and various modes of badness on the other. In real (exterior) life men are on both sides: which means a motley alliance of orcs, beasts, demons, plain naturally honest men, and angels.[153]

Tolkien indeed had a mixed picture of the historical Theodoric. Once he noted:

> Theodoric the Gothic king ruled Italy from Ravenna and passed into the legends of Germanic-speaking peoples as Theodric (Dietrich von Bern), and into history as a good ruler whose repute has however been much damaged by his probably unjust and certainly cruel torture and execution of Boethius, A.D. 524.[154]

Tolkien made this statement when he dealt in depth with the historical figure of Boethius in connection with the work of Geoffrey Chaucer.[155] Boethius was a Roman philosopher who rose to become one of the highest-ranking servants under Theodoric (consul and *magister officiorum*). But then he fell into disfavor and was captured and killed by the king. Like Gandalf, he was locked up in a tower in Pavia for a long time before his death.[156]

Using Theodoric as his protagonist model, Tolkien thus seems to have processed the inner struggle between good and evil in *The Lord of the Rings*. This fits Tolkien's inspiration from Dante's *Divine Comedy*, which follows Dante's deviation from the right path and contains the three parts *Inferno (Hell)*, *Purgatorio (Purgatory)*, and *Paradiso (Paradise)*. These elements, Tolkien also seems to have used as a framework for *The Lord of the Rings*, simply in a different order. Hell—Moria—is followed by a vision of (earthly) Para-

---

[152]   *Letters of Tolkien*, no. 165: "[The LOTR] is not 'about' anything but itself. Certainly it has no allegorical intentions, general, particular, or topical, moral, religious, or political."

[153]   *Letters of Tolkien*, no. 71; see also *Letters of Tolkien*, nos. 109 und 131.

[154]   Bowers (2019), 145.

[155]   See Bowers (2019), 143 ff.

[156]   So already Bowers (2019), 146.

dise—Lothlórien—and only then by Mount Purgatorio with its seven levels of spiritual growth—Minas Tirith (and Mount Doom). The linking of Dietrich von Bern with Dante's *Divine Comedy* may have been due to the fact that Dante wrote a large part of his work in Verona, that is Bern. And so it seems that we follow, guided by Dante, Theodoric's spiritual path in *The Lord of the Rings*—which makes sense since Bilbo has grown old.

The Dietrich legend's connection to Switzerland is merely indirect, on the one hand through the natural associations with the name Bern and on the other hand through the Virginal part that is reminiscent of the Eiger, Mönch (Monk), and Jungfrau (Virgin) mountain trinity. The giant Orkise blackmails Virginal, Queen of the Mountains, just as the Eiger or Ogre in popular parlance harasses the Virgin, protected by the Monk. Tolkien might have made similar connections and therefore overlaid his journey with Dietrich's adventures: the Lauterbrunnen Valley lying under the Jungfrau became the Land of the Elves of Virginal. It even seems that the saga complex around Dietrich von Bern, along with Tolkien's journey through the Bernese Oberland and the Valais, served somewhat as a framework for the plot in *The Hobbit*. And later, in *The Lord of the Rings*, Tolkien linked this structure to Dante's *Divine Comedy*.

Apart from this, it is remarkable that the brothers Sintram and Bertram appear in a legend about the foundation of Burgdorf, a Bernese town. In that legend, Sintram cuts his brother out of a dragon's belly—quite like in the corresponding episode in the Dietrich legend. The Swiss pastor and writer Jeremias Gotthelf wrote an embellished version of the legend with the title *Die Gründung Burgdorfs oder Die beiden Brüder Sintram und Bertram (The Foundation of Burgdorf or The Two Brothers Singram and Bertram)*, a tale well worth reading. It is not easy to determine whether this tale's connection with the Dietrich legend is original and was later detached from it, or whether the two were later connected, since the myth of the foundation of Burgdorf was already recorded in the fifteenth century.[157] In any case, it seems like the name Bern already aroused false associations in the Middle Ages; and it would therefore also be conceivable that the story of Virginal, Queen of the Mountains, found its way into the Dietrich legend only in this way.[158]

---

[157] Heinzle (1999), 141.

[158] However, in the poem the Tyrolean mountains are mentioned, which also fits the journeys of Theodoric and Alboin better; see, by the way, Schiller's Berglied, where he probably referred to the Jungfrau in the last part.

Dark Creatures with a Possible Swiss Connection

The preceding chapter brought to light evidence that Switzerland's influence on Tolkien's imaginary world goes beyond a mere impact on its landscape. Some of its well-known characters, too, seem to have been inspired by stories connected to Switzerland. This raises the question of whether there is also a connection between Middle-earth's dark creatures and Switzerland. In the chapter "The Misty Mountains," some possible links have already been pointed out; I will explore this in more detail now.

I. Orcs and Goblins

Orcs and goblins are the simple evildoers of Middle-earth. To see a possible connection to Switzerland in a better context, it is essential first to look at two works: George MacDonald's *The Princess and the Goblin* and William Morris' *The Roots of the Mountains*.

1. George MacDonald's *The Princess and the Goblin*

Tolkien once mentioned that the goblins in *The Hobbit* owe a good deal to the goblin tradition, especially as it appears in George MacDonald's stories.[159] And from the biographer Humphrey Carpenter we learn that Tolkien was very fond of MacDonald's Curdie stories, *The Princess and the Goblin* and *The Princess and Curdie*, in his childhood and that Tolkien later read these stories to his children.[160]

The Princess and the Goblin tells the story of an eight-year-old princess, who lives a rather lonely life in a large house, which was half castle and half farm, in a mountainous kingdom. Her father, the king, is hardly ever present, and her mother had died years ago. Not far from the castle, danger lurks in the shadows because goblins live in a nearby mountain. Legend has it that the goblins had once lived above ground and had been very similar to other peo-

---

[159] *Letters of Tolkien*, no. 144.

[160] Carpenter (1977), 30, 167.

ples. However, for a reason no longer known, the goblins were harassed by the king. So they retreated into underground caves, which they left only at night, if at all. Over generations, living in the caves caused their appearance to change, and they increasingly took on a disgusting and grotesque appearance. The goblins also became smaller, but this did not diminish their strength; only their feet became very sensitive—an element Tolkien did not find convincing.[161] Moreover, the goblins became cruel and cunning, always waiting to take revenge.

One evening, the princess and her nanny are surprised by the onset of darkness. They race to reach the castle's protecting walls, but goblins appear and chase them—a bit like the hyenas in *The Lion King*. Just as hope is fading, Curdie, a young miner boy, shows up and saves them. Over the next few days, Curdie and other miners advance from the existing mines deeper into the mountain, getting closer and closer to the goblins, until one day Curdie overhears the goblins through the rock. Curdie follows the goblins deep inside the mountain to their main hall, but there, he is discovered and captured. Fortunately, the princess has a magic thread that leads her to Curdie, and so this time, she frees him.

Back in the mines, Curdie overhears the goblins again and learns that they are digging a tunnel to the castle to kidnap the princess. He hurries to the palace to warn the guards, but instead of listening to him, they capture him. So, when the goblins enter the palace through the palace floor, the guards are not prepared. Luckily, Curdie frees himself in time and makes the goblins flee by stepping on their sensitive feet. As a reward, the king offers him a job as a bodyguard, but Curdie refuses, as he prefers staying with his parents.

Apart from the goblins' appearance, the fairy tale bears some similarities to Tolkien's stories in Middle-earth. There is the episode in *The Hobbit*, for example, in which

28 Curdie and the Goblins, illustration by Jessie Willcox Smith in George MacDonald's *The Princess and the Goblins*, David McKay Company edition, 1920.

---

[161]   *Letters of Tolkien*, no. 144.

Bilbo and the dwarves are surprised and captured by goblins but then manage to escape. And there is also the episode in *The Lord of the Rings* in which Sam first eavesdrops on Orcs and then rescues Frodo from the tower of Cirith Ungol, just like Curdie eavesdrops on the goblins. Furthermore, there are parallels with the Dwarves of Moria, who had dug too deep under Durin VI and thus awakened the Balrog that sealed their end. However, in this respect, there is probably an even stronger connection to the legend of the Lords of the Red Valley.[162] Finally, the way the goblins' appearance adapted to life in a cave is reminiscent of the similar Lamarckian underground transformation of Sméagol or Gollum.[163] MacDonald's influence on Tolkien's work should certainly not be underestimated.

Although MacDonald was mentioned here primarily because of the context, even his goblins might be connected to Switzerland. MacDonald once went on an inspiring trip to Switzerland himself, and he described this trip in his autobiographical story *Wilfried Cumbermede* from 1872—the same year in which he also published *The Princess and the Goblin*.[164] MacDonald and his companions had sailed from Thun to Interlaken when he had a divine vision, he recounted. As they passed through wafts of mist, a friend's scream caused MacDonald to look up, and he saw a wonderful window in the mist opening before him. The Jungfrau rose above the clouds; the sight left him speechless, and just an instant later, she disappeared again in the mist.[165] MacDonald describes this vision as something that raised him above his former self and gave him a longing to rise even higher. The vision had awakened his belief in the incomprehensibly divine, and later, whenever he had doubts, the Jungfrau appeared to him, looking directly into his very soul. After that, MacDonald went on to Lauterbrunnen, Mürren, and Grindelwald, quite like Tolkien some decades after him.[166] Grindelwald lies at the foot of the Eiger, and from there, MacDonald and his companions walked to an ice cave. Although speculative, it is thus quite conceivable that the Eiger (or Ogre) and the Jungfrau (or Maiden) inspired MacDonald to write the story *The Princess and the Goblin*, set in a mountain kingdom.

While Tolkien was very fond of MacDonald's stories in his childhood, his attitude towards him gradually changed. This was mainly due to the moral

---

[162]   Above, pp. 42 ff.

[163]   Cf. above, pp. 63 f.

[164]   Cf. Hein (1993), 172 f., 219.

[165]   MacDonald (1872), chap. XV.

[166]   Hein (1993), 172 f.; for Grindelwald see MacDonald (1872), chap. XV.

allegories that Tolkien increasingly despised.[167] At the same time, the image of the Goblins changed: the rather humorous Goblins of *The Hobbit* became gloomy Orcs in *The Lord of the Rings*—although Tolkien did not consider them to be different creatures.[168]

This change can also be seen in two of Tolkien's letters. While he still referred to the goblin tradition and the Orcs' similarities to MacDonald's goblins in a letter dated April 25, 1954—and thus shortly before the publication of the first volume of *The Lord of the Rings*—he more strongly distinguished the Orcs from these goblins in a letter dated September 18 of the same year. More specifically, he explained:

> Your preference of *goblins* to *orcs* involves a large question and a matter of taste, and perhaps historical pedantry on my pan. Personally I prefer Orcs (since these creatures are not 'goblins', not even the goblins of George Mac-Donald, which they do to some extent resemble).[169]

The fact that Tolkien, nevertheless, still referred to George MacDonald at this time is remarkable. For unlike the Goblins from *The Hobbit*, the Orcs from *The Lord of the Rings* no longer bear much resemblance to MacDonald's goblins. Rather, they mirror threatening figures from William Morris' *The Roots of the Mountains*.

2.   William Morris' *The Roots of the Mountains*

With his novels *The House of the Wolfings* and *The Roots of the Mountains*, William Morris also significantly influenced Tolkien. Tolkien himself acknowledged this when he, asked about the impact of the two world wars, instead referred to these two novels.[170] Already the title *The Roots of the Mountains* is reminiscent of *The Hobbit* since, in *The Hobbit*'s prehistory, the Dwarves find the Arkenstone at the Lonely Mountain's roots. In addition, the landscape and place names in the two novels bear resemblances. The plot in *The House of the Wolfings* is mainly set on a river in a forest called Mirkwood,[171] and *The Roots of the Mountains* is set in Burgdale, a village in a valley called Dale. Morris did not invent these terms—Mirkwood and *The*

---

[167]   See Fisher (2006).

[168]   See also the following paragraph.

[169]   *Letters of Tolkien*, no. 151.

[170]   *Letters of Tolkien*, no. 226.

[171]   For further parallels see below, pp. 104 f.

Roots of the Mountains originate in Germanic-Norse mythology,[172] and Dale is an old English term for valley.[173] However, these names were probably inspired primarily by Morris, given the number of identical names and Tolkien's explicit reference to him.

An inspiration for the Orcs is also likely, for in *The Roots of the Mountains*, more and more shady human-like figures show up around Dale. Morris calls them the Dusky Men and describes them as "short of stature, crooked-legged, long-armed, very strong for their size: with small blue eyes, snubbed-nosed, wide-mouthed, thin-lipped, very swarthy of skin, exceeding foul of favour."[174] Tolkien, for his part, described the Orcs in a letter as "squat, broad, flat-nosed, sallow-skinned, with wide mouths and slant eyes: in fact degraded and repulsive versions of the (to Europeans) least lovely Mongol-types."[175] And in *The Lord of the Rings*, Sam once told Frodo that he would make a better orc if he had longer arms and were bow-legged.[176] It should come as no surprise that Tolkien was already criticized for racism because of this, even though he always distanced himself from racist and anti-Semitic positions.[177] In any case, Morris' Dusky Men and Tolkien's Orcs resemble each other.

Apart from their appearance, there is another commonality in their tolerance for the sun. When the dusky creatures first appear in Morris' novel, the protagonist's grandfather raises the question of whether they are humans or trolls. Finding the answer is important, he says, for trolls, unlike humans, have to avoid daylight, which makes them less of a danger.[178] Similarly, in *The Lord of the Rings*, the wizard Saruman is said to cross Orcs with humans and thus breed the Uruk-hai, who, unlike the Orcs, do not mind daylight.[179] Furthermore, the number and power of these sinister figures increase in both works, so there is an urgent need for action by the protagonists.[180]

From a historical point of view, Morris' Dusky Men were probably inspired by the Huns. In the least, Tolkien identified them as such, and this is

---

[172]   See for example *Prose Edda, Gylfaginning*, chap. 34.

[173]   See "dale," Wiktionary, https://en.wiktionary.org/wiki/dale.

[174]   Morris (1893), 90.

[175]   *Letters of Tolkien*, no. 210.

[176]   *The Return of the King*, Book 6, chap. I.

[177]   See for example *Letters of Tolkien*, no. 29, 30, 61, 71, 81.

[178]   Morris (1893), 174 f.

[179]   See *The Two Towers*, Book 3, chaps. IV and VII.

[180]   Cf. Morris (1893), 130.

also relevant to the historical background of Tolkien's novels.[181] The Hun horsemen, who in late antiquity advanced westward from the Central Asian steppes, aroused fear and terror in Romans and Germanic peoples alike. Accordingly, they were described in a demonic way, even orkish, by ancient authors such as Jordanes. In Jordanes' *Gothic History*, we read that the Huns allegedly dwelt first in the swamps and that their scarcely human-like appearance alone spread fear. Their heads, he wrote, were a shapeless lump with pinholes rather than eyes, and they cut their children's cheeks so that they would get used to pain from a very young age.[182] When the Europeans became increasingly interested in their own past in the nineteenth century, the Huns were also stylized as the envoys of evil par excellence and portrayed accordingly by painters.[183]

Apart from the place names and the Orcs, other parallels are remarkable. In *The House of the Wolfings*, the main character, like Bilbo, is given a magical hauberk (shirt of mail) forged by dwarven hands; and in *The Roots of the Mountains*, the elves and other mystical creatures of the forest disappear before the coming war, as do the Elves in *The Lord of the Rings*. Moreover, the inhabitants of Burgdale are protected, without knowing it, by descendants of the Wolvings, who wear down smaller groups of the Dusky Men, just as the Hobbits of the Shire are protected, without knowing it, by Aragorn and the Dúnedain.[184] And Morris' protectors, like Tolkien's Dúnedain, have a slowly fading heroic past.[185] In addition, there is also a love story in *The Roots of the Mountains* that bears similarities to the one of Aragorn, Arwen, Eowyn, and Faramir; and, finally, it is certain that Morris' narrative style of interspersing prose with chunks of poetry inspired Tolkien, as Tolkien himself stated it in a letter of 1914.[186]

Again, there might also be an indirect connection between the Orcs and Switzerland since *The Roots of the Mountains* is set in the Migration Period, and its mountains are probably the Alps, into which Germanic tribes advanced in the course of the migration. In any case, Morris' depiction of the mountains recalls the Alps rather than the Carpathians. Although Morris was

---

[181]   *Letters of Tolkien*, no. 226.

[182]   Jordanes (ca. 550), nos. 122 and 127 ff.; probably, he was mistaken, see Maenchen-Helfen (1973), 361 ff.

[183]   See below 170.

[184]   Cf. Morris (1893), 130.

[185]   Morris (1893), 109 ff.; Morris (1889).

[186]   *Letters of Tolkien*, no. 1.

29 William Morris; photo: Frederick Hollyer, 1888.

perhaps inspired primarily by the Italian Alps,[187] the main scenery in the valley of Dale shows remarkable similarities to the Lauterbrunnen Valley—with green meadows on the valley floor, vertical rock faces on the sides, and a view of the high mountains. It is therefore conceivable that Tolkien felt transported to Morris' world on his trip to Switzerland, especially since there is a rock face called Hunnenfluh (Hun-rock) at the entrance to the Lauterbrunnen Valley, and according to legend, the Val d'Anniviers he later visited is associated with the Huns.[188] Thus, autobiographical elements of Tolkien's trip to Switzerland might have been mixed naturally with Morris' stories, and perhaps Morris was even inspired by them himself.

Morris was a fascinating personality, by the way. Today, he is known less as a pioneer of modern fantasy literature and more as the father of the Arts and Crafts movement, the founding of the Socialist Party in England, and the wallpaper patterns he designed.[189] Apart from that, he studied Icelandic and translated the Völsunga saga, which is also the subject of Tolkien's book *The Legend of Sigurd and Gudrún.* In other words, Morris may have served as a role model for Tolkien even beyond his novels.

3. Possible Direct Sources of Inspiration in Switzerland

3.1   *The Eiger and Postcards by Emil Nolde*

The Orcs' relationship to Switzerland and the Alpine region is probably primarily indirect: on the one hand, through the works that inspired Tolkien, and on the other hand, possibly through trigger experiences that reminded

---

187   Where the Huns conquered large areas during Attila's Italian campaign; however, the Goths only settled there permanently after the Huns invaded.

188   Below, pp. 186 ff.

189   See for example "William Morris," The William Morris Society, https://williammor rissociety.org/about-william-morris.

Tolkien of the stories of MacDonald and Morris during his journey in Switzerland. However, there would be enough sources of inspiration for Orcs in Switzerland. The Eiger (Ogre) and the postcards of Emil Nolde have already been mentioned. As far as the Eiger is equated with an ogre, there is an obvious connection. Tolkien himself stated that the word *Orc* comes from the Old English word *orc*, as it can be found in *Beowulf*, and he translated it himself with the word "orgr."[190] There is also a mountain near Sion called Mont d'Orge or Montorge, where a connection with Orcs would not seem very farfetched either.[191] It would be a mountain of Orcs—or perhaps Minas Morgul, Gondor's fortress at the feet of the Mountains of Shadow, which is occupied by forces of Mordor during the War of the Ring.

3.2   Swiss Customs: *Ubersitz, Tschäggättä, and Fasnacht*

Also conceivable is an influence by a number of Swiss customs still practiced today in which the mountain inhabitants give themselves an orkish appearance. Examples are the *Ubersitz* in Meiringen, the *Tschäggättä* in the Lötschen Valley, and the Swiss *Fasnacht* (Carnival) in general.

At the Ubersitz, the inhabitants chase away the evil spirits in the week between Christmas and New Year's Eve with drums and cowbells to keep them away from the villages.[192] Beat Kohler, a journalist for the *Jungfrau Zeitung* (a local newspaper), wrote in an article about one such event that the drummers from Meiringen had marched in "like the armies of Mordor."[193] This, of course, does not mean that Tolkien was inspired by this event. First, it is quite likely that the marchers, for their part, were inspired by *The Lord of the Rings* when they dressed up for the event; and second, Tolkien was not in Meiringen in the week between Christmas and New Year's Eve. Nevertheless, the journalist's analogy is perhaps no coincidence. Tolkien might very well have seen horrible masks when hiking through Switzerland, for example masks hung on the walls. The population probably practiced the customs more than today, and an English counterpart with similar masks is not known to me, so such masks were likely something special for Tolkien.

Perhaps an even more remarkable custom still practiced today is the Tschäggättä in the Lötschen Valley, where people dressed up as orkish mon-

---

190   "I originally took the word from Old English *orc* [*Beowulf* 112 *orc-nassand* the gloss *orc* = *pyrs* ('ogre'), *heldeofol* ('hell-devil')];" see Tolkien and Tolkien (1975), 9; see also *Letters of Tolkien*, no. 144.

191   Cf. below, pp. 153 ff.

192   For additional information see www.meiringen.ch.

193   Kohler (2012).

30 Lötschental mask, © Museum Rietberg Zurich, Photo: Rainer Wolfsberger.

sters chase after anyone they come across in a particularly sinister carnival tradition.[194] Tolkien hardly experienced this himself, since the Tschäggätta takes place in February, but as in Meiringen, he may have seen wall masks there as well (see Figure 30). Although it is not sure whether Tolkien was in the Lötschen Valley, there has been speculation that he may have returned to the Bernese Oberland via the Lötschen Pass at the end of his journey.[195] And if this is the case, he would also have passed through the Lötschen Valley. This hike past the south portal of the Lötschberg Tunnel, Moria, to the orkish masks in the Lötschental, and then over to the north portal of the tunnel would have been a very fitting autobiographical basis for *The Lord of the Rings*.

3.3 *Diseases Caused by Iodine Deficiency: Goiter and Cretinism*

Other possible autobiographical sources of inspiration were the iodine deficiency diseases goiter and cretinism, for they were widespread in the Valais in the nineteenth and the beginning of the twentieth centuries.[196] According to the English travel guide by Murray, goiter was so widespread in the Valais that hardly any woman was free from it, and those with no swelling were laughed at and called goose-necked.[197] More serious, however, was cretinism, since the disease leads to skeletal deformities and delayed mental development in adolescence. The travel guide described individuals with this disease—from today's point of view not at all correct—as "idiot[s] of the worst sort, deformed in body as well as mind."[198] The heads were disproportionately large, the limbs crippled, and the affected individuals could hardly ar-

---

[194]   Cf. www.loetschental.ch/de/kultur-/tschaeggaettae--fasnacht/brauchtum-9.

[195]   Lewis and Currie (2019), 194.

[196]   Murray (1886), lxxvi.

[197]   Ibid.

[198]   Murray (1886), lxxvii.

ticulate words nor do any work. Instead, the guide stated, they would spend their days as clamorous and importunate beggars, assailing strangers while basking in the sun.

Begging Swiss as an inspiration for the Orcs? Well, Switzerland was not always as wealthy as it is today. In any case, although speculative, it is quite possible that the Orcs were influenced to a certain degree by cretinism and goiter. Even though cretinism had become rare at the time of Tolkien's trip according to the guidebooks of Murray, the Valais was still known as a "pronounced goiter region."[199] In 1912, an academic even suspected an inherited lack of resistance in the people from the Valais;[200] and only since the 1920s has salt been enriched with iodine in Switzerland to counteract these deficiency symptoms.[201] Tolkien thus probably came into contact with sick people, who possibly also ran after him, begging and harassing. The flight from the Orcs would have an autobiographical element in the Valais on the other side of the Misty Mountains.

The guidebook of Murray then comes to a completely different topic, the prehistoric lake dwellings in the Swiss lakes, but more on this later.

3.4   Hans Christian Andersen's The Ice-Maiden

Tolkien would not be the first writer to take note of these diseases in the Valais. Another one is none less than Hans Christian Andersen in his fairy tale *The Ice-Maiden*. When its main character, the boy Rudy, arrives in the Valais for the first time, he meets strange people there, misshapen, pitiful creatures with yellow skin and dark, ugly outgrowths hanging down from their necks like sacks. Rudy already wonders if these are the people he would be living with in his new home, but this is not the case. In the further course of the story, Rudy is constantly pursued by the Ice-Maiden, for she wants to kiss him and take him to her ice palace on a mountaintop, which—warning, spoiler alert!—she finally succeeds in doing.[202]

Tolkien stated in a letter that he had often read Andersen's stories in his childhood, so probably this included *The Ice-Maiden*.[203] And even though he did not like Andersen much, he once compared Frodo to Andersen's ugly duckling.[204] Moreover, Andersen's *The Ice-Maiden* is set mainly in the

---

[199]   Wacker (1912), 495.

[200]   Ibid.

[201]   Germann (2017), 17.

[202]   Which means his death.

[203]   *Letters of Tolkien*, no. 234.

[204]   *Letters of Tolkien*, no. 180.

Bernese Oberland and the Valais, precisely the same area that inspired Tolkien in the creation of Middle-earth. So, it would almost be surprising if Tolkien did not know the story.

By the way, Andersen's *The Ice-Maiden* possibly loosely inspired the makers of Disney's *Frozen*, together with Andersen's more famous fairy tale *The Snow Queen*. For example, unlike the Snow Queen, the Ice-Maiden has her palace on a mountaintop, the Jungfrau. And the plot of Disney's *Frozen* reminded me a bit of the first ascent of the Jungfrau in 1811 and the year without summer, a volcanic winter, in 1816.

II.   Dubious Dwarves: An Unexpected Party

A possible connection between the Orcs and Switzerland is admittedly indirect and vague, and this also applies to other possible Swiss links to dark creatures and plot elements. Nevertheless, these connections seemed to me sufficiently remarkable to deserve mention here.

As already indicated, I came across a book during my research in which I immediately felt like I was in Middle-earth, the book *Berner Oberland in Sage und Geschichte (Bernese Oberland in Legend and History)* by Hermann Hartmann. Starting with a character reminiscent of Gandalf, there are legends in this book that tell of vanished golden cities, of dwarfs and dragons, and of dark creatures and ghostly processions. Alone, these legends are hardly sufficient to believe they were an inspiration to Tolkien. But combined, and since Tolkien was also inspired by the landscape in which the tales take place, they are nevertheless worth noting. Moreover, the book was published in 1910, exactly one year before Tolkien visited Switzerland.

"The Lords of the Red Valley," concerning the expelled Lords of Moria, is one of the book's legends, and another reminded me of the beginning of *The Hobbit*.[205] It tells of what is commonly known as the Wild Hunt or the Wild Army. In Hartmann's version of this folklore motif, this is a ghostly procession, which often roams through the valleys and over the heights of the Bernese Oberland on dark, stormy nights but does not harm anyone unless you stand in its way. Therefore, whoever encounters this procession stands aside and lets the whispering figures move on. And the doors to the stables and chalets are left open since these creatures often stop there.

Hartmann recounts a tale, according to which an alpine dairyman once heard strange voices as he slept in the hay on a gallery in the stable, and so he

---

[205]   Hartmann (1910), 35 f.; Aeby et al. (1865), LVIII ff.

cautiously crept to the food gap to look down. The night folk were in his hut, and the strange creatures had made themselves comfortable. Some sat around the sooty stove, where they had lit a blazing fire, while others untied Spiegel, the most beautiful cow in his barn, then slaughtered and roasted her, and ate her flesh with pleasure. The insolence annoyed the dairyman in his innermost being. He jumped up to intervene, but he reconsidered in time and remained silent.

However, at that very moment, one of the mysterious creatures turned its eye on him and offered the dairyman a bite of meat from his own property. The dairyman could not refuse and ate the piece without saying a word. After they had finished the meal, the night folk disappeared again, the fire went out, and the alpine dairyman, still paralyzed with fear and anger, crawled back to his camp.

When the dairyman descended into the stable the next morning to look after the cattle, he was startled to find Spiegel standing again at her usual place, greeting him with the typical morning greeting. Only something was strange: the cow was missing a piece of meat. On closer inspection, the dairyman realized it was exactly the piece he had eaten during the night.

Similar to this legend, dwarves make themselves comfortable in the surprised Bilbo's home and help themselves in his food chamber in the first chapter of *The Hobbit*. Although the Wild Army or Wild Hunt appears in many places in Europe's world of legends, Hartmann's version seemed special to me; elsewhere, the stories are more reminiscent of the Nazgûl or the Battle of Helm's Deep.

III. The Nazgûl and the Lords of Gafertschinken

Another legend in Hartmann's collection can be attributed to the folklore motif of the Wild Army or Wild Hunt—and probably corresponds more to the norm.[206] It tells of the Lords of Gafertschinken, former lords of the Simmental Valley, who allegedly keep the land in terror even today. When clouds gather threateningly on the mountains and the black snails appear on the hedges in the valleys below, when the Hauri (a mountain spirit) lets his wailing sounds resound through the valleys at dusk, then, whoever can, takes shelter under a safe roof. Even the cattle become restless and run like mad

---

206   Hartmann (1910), 36 f.; Gempeler-Schletti (1904), 340 ff.

towards the stables. "The Tschinggen Riders are coming," you hear people saying, according to Hartmann's account of 1910.[207]

At midnight, a horseman appears over the rocks in a fiery red coat and with a huge horn. Into that horn, he blows three times. Thereupon, a mighty screaming starts, shaking anyone who hears it to the core, the storm wind roars and blows down even the sturdiest fir trees, stones fly through the air, and a crash and rumble can be heard from within the rocks, a sound as terrible as the bloodiest battle raging. Then, a ghostly procession sets itself in motion, led by the red horseman with his glowing red eyes. Under the howling of the air, the eerie posse moves to the mountains' highest peak and finally stops at a place called Rosengarten, where a veritable hellish noise begins. The nocturnal horsemen strike the rocks with their spears and skewers, breaking out large blocks and throwing them with terrible force through the gullies down into the valley. When, during this dreadful roar, a flash of lightning suddenly illuminates the area, the many escorts of the horsemen can be seen here and there. Only when the morning moves into the valley does the gruesome procession start to disappear. By twilight, the last of the ghostly figures—a black horse and on it, fluttering high, a cloak of which it cannot be said whether it envelops a rider—finally disappears.

Is this a Nazgûl? In Tolkien's legendarium, the Nazgûl are former lords who fall under Sauron's power and, as spirits, ascend to be his highest servants. As black horsemen, they seek the One Ring for him. Invisible to normal eyes, Frodo and the other hobbits see only black cloaks on black horses, and the cries of the Nazgûl make their blood freeze.[208] Similarly, the riders of Gafertschinken are former lords who, as spirits riding black horses, spread fear and terror and shake people to the core with their cries. And at least at the end of the legend, the rider himself is invisible, like the Nazgûl; only a cloak on a black horse can be seen.

Apart from the Nazgûl, the legend is reminiscent of the Battle of Helm's Deep, which also takes place during a nocturnal thunderstorm. Tolkien wrote there:

> It was now past midnight. The sky was utterly dark, and the stillness of the heavy air foreboded storm. Suddenly the clouds were seared by a blinding flash. Branched lightning smote down upon the eastward hills. For a staring

---

[207] "Tschingg" is a pejorative term for an Italian; however, the term probably means *rock* or *ledge* here, see "Ruine Gaffer Tschinge," Wikipedia, https://de.wikipedia.org/wiki /Ruine_Gaffer_Tschinge.

[208] See for example *The Fellowship of the Ring*, Book 1, chaps. III and IV; *The Two Towers*, Book 3, chap. I.

moment the watchers on the walls saw all the space between them and the Dike lit with white light.[209]

And so, the defenders of Helm's Deep can briefly see the countless Orcs streaming toward their walls. In the legend, the riders' escorts are similarly shown to the observer in a flash of lightning. And the battle then also follows screams and trumpets and is over again in the morning.

Caution is certainly advised as Tolkien and the author of the tale of "The Lords of Gafterschinken" may have been inspired by similar sources. The folklore motif of the Wild Army or Wild Hunt is widespread in Europe, and the tale is probably, first and foremost, an example for why Wilhelm Grimm saw a connection between the Dietrich legend and the Wild Hunt. Furthermore, the Nazgûl are also somewhat reminiscent of the Bible's Horsemen of the Apocalypse, who, however, ride on horses of different colors. Nevertheless, it is worth noting that the legend appears in Hartmann's collection directly before the tale of "The Lords of the Red Valley," a story which does

31 These illustrations by Arthur Rackham are other possible sources of inspiration for the Nazgûl, and perhaps they can also be viewed as illustrating a bit the legend of the Lords of Gafterschinken. Left image: Wotan (Odin); right image: Valkyries; both from Richard Wagner's *The Rhinegold and the Valkyrie*, 1910.

---

[209]   *The Two Towers*, Book 3, chap. VII.

seem to have influenced Tolkien. And besides, the Horsemen of the Apocalypse could also be linked to Switzerland, for Byron once compared Staubbach Falls with the tail of the white horse on which Death rides in the apocalypse.[210] Staubbach Falls is the most famous waterfall in the Lauterbrunnen Valley, and so it may not be a coincidence that the Nazgûl are washed away by the river Bruinen in *The Lord of the Rings*. Since Tolkien was probably inspired by Byron's *Manfred*, such additional inspiration by Byron would come as no surprise.

IV. Grindelwald and *Beowulf*

It has also been suggested that the village of Grindelwald with the towering Eiger or Ogre may have reminded Tolkien of the epic poem *Beowulf*, in which there is a monster called Grendel.[211] *Beowulf*, in turn, probably influenced *The Hobbit*, for Grendel seems to have co-inspired Gollum, and there is also a theft of a cup from a dragon's cave and subsequent devastations by the dragon. When asked about this, however, Tolkien stated in 1938:

> *Beowulf* is among my most valued sources; though it was not consciously present to the mind in the process of writing, in which the episode of the theft arose naturally (and almost inevitably) from the circumstances. It is difficult to think of any other way of conducting the story at that point. I fancy the author of *Beowulf* would say much the same.[212]

In other words, Tolkien seems to have been, at most, unconsciously inspired by *Beowulf*. In another letter, he attributed a more significant role to the dragon Fafnir from the Nibelung saga.[213] This reference makes it all the more speculative to assume that an association of the place name Grindelwald with *Beowulf* led Tolkien to link his trip to Switzerland with this epic poem when writing *The Hobbit*.

Nevertheless, it might still be worth noting that Grindelwald's word part *grindel* is traced back to a Middle High German *grendel*, and Tolkien explicitly mentioned the place in his letter of 1967.[214] Moreover, Tolkien was a phi-

---

210   Moore (1830), 234.
211   Lewis (2013); Sears (2014).
212   *Letters of Tolkien*, no. 25.
213   *Letters of Tolkien*, no. 122.
214   *Letters of Tolkien*, no. 306.

lology professor who owned numerous books on the origin of place names[215] and who, as seen, also processed the village of Lauterbrunnen (Loudwater, Bruinen) and the Silberhorn (Silvertine, Celebdil) in Middle-earth. Perhaps, Tolkien simply could not remember the association or did not want to admit it. But at the latest, when he wrote *The Lord of the Rings,* he was probably consciously co-inspired by *Beowulf* for the Riders of Rohan.[216] Besides, Tolkien would not be the only famous writer inspired by the name Grindelwald as the Harry Potter character Gellert Grindelwald suggests. And yet, whether the name Grindelwald inspired Tolkien remains highly speculative.

32 View from the Männlichen towards Grindelwald, the Grosse Scheidegg and the Wetterhorn; in this direction Tolkien hiked to Meiringen.

---

[215]   See Cilli (2019).

[216]   See the entry for Grindelwald at www.ortsnamen.ch; Tolley (2007); Shippey (2003), 124 ff.

The Dead Marshes at the Totensee

From Grindelwald, Tolkien hiked to Meiringen, and from there probably passed trough the Aar Gorge before hiking up through a stone world to the Grimsel Pass. When Tolkien was there, nature and the mountain spirit still ruled. But soon after, humans took over and left their mark with reservoirs and power pylons. Nevertheless, it is still an imposing world. At the Grimsel Reservoir, a view opens up on the right side to the Mini-Karakorum of Switzerland with the Unteraar Glacier and two four-thousand-meter peaks (more than 13,123 feet), the *Finsteraarhorn* (lit. Gloomy Aarhorn) and the *Schreckhorn* (lit. Horn of Horrors)—mountains which, by their names alone, would fit into Middle-earth. But the path to the Grimsel Pass leads left up to the Totensee, the Lake of the Dead, and this lake is of particular interest here.

33 The bridge over the Aar on the way to the Grimsel Pass would also be a beautiful Bridge of Khazad-Dûm. Aquatint by Gabriel Lory the Younger and Johann Hürlimann, *Pont sur l'Aar au passage du Grimsel*, 1822, digitized by the Swiss National Library, GS-GUGE-LORY-C-31; to my knowledge, the bridge no longer exists in this form.

The hypothesis has been put forward that this lake may have inspired Tolkien's Dead Marshes.[217] Similar to the Dead Marshes, the Totensee got its name from a battle that happened there a long time ago. In 1211, the Valaisans drove the army of the Duke of Zähringen into the lake.[218] And history was to repeat itself, for there was another battle in the summer of 1799 at the same place. The French general Gudin had received Napoleon's order to conquer the pass, which the Austrians held.[219] The venture seemed impossible and the massacre of the French inevitable. But the innkeeper of Guttannen allegedly boasted that he knew how to prevent this massacre. When this was reported to Gudin, he sent for the innkeeper at once and forced him to lead a troop of French riflemen over the mountains behind the Austrians' line, a daring undertaking—but it succeeded. The French caught the Austrians completely unprepared. Exposed to the hail of French bullets, they panicked and tried to retreat, but mostly in vain. After the battle, the Lake of the Dead was again filled with corpses. The French had forced some of the Austrians into the icy lake while still alive, and they later disposed of the remaining bodies there because of the hard, rocky ground of the mountains—the horrors of war.[220]

Lake Totensee lies at an altitude of 7,087 feet (2,160 meters) in a barren landscape. At this altitude, the biological decomposition of the corpses probably took decades. And even if it is unlikely that Tolkien himself saw the Austrians' bodies in the lake 112 years later, the reports about it may well have inspired him for the Dead Marshes. It is true that Tolkien once stated that the Dead Marshes owe something to Northern France after the Battle of the Somme, this horrible battle of World War I, in which he had fought himself.[221] It is one of the bloodiest battles in world history with over a million dead—an unbelievable nightmare and hard to even imagine.[222] Two of the four members of Tolkien's Tea Club were among the victims; only one of his childhood friends survived.[223] Nevertheless, an influence by the Battle of the Somme does not necessarily rule out a co-influence by Lake Totensee: the

---

[217]   Frías Sánchez (2009), 11; User *Eowyn of Penns Woods* in a forum post of July 2, 2008, available at http://newboards.theonering.net.

[218]   See, e.g., B. Meyer, "Mutige Walliser und schlaue Berner," Nationalmuseum-Blog, https://blog.nationalmuseum.ch/2018/12/mutige-walliser-und-schlaue-berner.

[219]   Cf. Lohbauer (1838).

[220]   Lohbauer (1838), 36, 39.

[221]   *Letters of Tolkien*, no. 226.

[222]   On Tolkien's involvement see Garth (2003); Carpenter (1977), 88 ff.; *Letters of Tolkien*, nos. 5 and 165.

[223]   Carpenter (1977), 88 ff.

34 The view back from the Grimsel Pass: the stone wasteland has given way to a hydroelectric and motorbike wilderness. The reservoirs were all built after Tolkien's trip to Switzerland; they deprive the Aar of its former power.

corpses in the Battle of the Somme came from recent deaths, unlike in the case of Lake Totensee and the Dead Marshes, where the name and the preserved corpses tell the story of a battle that took place a long time ago.

Horrible stories—yes. It is always terrifying to see what human beings capable of, but this topic should not gain the upper hand here. So let us turn again to Tolkien's wonderful hike through the mountains, which he did when the world still seemed to be in order, in the *"annus mirabilis* of sunshine,"* as he wrote[224], when the shadow over Europe was only growing. To this place, he could retreat to in his thoughts in the dark times that followed, or so it seems.

A break at this point is certainly deserved, here on top of the Misty Mountain pass. It is also the divide between the Aar and the Rhône Valley. And so Tolkien and his companions are now leaving Arnor behind and looking down into Middle-earth's wild east, to Rhovanion—and Rohan.

---

[224]   *Letters of Tolkien*, no. 306.

Part 2: In the Valais
Rohan, Gondor, and Mordor

35 Sion, aquatint by Gabriel Lory the Younger entitled *Vue de Sion prise du côté du levant* (View of Sion taken from the east side), 1811, digitized by the Swiss National Library, GS-GUGE-125-62.

Tolkien's Way into the Valais

> We later crossed the Grimsell Pass down on to the dusty highway, beside the Rhone, on which horse diligences still plied: but not for us. We reached Brig on foot [...].[225] (J. R. R. Tolkien)

At the age of seventy-five, Tolkien described the first part of his journey through the Valais in detail and with quite some anecdotes. The route led him and his group from the Grimsel Pass down the Rhône Valley to Brig and then up to a "village at the foot of the Aletsch Glacier," where they spent a few nights in a "châlet inn."[226] According to Colin Brookes-Smith, this was the village of Belalp, and the châlet inn was probably the Hotel Belalp for lack of

36 Tolkien's long walk along the Rhône from the Grimsel Pass to Brig and then to Belalp. The map is based on: Bergfex OSM, © OpenStreetMap.org-Contributors, CC-BY-SA, see p. 286, no. 2.

---

225   *Letters of Tolkien*, no. 306.

226   Ibid.

37 View from Hotel Belalp towards the Aletsch Glacier; the glacier has retreated a long way but is still impressive.

alternatives, but unfortunately, its operator no longer has any registers from that year.[227] Since the Aletsch Glacier was then much larger than it is today, the hotel stood above the end of the Aletsch Glacier, which also fits Tolkien's description of the location "at the foot of the Aletsch Glacier." Apart from that, Tolkien's group would hardly have hiked all the way to Brig first if they had climbed to the Riederalp or Bettmeralp.

From Belalp, the path led them further through the Valais, but the exact route is not that clear. More than fifty years later, Tolkien himself explained that his memories of this part of the journey were less clear.[228] The rest of the trip as can be pieced together now is therefore based mainly on the explanations of Colin Brookes-Smith, who described the route in his memoirs based on a map from Dorothy Le Couteur. According to him, they went on from Belalp via the villages of Visp, Stalden, and St. Niklaus to Gruben in the Turtmann Valley, then over the Forcletta Pass into the Val d'Anniviers and to Grimentz, and finally over another pass into the Val d'Hérens and to Arolla, which served them as a base for the final part of their journey.[229] How-

---

227   Brookes-Smith (1982), 2; cf. Murray (1904), 258 ff., 262; inquiry by the author.

228   *Letters of Tolkien*, Nr. 306.

229   Brookes-Smith (1982), 2 f.; cf. Frías Sánchez (2009), 4; Morton and Hayes (2008), 71.

ever, unlike Colin Brookes-Smith, Tolkien also mentioned Zermatt, which calls into question Brookes-Smith's route description. Since Tolkien's signature is documented in the Bertol Hut near Arolla, the way Brookes-Smith described cannot be completely wrong, though.[230]

The easiest way to include Zermatt into Brookes-Smith's tour description would be a detour from St. Niklaus, and this is how I marked it on the maps.[231] However, it is possible that Tolkien's Swiss travel party split up, just like the Fellowship of the Ring did after crossing the Misty Mountains. For Tolkien—probably unlike other travelers—had not yet visited Zermatt and had not yet seen the Matterhorn. Tolkien could then have caught up with the

38 Tolkien's presumed route through the Valais, based on Colin Brookes-Smith's comments and Tolkien's signature in the Bertol Hut, possible variants dashed and dotted. The map is based on: Bergfex OSM, © OpenStreetMap.org-Contributors, CC-BY-SA, see p. 286, no. 2.

---

230   Lewis and Currie (2019), 166 f.

231   See Frías Sánchez (2009), 4; Murray (1904), 171 ff.

others, for example, by taking the train via Visp to Sion and from there to Arolla on foot, by carriage, or by horse. Apart from that, it is also conceivable that Tolkien hiked over glaciers and the Col d'Hérens to reach Zermatt only after his stay in Arolla or that he chose the opposite way from Zermatt to Arolla. Finally, it is also possible that Tolkien was never in Zermatt at all, for his memories of it could also refer to Arolla. In other words, the exact path cannot be determined with certainty at present. However, if additional signatures of the group participants are found in guestbooks or registers, this could change.

Although Tolkien only explicitly connected his Swiss journey with *The Hobbit*, the path through the Valais is more reminiscent of *The Lord of the Rings*: of Rohan, Minas Tirith, and Mordor, and of the plot in Books Three to Five. Looking at Tolkien's letters, there are perhaps two direct indications for this. First, he described a member of his hiking group as "one of the hobbits" when they were close to the Aletsch Glacier,[232] and several hobbits travel together only in *The Lord of the Rings*. Second, in a little-noticed letter, he hinted that the stony alpine wasteland had inspired him for scenes in and around Mordor.[233] These marginal hints are probably only the tip of the iceberg, though, but please see for yourself.

Since this second part of Tolkien's Swiss trip can be well connected to the journeys in *The Lord of the Rings*, I will systematically follow its plot. But before I set out on the tracks of Frodo, Sam, and Aragorn to Rohan, Minas Tirith, and Mordor, I would like to devote myself to Mirkwood, the great eastern forest that Bilbo and the dwarves cross in *The Hobbit*.

Mirkwood and the Wood-Elves

As a reminder: after crossing the Misty Mountains and a visit to Beorn, the skin-changer, Bilbo and the dwarves cross the great forest Mirkwood on their way to the Long Lake; but in the middle of the forest, they get off the path and overwhelmed by giant spiders, which wrap the dwarves with spider threads. Only Bilbo escapes capture, and he saves his companions with the

---

[232]   *Letters of Tolkien*, no. 306.

[233]   See *Letters of Tolkien*, no. 78; Tolkien was writing on *The Lord of the Rings* and had just crossed the pass of Cirith Ungol; see also *Letters of Tolkien*, nos. 72 and 140 ff.

help of the One Ring. A little later, the dwarves are captured again, this time by the Elvenking of the Woodland Realm, but once again, Bilbo frees them with the help of the Ring. The whole group then floats down the Forest River in barrels to the Long Lake.

The name and place *Mirkwood* was probably inspired in part by William Morris' novel *The House of the Wolfings*, which is set in a forest of the same name.[234] The Wolfings live there by a river near their blood relatives, the Elkings and the Bearings, who are reminiscent of the skin-changer Beorn. An invasion is imminent, the great Roman Empire stretches out its tentacles to the north, but the tribes beat back the advancing enemy with united forces. The story setting might be the Weser or the Elbe, and the historical background the Battle of the Teutoburg Forest (the so-called Varian Disaster) of around 9 AD. In this battle, Germanic tribes under Arminius ambushed and annihilated three Roman legions.[235] On the other hand, Morris also mentioned the Burgundians and Huns, which rather points to an event in late antiquity — the time of the last Roman advances across the Rhine and the time of the Nibelung saga and other legends. Ultimately, however, the novel is more fantasy than historical fiction, so these historical events should be seen as possible sources of inspiration rather than a precise historical background.

Although Tolkien probably chose the name Mirkwood because of Morris, the latter had not invented the term. In a letter to his son Michael, Tolkien himself pointed out that the word is of very ancient origin and weighted with legendary associations.[236] Mirkwood, he wrote, was probably the primitive Germanic name for the large mountainous forest regions that formed the southern barrier of the lands of Germanic expansion in ancient times.[237] And he added that in some traditions, the name also became used for the boundary between Goths and Huns.[238]

The large mountainous southern forest is the legendary Hercynian Forest, which, in ancient times, stretched from the Black Forest to the Bohemian-Bavarian forests and up to the Carpathian woods.[239] No giant spiders lived

---

[234]   Above, pp. 83 f.

[235]   Cf. P. Wright, "Place, Dates and Names in *The House of the Wolfings*," William Morris Archive, http://morrisedition.lib.uiowa.edu/houseofwolfingswright.html.

[236]   *Letters of Tolkien*, no. 289.

[237]   Ibid.

[238]   Ibid.

[239]   Cf. Woodburn Hyde (1918), 231; and the Gothic-Hunnish border of the Hervararar saga was, according to his son Christopher, in the Carpathian region, see Tolkien (1953), 142.

there—as far as we know—but other strange animals did if we believe Caesar's *Commentaries on the Gallic War*: a large stag with a single horn, large hornless goats with jointless legs, and aggressive wild bulls, only slightly smaller than elephants.[240] Pliny the Elder, a Roman philosopher and commander, also mentioned gigantic oaks and even a bird whose wings shone like fire in the night in his encyclopedic *Naturalis Historia (Natural History)*.[241] It is a mysterious world that the ancient authors tell us about, a world that aroused both fascination and horror among the inhabitants of the Mediterranean. The animals they mentioned could be the reindeer, the moose or European bison, the aurochs, and the barn owl, animals that—except for the barn owl—could not (or could no longer) be found in the Mediterranean.[242]

However, it is possible that Tolkien also found inspiration in Switzerland. Tolkien's sketches of the Elven palace could indicate this connection, for in these sketches, the palace is situated on a river with hills in the background.[243] Although these hills seem very abstract at first glance, the Tolkien researcher Denis Bridoux suggested that Tolkien might have been inspired for them in the upper Rhône Valley, where hills of a similar shape are found.[244] The hills in Goms are indeed somewhat reminiscent of Tolkien's drawing of the Elven palace. This would fit the plot in *The Hobbit* for Tolkien walked through the upper Rhône Valley after crossing the Misty Mountains on his way to the Matterhorn, a possible source of inspiration for the Lonely Mountain. Furthermore, Tolkien mentioned in his letter of 1967 that at least for the glissade down into the pine woods on the other side of the Misty Mountains, he was inspired by his Swiss journey.[245]

Apart from this, it is also conceivable that Tolkien found inspiration in Switzerland for the escape from the Elven palace. As he himself noted, the way from the Grimsel Pass to Brig was long, over thirty miles (fifty kilometers) if measured, and Tolkien's group covered the entire distance on foot. In his letter of 1967, Tolkien mentioned only horse "diligences" as an alternative, but there was perhaps another, far more adventurous one: rafts. In those days, the wood from felled trees was often tied together into rafts and trans-

---

[240] Caesar (ca. 50 v. Chr.), 25–28.

[241] Pliny the Elder (ca. 77 AD), Books 10.67 and 16.2.

[242] See for example Woodburn Hyde (1918), 234 ff.; Masterson (2018).

[243] *Artist & Illustrator*, 127; Tolkien had already drawn it in an earlier sketch (*Nargothrond*), see *Artist & Illustrator*, 60.

[244] Bridoux (2016), who shows in his presentation that these hills can also be found on other drawings, namely those of Nargothrond.

[245] *Letters of Tolkien*, no. 306.

ported down the waterways, sometimes with goods and passengers and usually manned.[246] On the Rhône, this rafting was still practiced at the time of Tolkien's journey between Oberwald and Brig, but it is not entirely clear whether rafts were used there, or whether the logs (and perhaps barrels) were just loosely drifted. Crewed rafting would have been quite spectacular there.[247] Of course, Tolkien could have been inspired for this episode in England or elsewhere. Although I am not quite sure how widespread rafting still was in England at that time, it is striking that this waterway follows the crossing of the Misty Mountains in both *The Hobbit* and *The Lord of the Rings*. And this fits extremely well with the rafting on the Rhône.

By the way, the Mirkwood of *The Hobbit*'s movie adaptation also has connections to Switzerland, perhaps clearer ones, but more about this later.[248]

39 Nineteenth century forestry rafting on the Rhône, here in the lower part of the Valais; detail from: Gabriel Lory the Younger, *Le Pont de St-Maurice* (The Bridge of St-Maurice), 1811, digitized by the Swiss National Library, GS-GUGE-125-50.

---

246   Walther (1997), 115; Dubler (2009).

247   See Walther (1997), 143 ff., 147 f., who, however, pointed out that there was a decline of this method at the time of Tolkien's Swiss trip; see also Dubler (2009).

248   Below, pp. 232 ff.

Rohan and the White Mountains

I. The Upper Rhône Valley as Rohan and the Weisshorn as the White Mountains

In Middle-earth, southwest of Mirkwood lies Rohan, the green plain inhabited by an equestrian tribe at the foot of the White Mountains. Rohan first of all recalls the Pannonian Plain, where riders from the east settled down repeatedly in historical times, and Tolkien once hinted at such an inspiration when he connected Minas Tirith with the Belgrade area.[249] From there, the Pannonian Plain lies in the northwest—like Rohan from Minas Tirith. Again, however, I suspect that Tolkien overlaid parts of the European map with his hiking adventure in Switzerland.[250] More precisely, I believe the upper Rhône Valley might have served as a source of inspiration for Rohan and the Weisshorn for the White Mountains (*Ered Nimrais*), the mountain range that lies south of Rohan and forms the border with Gondor.[251]

First, the word image indicates such an influence. While it speaks for itself in the case of Rohan—Rhône, the word *White Mountains* looks like a generic name at first. However, exactly translated, *Ered Nimrais* does not mean "White Mountains" but "Whitehorn Mountains," strengthening the Weisshorn hypothesis.[252] With its 14,780 feet (4,505 meters), this white mountain is one of the highest and most dominant Alpine peaks, and it was Tolkien's constant companion on his journey through the Valais. It rises particularly majestically from the Goms region above the green plain. And there, Tolkien not only spent a great deal of time, but he also walked constantly towards this mountain on his thirty-mile march from the Grimsel Pass to Brig. And from Belalp and Zermatt and on he way from St. Niklaus to Arolla, the Weisshorn can also be seen magnificiently. However, this mountain would then have

---

[249] www.tolkiensociety.org/wp-content/uploads/2015/11/transcribed-map.jpg.

[250] As well as with the worlds of Morris and the Anglo-Saxon Cotton world map, see https://thijsporck.com/tag/cotton-world-map.

[251] User18337238 at wattpad.com is perhaps the only one who has suggested this, see www.wattpad.com/555358038-guide-du-tour-tolkien-la-carte-de-jrr-tolkien-pour.

[252] Tolkien (1980), Index, according to which *Ered Nimrais* means "White-horn Mountains" (actually "White-horns Mountains").

40 The valley of the Rhône and the Weisshorn in the background; they are probable (but of course not exclusive) sources of inspiration for Rohan and the White Mountains. In this direction, Tolkien hiked for probably about two days to Brig. Photo: User Flöschen at wikivoyage shared, *The village of Ulrichen in Goms*, detail, slightly edited. CC-BY-SA 3.0.

given its name to the whole chain of the southern Alpine ridge in Middle-earth, which is, apart from its descriptive name, perhaps due to the mountain peak's omnipresence during Tolkien's trip.

However, Tolkien once mentioned that he derived the name *Rohan* from the older word *Rochand*, which he created from the Elvish word **rokkō*, meaning "swift horse for riding."[253] Moreover, Tolkien was familiar with the Breton House of Rohan; he liked the name of the noble family and saw that he could linguistically incorporate it into his world in a meaningful way; however, the Elvish horse-word he had created much earlier and without any influence from the House of Rohan.[254] These references may make a connection between Rohan and the Rhône seem somewhat doubtful, but it also does not preclude such a link, for as we can see, Tolkien liked to associate different words with each other.

The location of the upper Rhône Valley and the plot of *The Lord of the Rings*, aside from the name of the river, speak for an influence on Rohan. If

---

[253]   *Letters of Tolkien*, no. 297.

[254]   Ibid.

Tolkien autobiographically followed his path through Switzerland in *The Lord of the Rings*, Rohan should be located there. The upper Rhône Valley lies beyond the Bernese Oberland Alps, which inspired Tolkien's Misty Mountains, and the Lötschberg Tunnel, which probably inspired Tolkien for Moria, leads into this region. In addition, after his hike through the Upper Valais, Tolkien visited places that probably inspired him for Mordor and Minas Tirith, but more on this later.

Aragorn's view over the plain of Rohan to the White Mountains also recalls the perspective shown in Figure 40:

> [In the East,] the red rim of the sun rose over the shoulders of the dark land. Before them in the West the world lay still, formless and grey; but even as they looked, the shadows of night melted, the colours of the waking earth returned: green flowed over the wide meads of Rohan; the white mists shimmered in the water-vales; and far off to the left, thirty leagues or more, blue and purple stood the White Mountains, rising into peaks of jet, tipped with glimmering snows, flushed with the rose of morning.[255]

However, to see this, you have to get up early in summer.

If you look closely at Tolkien's letter to his son Michael, you may find some clues there, too, for he wrote: "We later crossed the Grimsell Pass down on to the dusty highway, beside the Rhône, on which horse 'diligences' still plied: but not for us. We reached Brig on foot [...]."[256] So not only did Tolkien remember the Rhône; he also associated it with horses in the same sentence. As early as 1911, it was already extraordinary for Tolkien that horse-drawn carriages were still in use there. The railroad only went as far as Brig, and local people in the Upper Valais could not afford cars at that time — those devilish machines of the rich with which, according to contemporary media reports, they ran over poor people and then made off.[257] Besides, the cars of that time probably did not cope well with the terrain and gravel roads in the Upper Valais, and they were prohibited in most of the Valais' side valleys.[258] Therefore, at least those better off must have still used horses as an individual means of transport: Tolkien's experience was perhaps similar to how I experienced it in Kyrgyzstan a few years ago. It is also noteworthy that in *The Lord of the Rings*, Aragorn, Legolas, and Gimli reach Rohan on foot, just as

---

[255]   *The Two Towers*, Book 3, chap. II.

[256]   *Letters of Tolkien*, no. 306.

[257]   See for example the article "Noch einmal die graubündnerische Automobilabstimmung" in *Briger Anzeiger*, March 25, 1911.

[258]   Siehe Recueil des Lois, Décrets et Arrêts du Canton du Valais de 1899 à 1902, 76 ff.

Tolkien himself got to Brig, on a long and dry path as they pursue the captors of Pippin and Merry.[259]

The Upper Valais did not inspire Rohan alone, of course. The inhabitants of Rohan, the Rohirrim, were primarily inspired by the Goths and Anglo-Saxons (and perhaps also a bit by the Lombards).[260] Their language is based on Old English (Anglo-Saxon), and the names are of Anglo-Saxon and Gothic origin — Tolkien learned both languages in school and later became a professor of Anglo-Saxon.[261] Conversely, Tolkien made it clear that — despite the name deriving from the Breton noble family — nothing in the history of Brittany would throw any light on the Riders of Rohan.[262]

According to the Roman historian Jordanes, who lived in late antiquity, the Goths came from the northern island of Scandza (probably Scandinavia) and settled north of the Black Sea after various intermediate stays. There, at the edge of the Eurasian steppe with its equestrian tribes, they themselves became riders (a process of *Verreiterung* in German), and thus they became the Riders of Rohan. After Attila's death — at the latest, but perhaps earlier — they settled in the Pannonian lowlands, the European Rohan, before they conquered Italy under Theodoric — the omnipresent Dietrich von Bern, who, it seems, has his fingers in the pie with all peoples and characters of Middle-earth. Apart from the Anglo-Saxons and the Goths, Tolkien may also have been inspired by Iron Age hill settlements, especially Celtic ones, such as those on the Malvern Hills,[263] and in general, like Morris, by historical sources on Germanic tribes and their royal halls.

In any case, the Rohirrim are not an eastern but a Germanic-Norse equestrian people. This is shown not only by their language and their names but also by their northern origin. In this respect, however, the settlement history of the Upper Valais shows remarkable parallels with Rohan. Alemanni, a Germanic tribe, migrated into the Upper Valais from the north from about 800 onwards — after having already crossed the Hercynian Forest earlier. There, they pushed back the existing Gallo-Roman — or Celtic — population, at least culturally; this is why the Upper Valais is German-speaking today, unlike the Lower Valais. You may say that a southward Germanic migration

---

259   *The Two Towers*, Book 3, chap. II; *Letters of Tolkien*, no. 306; see also Morton and Hayes (2008), 70, for a corresponding statement by Brookes-Smith.

260   See for example Shippey (2003), 16 ff., 140 ff.; *Letters of Tolkien*, no. 193.

261   For the language see for example *Letters of Tolkien*, nos. 144, 190, 193, and for the school no. 163; see also Carpenter (1977), 42 f.

262   *Letters of Tolkien*, no. 297.

263   Cf. Garth (2020), 89.

was the rule rather than the exception during the Migration Period—and, of course, you are right; this is particularly true for the Goths and Lombards. But Tolkien probably never experienced this as closely as he did in the Valais, where he hiked from the Germanic to the Latin world—from the Germanic *dale* (as in *Lauterbrunnnental*) to the Latin *valley* (as in *Valais*). Apart from this, it is also quite conceivable that, in the Upper Valais, Tolkien felt transported to William Morris' *The Roots of the Mountains*. For in this story, the Germanic tribes no longer live in the Mirkwood forest in present-day Germany as in the prequel *The House of the Wolfings*. Instead, after a southern migration, the tribes reside in valleys of the Alps or Carpathians; there, the main tribe had settled in an east-west valley.[264]

With his reference to horse diligences, Tolkien hinted that he might have felt able to look into the past a bit in the Upper Valais. Perhaps, he even believed that he could find something of these old Germanic tribes among the local population. The budding philologist might have noticed that the Upper Valais dialect preserved elements of Old High German that were lost in Standard German, and perhaps he even saw commonalities with Gothic and Anglo-Saxon.[265] Or he saw the image of the Georg Supersaxo, a local fifteenth century politician and rebel, on the altar wing of the Gothic pilgrimage church in Glis.[266] And maybe, even the tonality of the language may have served as a source of inspiration. According to Tolkien, the language of the Rohirrim was archaic and relatively untouched by Eldarin (an Elven language) since they were newcomers out of the North.[267] Compared to the language of modern "urbans," it was spoken with a slower tempo and more sonorous articulation.[268] While such a slower pace may be typical for the language of rural populations in general, it perfectly fits the melodic Upper Valais dialect, with which even *Üsserschwiizer* (Outer-Swiss)[269] have trouble.

II.   Brig as Edoras

If Rohan was partially inspired by the upper Rhône Valley, the question arises whether a source of inspiration for Edoras can also be found there. In

---

[264]   Cf. *Letters of Tolkien*, no. 226.

[265]   Moulton (1941), 9 ff.

[266]   Cf. Murray (1904), 131.

[267]   *Letters of Tolkien*, no. 144.

[268]   *Letters of Tolkien*, no. 193.

[269]   Valaisan term for the inhabitants of the rest of Switzerland.

The Lord of the Rings, Legolas gives us the following picture of Rohan's capital:

> I see a white stream that comes down from the snows. Where it issues from the shadow of the vale a green hill rises upon the east. A dike and mighty wall and thorny fence encircle it. Within there rise the roofs of houses; and in the midst, set upon a green terrace, there stands aloft a great hall of Men.[270]

The most obvious candidate for Edoras in the region would be Brig, the largest town in the Upper Valais. Although Tolkien did mention Brig in his letter, his description hardly suggests any inspiration at first glance, for he was not very enthusiastic about the noisy trams: "We reached Brig on foot, a mere memory of noise: then a network of trams that screeched on their rails for it seemed at least 20 hrs of the day."[271] The shock must have been great after weeks in the mountains and the idyll of the Goms region.

Nevertheless, apart from its relative size to the surrounding villages, there are indications that there is a connection between Edoras and Brig. An important one is the name Brig, for it is generally believed to come from the Celtic word *briga*, which means "hill" or "hill fortress"—a detail that certainly caught the philology professor's attention, who still remembered the name over fifty years later.[272] The potentially Celtic name *Brig* thus recalls the Celtic hill towns, the *oppida*, and, despite the Germanic origin of the Rohirrim, so does Edoras.

However, it is not the Brig of today that would have been the source of inspiration for Edoras but a historical Brig derived from the name. Today's place does not fit the description of Edoras much. Although the church district and the Stockalper Palace are slightly elevated, they are not located on a round hill. But with the Brigerberg, there is a more convincing place for a historical Brig that might be reminiscent of Edoras. And there are Iron Age finds there, too, including a fortification on a hilltop called *Burgspitz*.[273]

Another indication of an influence of Brig on Edoras can be seen in the name of the king of the Rohirrim who had the great hall built, for he was called Brego. While this could also be a coincidence since Jordanes told of a legendary king of the Goths named Berig, the resemblance between Brig and

---

[270]   *The Two Towers*, Book 3, chap. VI.

[271]   *Letters of Tolkien*, no. 306.

[272]   According to another view, it comes from the late gallic **brigwa*, see "Brig," orts-namen.ch, https://search.ortsnamen.ch/de/record/802006002.

[273]   Meyer (2015); for a hiking tour map see www.ecomuseum.ch/data/Ressources/37_1-Flyer_Rundweg_Brigerberg.pdf.

41 Brig with the Brigerberg (wooded valley hill on the lower left) as a possible source of inspiration for Edoras, and the Glishorn (on the right).

Brego is remarkable, and perhaps Tolkien even connected the city with the Gothic king.

Brig, of course, did not alone inspire Tolkien for Edoras, as the Germanic hall or the Anglo-Saxon name Edoras show. Tolkien was probably also inspired by Celtic oppida in general, and specifically by the Bronze and Iron Age structures on the Malvern Hills.[274] Nevertheless, a co-inspiration by Brig, especially by the meaning of its name and in view of its location in Middle-earth, seems to me quite convincing.

By the way, there are no longer any trams in Brig—so you are safe—but the region is much more populated than in Tolkien's time. To recognize Rohan and Edoras, you therefore need some imagination: in your mind, you have to get rid of all the newer settlements in the valley and think of a historical hill town on the Brigerberg hill.

III. Belalp as Dunharrow

After a noisy night in Brig, Tolkien and his companions climbed up to a village at the foot of the Great Aletsch Glacier (*Grosser Aletschgletscher*), where

---

[274]   Cf. Garth (2020), 89, who, however, does not suspect a connection.

they spent a few nights in a châlet inn.[275] According to Colin Brookes-Smith, this village was Belalp.[276]

1. Tolkien's Fight against Spiders and Other Memories

In the 1967 letter to his son Michael, Tolkien described some memories of this inn. To begin with, the beds imprinted themselves in his mind: they had slept under them rather than in them, he recalled, the *bett* (bed) being a shapeless bag. And he also remembered that he was going to confession in Latin. The liberation from sins had to be earned, it seems.

Three other memories from Belalp can potentially be put into the context of his novels. The first is about a fight against spiders, harvestman spiders to be more precise, and shows the child in the nineteen-year-old Tolkien. More than fifty years later, he still remembered how he and others of the travel party had taken care of their "friends" (the spiders) in the chalet inn. They dropped hot wax from a candle onto the spiders' fat bodies, which the servants disapproved. In *The Hobbit*, the spiders then turn the tables and make the dwarves similarly immovable by wrapping them with spider threads. Did Tolkien possibly have the episode from Belalp in mind when he wrote this passage?

These descriptions by the seventy-five-year-old Tolkien are, by the way, in a certain contrast to those by the sixty-three-year-old Tolkien, who, when asked about his relationship with spiders, said that he did not dislike spiders particularly, felt no urge to kill them, and usually rescued those he found in the bath.[277] Well, it was apparently not always like that.

2. The Beaver Game: Dams, Ents, and Saruman

In the letter to his son Michael, Tolkien further mentioned that he and his hiking companions had played the "beaver-game" at the chalet in Belalp, a game that had always fascinated him. It was a wonderful place for it, he said, with plenty of water coming down in rills and material for the dam in abundance. Soon they had dammed up a lovely little pond containing at least 200 gallons (about 900 liters) of water, but then hunger smote them, and a hobbit of the group — maybe Tolkien himself — called "lunch" and wrecked the dam with his *alpenstock* (hiking stick). Only then they noticed that they had

---

[275] *Letters of Tolkien*, no. 306.

[276] Brookes-Smith (1982), 2; cf. Frías Sánchez (2009), 4.

[277] See *Letters of Tolkien*, no. 163.

dammed up a rill that ran down to feed the tanks and butts behind the inn. Just at that moment, as the foaming water soared down in great quantity, an older woman came out with a bucket to fetch some water. At the sight of the flood roaring toward her, she dropped the buckets and fled calling on the saints—perhaps the reason for Tolkien's confession. After that, Tolkien and his companions behaved as inconspicuously as possible ("we lay more doggo than 'men of the moss-hags'") before finally presenting themselves dirty and sweetly innocent at lunch.

The episode recalls the Ents, who build a dam to flood Isengard, Saruman's fortress and domain.[278] You might be hesitant to assume such a connection at first, for Tolkien mentioned that the beaver-game had always fascinated him. However, by referring to a hobbit who destroyed the dam, he explicitly referred to his novels—and probably *The Lord of the Rings*—since he wrote of "one of the hobbits." In Isengard, Saruman is no less astonished by the masses of water than the good old woman in Belalp. And after that, the hobbits Merry and Pippin help themselves innocently to Saruman's pantry, perhaps similar to Tolkien and his hobbit companions in the châlet inn.

42 Old Swiss stone pines in the Aletschwald forest.

---

[278]   *The Two Towers*, Book 3, chap. IX; see also Garth (2020), 89, who is, however, careful.

43 Illustrations reminiscent of the Ents; by Arthur Rackham from Nathaneo Hawthorne's *A Wonder Book*, 1922 (left) and Vernon Jones' *Aesop's Fables*, 1912 (right).

If you are looking for Ents near Belalp, you will find them in the *Aletschwald* (Aletsch Forest) with its up to one thousand-year-old, branched Swiss stone pines (in German *Arven*, a quite Elvish-like word). According to the organization Pro Natura, the oldest trees in Switzerland are to be found in this forest.[279] However, there is no direct evidence that Tolkien was inspired by this forest.

One documented source of inspiration for the Ents is Shakespeare's *Macbeth*. In it, Macbeth, King of Scotland, receives the prophecy that he shall never be vanquished until Great Birnam wood should come to high Dunsinane hill; and this seemingly harmless prophecy is fulfilled when Macbeth learns that the approaching English had made their bows from the wood of this forest. Tolkien found this passage bitterly disappointing in his childhood and longed to devise a setting where the trees might really march to war.[280]

Did Tolkien perhaps find such a setting in the Upper Valais of 1911? At the time, many beautiful old trees were probably felled and carried away over the small streams and the Rhône; and the trees suffered additionally since

---

[279]   See "Naturschutzgebiet Aletschwald," Pro Natura, www.pronatura.ch/de/natur schutzgebiet-aletschwald.

[280]   *Letters of Tolkien*, no. 163; see also Carpenter (1977), 35.

there was an exceptional heat and a drought.[281] Even today, unfortunately, hardly any forest in Switzerland is allowed to be natural, but the Aletsch Forest at least was placed under protection in 1933.

Another likely source of inspiration are trees depicted by the aforementioned illustrator Arthur Rackham (Figure 43).

3.   The Mountain Path and the Stone Giants

In his 1967 letter, Tolkien mentioned yet another event: the only event from Belalp he explicitly referred to as a source of inspiration for *The Hobbit*, and the only event from his Swiss journey he mentioned in two letters.[282] One day, he recalled, he and his travel companions had set out on a long march up the Aletsch Glacier when he came near to perishing. They had guides, but either the heat of this summer was beyond their experience, or they did not much care, or they were simply late in starting. In any case, by noon they were strung out in file along a narrow track with a snow-slope on the right going up to the horizon and a plunge down into a ravine on the left. The summer of this extraordinarily hot year had melted away much snow, and, Tolkien later assumed, exposed stones and larger boulders that were usually covered in snow. As Tolkien and his companions made their way along the narrow track, many rocks and stones began to roll down the slope, gathering speed as they went until they—anything from the size of oranges to large footballs, and a few much larger—were whizzing across the path and plunged into the ravine. Suddenly, the group member just in front of Tolkien gave a squeak and jumped forward as a large boulder shot past between them, only about a foot in front of Tolkien's "unmanly knees."

As a reminder: in *The Hobbit*, Bilbo and the dwarves first try to cross the Misty Mountains but then encounter stone giants who hurl stones and boulders at them.[283] This is why they seek refuge in the cave, where they are found and captured by goblins. A similar situation occurs in *The Lord of the Rings*: when the companions attempts to cross the Misty Mountains, a blizzard forces them to turn around and choose the path through the Mines of Moria instead. The Aletsch Glacier is located just at the back of Eiger, Mönch, and

---

[281]   Kuonen (2003); see above, pp. 104 ff.; there had been a Federal Forest Law, though, since 1876, guided by the principle of sustainability, see www.admin.ch/gov/de/start/dokumentation/medienmitteilungen.msg-id-8245.html.

[282]   So explicitly in *Letters of Tolkien*, nos. 306 and 232.

[283]   *The Hobbit*, chap. IV.

44 The Oberaletsch Glacier with the Nesthorn as a possible source of inspiration for the scenery of the mountain path in *The Hobbit*.

Jungfrau and thus at the back of the Mountains of Moria. And the Lötschberg Tunnel, which was under construction at the time, is also not far away.

It is not clear where exactly the ominous spot is that Tolkien is telling us about here. The most likely place to me is a passage near the Oberaletsch Hut (*Oberaletschhütte*), which in those days was visited from the Hotel Belalp as part of day excursions over the Oberaletsch Glacier.[284] The view on the path to the hut in the direction of the Nesthorn looks similar to Tolkien's painting *The Mountain Path*. And at this altitude, there might have been a snow slope even in summer. In this case, however, Tolkien would not have climbed up the Great Aletsch Glacier, but the Oberaletsch Glacier. Unfortunately, the operators of the Oberaletsch Hut no longer have any guest books from 1911, probably because the old hut was destroyed by an avalanche in 1925.[285] Thus, I could not find out for sure whether Tolkien went up to the hut, but it can be expected from someone who stayed a few days in Belalp at that time.

The localization of the event near the hut may be contradicted, at first glance, by the fact that Tolkien wrote in the other letter on the subject that they were "approaching the Aletsch" when the event occurred. However, Tolkien did mention a long march and a snow slope, so this incident must have happened further up in the mountains; it is possible to approach the Aletsch Glacier again and again from different sides.

It is also conceivable—Tolkien mentioned a long march—that the party crossed the tongue of the Great Aletsch Glacier and then walked on the right side of the glacier, on the so-called *Panoramaweg* (Panorama Trail), in the direction of the Märjelen Lake in order to return to Belalp over the glacier.[286] The topography there, however, is much less similar to the landscape described by Tolkien and painted by him in *The Mountain Path*. Furthermore, I cannot imagine that there were snow-slopes there in 1911 after the preceding heat in July and August.[287] For snow-slopes, they would have needed to climb much further up the glacier near to the Konkordia Hut, a very long way, for which they would have had to set out from Belalp at night. But Tolkien's signature could not be found in the guestbook of that hut. Therefore—and based on Tolkien's painting—I would rather lean toward the path to the Oberaletsch Hut, or perhaps the path that led down to the glacier behind the Oberaletsch Hut.

---

[284] Murray (1904), 262.

[285] Inquiry by the author.

[286] See also Murray (1904), 260.

[287] See https://map.geo.admin.ch.

4.   The Thunder-Battle

In the other of the two letters, in which Tolkien explicitly referred to his trip to Switzerland, he finally mentioned that what he called the "thunder-battle" in *The Hobbit* was also based on an event that occurred during his Swiss adventure.[288] On a bad night, they had lost their way and slept in a cattle shed. Thus, probably autobiographically, he wrote in *The Hobbit*:

> You know how terrific a really big thunderstorm can be down in the land and in a river-valley; especially at times when two great thunderstorms meet and clash. More terrible still are thunder and lightning in the mountains at night, when storms come up from East and West and make war. The lightning splinters on the peaks, rocks shiver and great crashes split the air and go rolling and tumbling into every cave and hollow; and the darkness is filled with overwhelming noise and sudden light.[289]

The battle of the stone giants in *The Hobbit* takes place during this thunder-battle. Thus, the two events form a unity in the novel, but according to Tolkien's letters, they are based on two different incidents in Switzerland. There are also differences, of course: in *The Hobbit*, the group does not find refuge in a stable, but in a cave, where they are discovered and captured by goblins — probably inspired by George MacDonald's *The Princess and the Goblin*.

During Tolkien's trip to Switzerland, heavy thunderstorms occurred throughout the country, especially on August 21.[290] Where exactly Tolkien was at that time is not entirely clear, but perhaps already on his way from Zermatt to Arolla, where he climbed to the Bertol Hut on August 25.

5.   Blizzard in a Mountain Pass

In *The Lord of the Rings*, the Companions are prevented from crossing the Misty Mountains also by forces of nature. In the least, three of the obstacles they face might have been inspired by events in Tolkien's own Swiss journey.

First, fallen stones block the Companions' path as they attempt to reach the Redhorn Pass:

> The Company set out again, with good speed at first; but soon their way became steep and difficult. The twisting and climbing road had in many places

---

288   *Letters of Tolkien*, no. 232.

289   *The Hobbit*, chap. IV.

290   See for example *Gazette du Valais*, August 24 and 31, both p. 3; *Walliser Bote*, August 26, 1911, p. 2.

> almost disappeared, and was blocked with many fallen stones. [...] The narrow
> path now wound under a sheer wall of cliffs to the left, above which the grim
> flanks of Caradhras towered up invisible in the gloom; on the right was a gulf
> of darkness where the land fell suddenly into a deep ravine.[291]

In his Swiss travelogue, Colin Brookes-Smith mentions a similar episode in
which the hiking group had to overcome projecting rocks that required
"some agile footwork to get round it" when there was an "apparently bottomless valley" on the side of the path, and he recalled how they overtook an
elderly lady who shuddered and hesitated each time she came to encounter
this kind of situation.[292]

Second, in *The Lord of the Rings*, a heavy snowfall becomes a blinding
blizzard that forces the Companions to turn around:

> They went on. But before long the snow was falling fast, filling all the air, and
> swirling into Frodo's eyes. The dark bent shapes of Gandalf and Aragorn only
> a pace or two ahead could hardly be seen. [...] Gandalf halted. Snow was thick
> on his hood and shoulders; it was already ankle-deep about his boots.[293]

A snowstorm in Switzerland seems to have served as a source of inspiration
for this scene. Colin Brookes-Smith reports that they once came to the snow
line and into a blizzard while climbing a pass.[294] He particularly remembered
the signpost at the top for it had spectacular icicles and seemed to be there to
direct anyone who had lost sense of direction in the snowstorm. But much to
Colin Brookes-Smith's amazement, as they quickly descended into the next
valley, the group emerged from the snowfall into bright sunshine, and the
haunting was suddenly over. Or in Tolkien's words in *The Lord of the Rings*:
"The threat of snow lifted; the clouds began to break and the light grew
broader."

Brookes-Smith did not mention where this event occurred, but if I had to
guess, I would choose the *Col de Torrent*. First, Brookes-Smith called the
pass *col* in his memoirs, and the Col de Torrent is the only pass most likely
walked by Tolkien that has *col* in its name. Second, Brookes-Smith mentioned
that they descended into the *next valley* afterwards, which suggests a succes-
sion of passes and valleys. This would fit the series of passes with the Augstbord Pass, the Forcletta Pass, and the Col de Torrent. And third, the Col de

---

291   *The Fellowship of the Ring*, Book 2, chap. III.

292   Brookes-Smith (1982), 3; cf. Morton and Hayes (2008), 71.

293   *The Fellowship of the Ring*, Book 2, chap. III.

294   Brookes-Smith (1982), 3.

Torrent is 2,916 meters high, so it is likely that it snowed there in the period after August 20, 1911.

The third obstacle the Companions encounter is falling stones:

> Stones began to fall from the mountain-side, whistling over their heads, or crashing on the path beside them. Every now and again they heard a dull rumble, as a great boulder rolled down from hidden heights above.[295]

This third scene once again recalls the event that Tolkien himself described in the letter to his son Michael, which, according to Tolkien, happened near the Aletsch Glacier.[296] Thus, he seems to have used this terrifying experience in both *The Hobbit* and *The Lord of the Rings*.

We have partially moved away a bit from the Aletsch Glacier in this section, but mentioning this topic at this point seemed to me most appropriate after the similar events in *The Hobbit*. And at least in terms of location, the Aletsch Glacier fits very well with the mountain pass in *The Lord of the Rings* as it lies on the back side of the Jungfrau not far from the Lötschberg Tunnel and thus very close to Moria.

6. Belalp, the War Alp Dunharrow

Thus, Tolkien remembered many anecdotes from Belalp late in his life, but he did not say whether the place itself inspired him for a specific place in Middle-earth. Dunharrow, the Rohirrim's refuge situated on a mountain terrace, would probably fit best. The hamlets of Mürren and Wengen have already been mentioned as possible sources of inspiration for Dunharrow[297] — and this may well be true — but Belalp seems to fit even better for two reasons: First, the relative position of Belalp to Brig is comparable to that of Dunharrow to Edoras, and second, the name *Belalp* could mean "war alp." At least, Tolkien may have suspected that the word part **bel* comes from the Latin *bellum* and means war, especially since he was going to confession in Latin at this place — Caesar's *Commentarii de Bello Gallico* are not about the beautiful Gaul, but about the Gallic War. Belalp, like Dunharrow, would therefore be an alp to retreat to in times of war.

By the way, an Army of the Dead would also not be far. You find it in the *Beinhaus* (ossuary, lit. "bonehouse") of Naters, where skulls and bones of

---

295   *The Fellowship of the Ring*, Book 2, chap. III.

296   Above, pp. 118 ff.

297   See for example Garth (2020), 89; Scull and Hammond (2017b), 1278; Lewis (2013).

more than 30,000 deceased are waiting for the resurrection—on the Day of Judgment.[298]

45 Skulls in the ossuary of Naters. Photo: Gabrielle Merk, *Ossuary in Naters near Brig*, slightly edited, CC-BY-SA 4.0.

IV. Rohan Under Attack: Fires in the Valais in August 1911

While Tolkien was probably still in Belalp, a fight against an inhuman enemy began in the valley below: forest fires. Tolkien did not tell us about it himself, but the local newspapers in the Valais were full of news about it, and the fires must have had an impact on Tolkien's experience.

1. A Major Fire at the Gateway to the Valais

Already on August 1, the mountain Le Grammont near Bouveret on Lake Geneva began to burn. The *Briger Tagblatt*, a local newspaper, reported about it in its issue of August 9: "In a fir forest on the Grammont, a bonfire of August 1 started a forest fire that could not yet be extinguished. From Bouveret, the mountain with its enormous cloud of smoke appears like an active volcano." According to another local newspaper, the *Walliser Bote* (in

---

124

its issue of August 23), the fire was still not extinguished more than three weeks later; every night, you could see the flames. But then the incipient rain was said to have finally brought the fire to an end.[299] Even so, the fire had raged for almost a whole month.

During this time, Tolkien hiked from Interlaken through the Bernese Oberland, over the Grimsel Pass to Brig and Belalp, and then probably via Zermatt to Arolla. So, he was always at a distance from this great fire at the gateway to the Valais, yet this fire was always there.[300] Tolkien might have seen the cloud of smoke now and then, and since the fire was to his west, breathtaking, bloody sunsets probably accompanied his journey. Besides, it is also conceivable that this fire inspired the following passage in *The Lord of the Rings*:

> 'There is ever a fume above that valley [near Isengard] these days,' said Éomer: 'but I have never seen aught like this before. These are steams rather than smokes [perhaps because of the incipient rain]. Saruman is brewing some devilry to greet us. Maybe he is boiling the waters of Isen, and that is why the river runs dry.'[301]

2. Large Fires near Brig in Tolkien's Immediate Vicinity

Fires also broke out in Tolkien's immediate vicinity, probably just as he was in Belalp.[302] In the afternoon of August 15, "under the influence of an extremely warm August sun," the first bush fire occurred on the Brigerberg hill: "The fire, which found rich nourishment in the old and withered grass, extended over the 'Bodini' on the border to Termen, mostly over heath with few trees."[303] This fire in Edoras must have been clearly visible from Belalp, but according to the *Briger Anzeiger* it could be extinguished quickly.

However, the danger was not cleared. On August 17, at ten o'clock at night, a fire broke out at the Glishorn on the opposite side of Brig as seen from Belalp. The *Briger Anzeiger* of August 19 reported:

> In a short time, the flames seized the logs [piled up by woodworkers] and flickered up the rocks of the Glishorn. In Glis and Naters, the bells were rung

---

[299] *Gazette du Valais*, August 24, 1911.

[300] For the Gap of Rohan see below, pp. 135 ff.

[301] *The Two Towers*, Book 3, chap. VIII.

[302] On August 5, he was in Obersteinberg at the head of the Lauterbrunnen Valley, and then on August 25, he was in the Bertol Hut near Arolla; see above, p. XIV.

[303] *Briger Anzeiger*, August 16, 1911.

nonstop, and quickly several auxiliary columns were organized and dispatched. But this crew was far from sufficient. At the moment, the fire is spreading in all directions and offers a gruesome picture.

On August 23, the *Briger Anzeiger* then reported that the united teams of Glis, Naters, Brigerberg, and Brig had finally succeeded in taming the extensive fire of hundreds of hectares of forest after an uninterrupted battle of four days. For a while, it had looked as if the whole forest would have to fall victim to "the glowing breeze," but then the responsible persons blew to a renewed rush:

> Once again, the dull chimes of the old St. Jodern Bell in Naters and the Mother of God Bell in Glis sounded over the fields of the surrounding villages and mixed with the glaring sounds of the fire horn from the streets of Brig. On Sunday morning before daybreak—in Naters, the holy mass was read at 2 am—a massive attack on the western flank of the extensive hearth of fire was carried out. There, the villagers from Naters fought with their courageous priest at the head, the ones from Glis and Brigerberg led by their municipal councils, and the people from Brig under Captain Walpen, all in all, without the food column, almost 200 men.

And so, the expansion of the fire was stopped with trenches and dams.

While Tolkien was perhaps still in Belalp, or Dunharrow, dramatic events thus were taking place down in the valley in Edoras, and the *Briger Anzeiger* gives a vivid picture of it, with the dull chiming of the bells, the glaring fire horn, and the priest, the councilors, and the captain heroically marching into battle. Yes, it seems like Tolkien did experience something like a war, in which the Lords of Rohan, far from a central state, fought their invisible enemy together in self-help; unfortunately, there are no reports of English hobbits as helpers, though.

Tolkien certainly did not experience the entire fire from Belalp; perhaps, he was even already back in the valley when the fire broke out and experienced the fire horn and church bells at close range. However, especially from Belalp, the sea of flames on the Glishorn must have been a tremendous and eerie spectacle at night.

The fire horn is another distinctive mark of the Rohirrim. Perhaps Tolkien also believed in this respect that he could look back into the past a bit in the Upper Valais, into a time when the war units blew their horns as they rode into battle or when danger was approaching. Remarkably, even the well-known medievalist and Tolkien researcher Tom Shippey mentions Switzerland in this context. He recalls the Swiss central cantons, as they went near Marignano into battle against the overwhelming force of the French under the sound of their battle horns: the *bull* of Uri, the *cow* of Schwyz, and the *calf* of Unterwalden.[304] Something like that Tolkien must have indeed experienced in Switzerland.

3.　Other Major Fires and the Epidemic

Another major fire occurred near Sierre between August 14 and 20. Tolkien must have first seen the rising cloud of smoke from Belalp, but then also on the road via Visp to St. Niklaus and on the way from St. Niklaus to Arolla, where he climbed to the Bertol Hut on August 25. After the forest fire had seemed extinguished on August 18, the population was again startled from sleep by the gruesome sound of the bells on Saturday, August 19, at half-past two in the morning; for another mighty fire had flared up from the Val d'Anniviers side. This fire was, though, extinguished the very next day.[305]

Finally, I would like to mention a big fire in the Goms region between Ulrichen and Geschinen. Although this fire probably only occurred after Tolkien had passed by this place (between the Grimsel Pass and Brig), the reports give us yet another impressive picture of the drought, the life, and people in the Upper Valais in those days. The *Walliser Bote* stated in its August 23 issue:

> Even in the upper Goms, where otherwise life is most beautiful in summer, we must suffer heavily this year. There is an almost unbearable heat so that soon everything: meadows and gardens and fields and even the people are looking at you in a blood-red way. There was a prayer procession for rain, and since then, it burns down even hotter from the sky. [...]
>
> A few days ago, the news suddenly reached us that a fire had broken out in a forest between Ulrichen and Geschinen, and that when the wind blows, forests and villages all around are in great danger. Immediately, the telegraph played and the church bells howled, and from the whole of the Upper Goms, from Niederwald to Oberwald, the men and boys hurried to the scene of the fire on carriages and carts and wagons, by bicycle, and on foot, armed with saws and axes and shovels and hoes etc. Also, the prefect E. Seiler of Münster and the schoolmaster Mr. Schmid of Geschinen were not the last to help with words and deeds.

Again, the local celebrities were thus fighting on the front line as the bush fire raged. But by digging trenches and beating with fir branches, the hundreds of

---

[304]　Shippey (2003), 244.
[305]　*Walliser Bote*, August 23, 1911.

helpers were finally able to extinguish the fire. Suddenly, the women climbed up the steep and slippery slopes, loaded with many heavy buckets filled not with water but with a revitalizing drink. And so they celebrated like at the final feasts in Asterix.

In addition to these major fires, many smaller ones must have shaped Tolkien's Swiss adventure. According to the *Walliser Bote* of August 30, 1911, there were 213 fires recorded throughout Switzerland in the three preceding weeks, allegedly more than ever before. So it is possible that even as Tolkien hiked through the Goms region, there were small bush fires, and Tolkien may have used these impressions in *The Lord of the Rings*. For, when Aragorn, Legolas, and Gimli track the Uruk-hai and Orcs to Rohan, they see how they had bruised and blackened Rohan's sweet grass in passing, leaving an ugly slot.[306] But also apart from that, the drought is particularly evident in this part of the story: brown leaves and the dried-up spring of the river Isen are men-

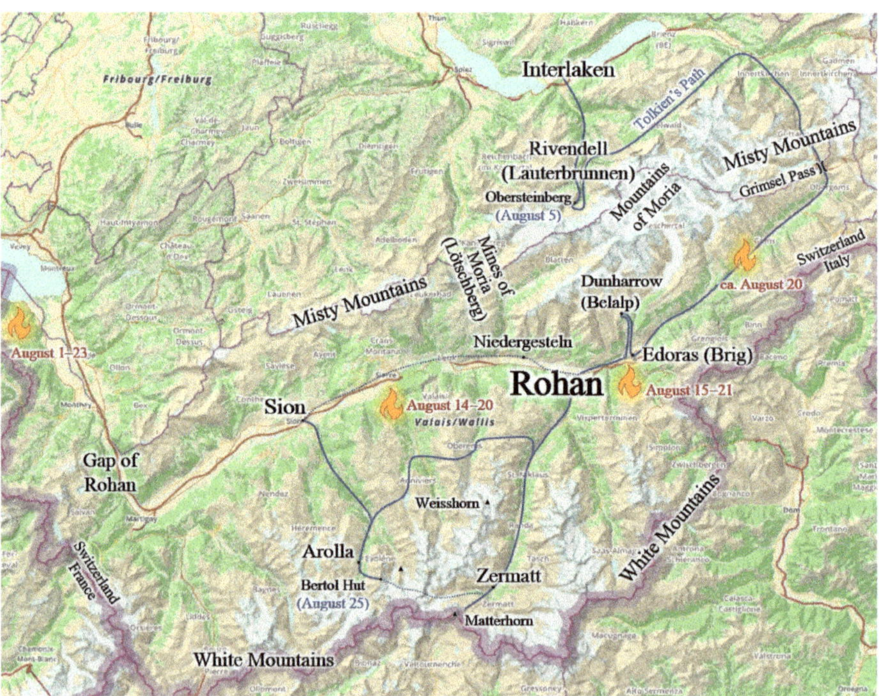

46 Rohan wavers, the Rhône Valley fires of August 1911, Tolkien's route and his known whereabouts (blue) and the dates of the fires (red). Map data: © OpenStreet Map.org-Contributors, see p. 286, no. 1.

---

306 *The Two Towers*, Book 3, chap. II.

tioned, likely autobiographical perceptions.[307] And Tolkien himself recalled the dryness of the year 1911 in the second sentence of the letter to his son Michael, before talking about his Swiss adventure in detail.[308]

Apart from the fires, there was yet another enemy on the advance: the foot-and-mouth disease. In its issue of August 19, the *Briger Anzeiger* mentioned that the disease had advanced from the south already to the Simplon, the main pass between Brig and Italy. Because of the disease, the pass was closed to "cattle traffic," and the Brig-Simplon-Zermatt Alpine hiking course was canceled. With the current coronavirus pandemic, this seems a little too familiar to us all now.

V.   Further Locations of Interest

From Belalp, Tolkien went on, I believe, via Visp and St. Niklaus to Zermatt. But before I follow him on this path, I would like to visit four more places, which, although it is not sure whether Tolkien was there, fit suspiciously well into Middle-earth.

1.   The Gestelnburg as Helm's Deep

The first of these places is the Gestelnburg castle ruin. Not far from Visp, down the Rhône Valley, a crevice opens up on the right side, giving the impression that a giant, long ago, cut through the rock here with a huge saw; and in front of the wall on the right side, there is a rocky outcrop, on which a medieval castle ruin sits. The site recalls Helm's Deep, the impregnable fortress of the Rohirrim, and all the more so if you consult Tolkien's sketch of the place.[309] As impregnable, the Gestelnburg castle was also considered in medieval times; and, where a cross now rises, reconstructions show that a round tower once stood, as in Tolkien's sketch of Helm's Deep. Furthermore, already the name of the castle of Helm's Deep, the Hornburg, almost suggests a source of inspiration in Switzerland, for it means "mountain castle" in German.[310] And the Gestelnburg is located in the area that probably influenced Rohan, not far from presumed sources of inspiration for Edoras and

---

[307]   *The Two Towers*, Book 3, chap. IV and V (dry leaves and ground), chap. VII (regarding the Isen), although this is probably due to the Ents damming the river.

[308]   *Letters of Tolkien*, no. 306.

[309]   *Artist & Illustrator*, 165.

[310]   However, there are places in Germany with that name.

Dunharrow. These are, I would say, quite some indications that the Gestelnburg was a source of inspiration for Helm's Deep.

The name *Gestelnburg*, by the way, means "castle-castle," a combination of the Latin *castelliōne* and the German *Burg*.[311] On the way up to the castle, wooden statues of the Barons of Turn, the castle's medieval lords, were erected a few years ago. The Barons of Turn were an important Valaisan noble family in the thirteenth century. They were under the direct authority of the Holy Roman Emperor (status of imperial immediacy) and thus enjoyed a high degree of independence. Astonishing, though, is the territory they ruled over. It consisted of a narrow stretch of land from the Gestelnburg Castle over the Lötschen Pass and the high mountains to Kandersteg and Frutigen in the Bernese Oberland. Like the dwarf kingdom of Moria, the territory thus extended from one side of the Lötschberg Tunnel to the other, only over the mountain, not under it; the castle in Niedergesteln was the only place where their dominion extended into the main valley of the Valais.[312]

While it is not clear whether Tolkien passed by the Gestelnburg Castle or had a postcard of the place, a detour from Visp is conceivable. And a visit at that time would have been extraordinary, for not only did the forest above

47 The Gestelnburg as a likely source of inspiration for Helm's Deep.

311   See the entry for Niedergesteln at www.ortsnamen.ch.

312   See, e. g., "Die von Turn," Niedergesteln community website, www.niedergesteln.ch /geschichte-portrait/dievonturn.php; "Herren von Turn," Wikipedia, https://de .wikipedia.org/wiki/Herren_von_Turn, with further references.

Brig burn further up the valley (August 17–21) but also the ones above Sierre down the valley (August 14–20). Especially at night, there must have been a gruesome spectacle: the flames and the sound of the bells that woke up the people of Brig and Sierre in the nights of August 19 and 20, mixed with the glaring sound of the fire horn, the war horn of the Rohirrim.[313] Maybe there was talk of the fire devil and the armies of the dead during these nights, for these also appear in many places in the Valaisan world of legends. Between Niedergesteln and Raron, for example, the spirits of Napoleon's armies were said to be making their mischief.[314] Perhaps, there were also lightning bolts, for the weather changed around August 20–21, and heavy thunderstorms occurred. That might be why the group passed by the Gestenburg Castle in the first place. The weather might have forced them to skip the Augstbordpass with its 5,800 feet (1,768 meters) of elevation difference and to pass through the main valley of the Valais instead.[315] But after the thunderstorm of August 21, the haunting was over again.

So, it seems the Battle of Helm's Deep contains a strong autobiographical note. It may be somewhat hypothetical, but in one form or another, Tolkien must have experienced these fires and thunderstorms on his way through the Valais, for on August 25, he was in the Bertol Hut near Arolla. And, in addition, a terrifying nightly thunderstorm experience in Switzerland also found its way into *The Hobbit*.[316]

Incidentally, the Lötschental Valley with its Tschäggättä custom is near Niedergesteln. Tschäggättä is the eerie carnival custom in which the inhabitants disguise themselves as orkish monsters and scare and pursue anybody they meet.[317]

2.   Leuk as Lothlórien

A few miles further down the Rhône Valley, on the right side and slightly elevated, lies the village of Leuk. So far, Leuk has been the site of five Middle-earth Festivals, and the town seems — probably not by chance — to be predes-

---

[313]   For the fires, see above, pp. 125 ff.

[314]   Gattlen (1948), 47, 67.

[315]   See for example *Gazette du Valais*, August 24 and 31, 1911, both p. 3; *Walliser Bote*, August 26, 1911, p. 2; see also the entry for Sitten at www.meteoschweiz.admin.ch /product/input/documents/annals/annalen-1911.pdf.

[316]   *Letters of Tolkien*, no. 232.

[317]   For the original legends see www.loetschental.ch/de/kultur-/tschaeggaettae--fas nacht/brauchtum-9.

tined for such events. Leuk is a perfect place since the Rhône Valley is still a bit more natural here than elsewhere, with the Pfynwald Forest covering the plain down the valley at the German-French language border. However, if Tolkien took the route assumed in this book, he only passed by here on his way back, if at all.

48 Did a river goddess or water spirit like Undine, depicted here, once live in the Dala stream near Leuk? Illustration by Arthur Rackham from Friedrich de la Motte Fouqué's *Undine*, 1909.

The name Leuk is of particular interest: while *leucos* is said to mean "luminous" or "white" in Old Celtic, *loucos* stands for "forest."[318] Linguistically, and in terms of its location behind the Misty Mountains only a short distance away from the Lötschberg Tunnel—that is, Moria—the name Leuk could therefore evoke memories of Lothlórien, the Golden Wood.[319]

Is Galadriel thus from Leuk? Well, that goes a bit far. Lothlórien was probably inspired by medieval visions of paradise, the English woods, and the Hall of the Volsungs built around a tree.[320] And Galadriel also shows parallels with figures from Arthurian legend such as the Lady of the Lake and Guinevere.[321] Nevertheless, Leuk's Celtic name fits a last Elven retreat at this place at the language border, and Galadriel does seem to have a connection to Switzerland, as shown.[322] Besides, Tolkien might have experienced glowing forests in Switzerland, as the foliage on the trees began to change color as early as August in 1911 due to the heat

---

318   See www.heinrich-tischner.de/22-sp/1sprach/kelt/akelt.htm.

319   However, regarding Tolkien's journey, Oberwald in the Obergoms would perhaps fit even better.

320   Cf. Garth (2020), 118 ff.; Shippey (2003), 247.

321   Snyder (2013), 137 f.

322   See above, pp. 58 ff.

and drought.[323] And the Lauterbrunnen Valley did inspire Rivendell, and a place in the upper Rhône Valley likely inspired the area of the Woodland Realm in Mirkwood. A connection between Lothlórien and Leuk or another location in the Valais would therefore not be surprising.

By the way, the name Leuk is indeed derived from the Celtic word for "luminous" or "white." A body of water, such as a white creek like the Dala, is proposed as the source of the name.[324] But in the past, a connection with a river goddess was also suggested, and this reminded me of the water spirit of Undine depicted in Figure 48.[325]

3.   The Rhine Falls as the Falls of Rauros

From Lóthlorien, the Fellowship of the Ring travels down the Silverlode and then down the Anduin past the Pillars of Argonath to the Falls of Rauros. For these waterfalls, I also suspect a source of inspiration in Switzerland. Not, however, in the Bernese Oberland or the Valais, but near Schaffhausen—the Rhine Falls.

I may be a bit biased in this matter, for I grew up only twelve kilometers from the Rhine Falls. Other waterfalls such as Niagara Falls between the U.S. and Canada, the Blue Nile Falls in Ethiopia, and Victoria Falls in Zambia may also have helped inspire the Falls of Rauros. In particular, René-Robert Cavelier's expeditions in North America to Niagara Falls and the Mississippi River should be considered, and those of David Livingstone in Africa to Victoria Falls and the sources of the Nile. Nevertheless, I believe that the Rhine Falls was the primary source of inspiration for the Falls of Rauros.

First of all, the Rhine is the right river, for it likely co-inspired the Anduin. Not only do the rivers have similar locations in their respective worlds (the Rhine next to the Black Forest and the Anduin next to Mirkwood), but the Rhine also stages the Nibelung saga, which most probably inspired Sméagol's seizure of the Ring on the banks of the Anduin. Although the Rhine was not the only source of inspiration for the Anduin—since the Danube, the Po, the Rhône, and the Nile probably also had an influence—the Rhine is probably the main one for the Anduin's northern half.

---

[323]   Erich Liechti, "Der Waldbrand an der Simmenfluh 1911," Wimmis comm. website, www.wimmis.ch/wp-content/uploads/2020/09/Simmenfluhbrand_1911.pdf; *Briger Anzeiger*, August 19, 1911, p. 2.

[324]   See the entry for "Leuk" at https://search.ortsnamen.ch.

[325]   Ibid.

Furthermore, the location of the Rhine Falls south of the Black Forest and north of the Alps also speaks in its favor, for the Falls of Rauros lies south of Mirkwood and north of the White Mountains.[326] The Roman Empire once extended into these northern regions, much like Gondor in Middle-earth.[327] And with the high rock dividing the Rhine Falls, there is a feature that recalls the mountain dividing the Falls of Rauros: the Tol Brandir.

For the gorge above the Falls of Rauros with its Argonath, the Pillars of Kings, I suspect that Tolkien's boat trip from Cologne to Frankfurt on his way to Switzerland was a significant source of inspiration. The passage through the Rhine Gorge in the Upper Middle Rhine Valley between Königswinter (Kingswinter) and Mainz evokes memories of the river gorge in *The Lord of the Rings*. Tolkien seems to have combined his memories of this boat trip with elements of the adventures of the Argonauts and Odysseus in Greek mythology, stories about Native Americans such as *The Last of the Mohicans*, and, perhaps, with accounts of adventurers, such as Livingstone.[328]

49 The Rhine Falls near Schaffhausen.

---

[326] Cf. for the connection between Mirkwood and the Schwarzwald above 104 ff. and for the connection between the White Mountains and the Alps 108 ff.

[327] Cf. for the connection between the Roman Empire and Gondor below 156 ff.

[328] For the latter, see Shippey (2003), 393.

50 James Duffield Harding, *The Rhine Falls near Schaffhausen*, before 1863, © Museum zu Allerheiligen Schaffhausen, deposit of the Sturzenegger-Stiftung, Photo: Jürg Fausch.

Whether Tolkien made a detour to the Rhine Falls after this boat trip on his way to Switzerland is not known, but it would definitely fit the plot in *The Lord of the Rings*.

4. The Gate to the Valais as the Gap of Rohan and Bex as Isengard

Following the Rhône further across the language border and through the French-speaking Lower Valais, you finally reach a gorge-like narrowing at Saint-Maurice before the valley opens up towards Lake Geneva. This narrow gateway is the place you would look for the Gap of Rohan in Switzerland.[329] If you do not want to cross a high mountain pass or a long tunnel, you have to pass through this narrow gap to enter the Valais.

---

[329] Since Tolkien to some degree overlaid the European map with his Swiss journey, strictly speaking there is a second place in Switzerland that may have somewhat inspired the Gap of Rohan, and that is Geneva. Geneva lies where the Alps and the Jura meet, and it is the place where Caesar prevented the Helvetians from leaving their lands in 58 BCE.

The search for a suitable Tower of Isengard (*Orthanc*) leads to Bex, where a round tower called *Tour de Duin* stands on a hill in the middle of the valley. It does not look very imposing, and it also does not look very similar to the Tower of Isengard. However, it was mentioned by Hans Christian Andersen in his fairy tale *The Ice-Maiden*. Like the guardian of the Canton of Valais, the tower stands there, Andersen wrote, surrounded by beautiful forests of chestnut and walnut trees. Tolkien read Andersen's fairy tales in his youth, and although he did not like them very much, perhaps it was through them that he became aware of this tower at the gateway to the Valais.[330]

The tower's history could also be a source of inspiration. In the fifteenth century, Jean Arambourg of Bex was imprisoned there; he had been found guilty of witchcraft but was later released by his guards, which incurred their feudal lord's wrath.[331] Similarly, after the Ents' uprising, Saruman was first confined in his tower but later released by his entish guards. And if you go there, it now really seems that the Ents have recaptured the area: beautiful old chestnut trees still stand there, apparently as they had in Andersen's time.[332] Unfortunately, the tower and its immediate surroundings are privately owned and cannot be visited.

The trial of Jean Arambourg of Bex is an example of the witch-hunts of the the early modern period (fifteenth to eighteenth century), a very dark chapter of European history, which was ingloriously opened in the Valais. Hundreds were tried there in the fifteenth century for an alleged pact with the devil, as Saruman is, and many were executed or tortured to death.[333] The only bright spot—if you can call it so—is that

51 The *Tour de Duin* near Bex.

---

[330]   Above, pp. 89 f.

[331]   See "Turm von Duin (Bex)," Swiss Castles, www.swisscastles.ch/Vaud/chateau/duins_d.html.

[332]   Ibid.

[333]   Cf. Modestin (2005).

the Valais trials were not specifically directed against women; witches and sorcerers—and even werewolves—were equally persecuted.[334] However, the Tower of Bex is not the only witcher tower in the Valais. In Sion, for example, there is a *Tour des Sorciers*, but the Tower of Bex certainly fits better to the Tower Orthanc of Isengard in terms of location and history.[335]

The name Isengard means "iron castle."[336] Tolkien obviously did not get it from Bex; both terms, *isen* and *gard*, are derived from Old English. However, the Old English form *isen* strikes the eye of any German-speaking Swiss since the very similar form *ise* is found in Swiss German. The philologist Tolkien probably noticed this, for example, when he passed the village of Isenfluh on his way to Lauterbrunnen. And perhaps he saw other similarities between Old English and Swiss dialects, which led him to link the language from the people of the Upper Valais with Anglo-Saxon. Another example could be the Swiss-German *Ross*, which is related to the English *horse* (Old English *hors* and proto-Western Germanic *hross*[337]), while the standard German *Pferd* has a Latin root.

Incidentally, near the Tower of Bex, there are salt mines that stretch for more than third miles underground,[338] and with a little imagination, you can find the production plant for the Uruk-hais there, the hybrids between Orcs and humans. While I doubt that Tolkien was inspired by these mines, it would not be a bad fit, for the enrichment of salt with iodine from the 1920s onward eliminated the diseases goiter and cretinism that might have co-inspired the Orcs. Perhaps, Saruman did not crossbreed Orcs with humans but gave them iodine to cure them. He might have been the good guy.

Finally, the *Grotte aux Fées* near Saint-Maurice is remarkable. Its name would be a suitable place for Elves, and with its underground lake, possibly for Gollum—not least since this cave lake already existed at the time of Tolkien's journey, unlike the large underground lake of St-Léonard. However, Tolkien once remarked that he was very displeased when his work was pulled toward the style and character of the *contes des fées*, the French fairy tales.[339] And the cave is also not very worth seeing, partly because the stalactites were all broken off and taken home as souvenirs by early tourists.

---

[334]   Modestin (2005), 405 f., 406.

[335]   The tower in Sion may be associated with the Witch King of Angmar, see Lewis and Currie (2019), 150.

[336]   *The Silmarillion*, Index of Names, entry for *Angrenost*.

[337]   See "horse," Wiktionary, https://en.wiktionary.org/wiki/horse#Etymology_1.

[338]   See www.seldesalpes.ch/de.

[339]   *Letters of Tolkien*, no. 210.

52 The salt mines of Bex; Photo: Wikimedia Commons user Souvaroff, *Mines de sel de Bex*, detail, slightly edited, CC-BY-SA 4.0.

Mordor

I.   Tolkien in Zermatt

Tolkien's path after Belalp is not as clear anymore, but I assume that it led via Visp first to Zermatt.[340] Tolkien himself described his memories more than fifty years later as follows:

> [After our stay near the Aletsch Glacier] we went on into Valais, and my memories are less clear; though I remember our arrival, bedraggled, one evening in Zermatt and the lorgnette stares of the French bourgeoises dames. We climbed with guides up to [a] high hut of the Alpine Club, roped (or I should have fallen into a snow-crevasse), and I remember the dazzling whiteness of the tumbled snow-desert between us and the black horn of the Matterhorn some miles away.[341]

---

340   Cf. above, pp. 101 ff.
341   *Letters of Tolkien*, no. 306.

Zermatt's hut that would fit Tolkien's description best is the old Monte Rosa Hut (Bétemps Hut). It was built in the year 1885 and, in the meantime, has given way to a somewhat controversial new construction.[342] The way to the hut still leads over the Gorner Glacier, but the latter is much smaller and thinner today; a dizzying ladder now leads down to the glacier. As always when crossing a glacier, I strongly recommend a guided tour. Tolkien himself admonished us to do so; he would have fallen into a snow-crevasse, he said, if he had not been roped. And when I myself explored the area in the summer of 2020, it was in the headlines that a Russian tourist involuntarily spent two nights in shorts in a crevasse near the hut; fortunately she survived. At the hut, you are rewarded with a breathtaking view over the tumbled snow-desert to the black cone of the Matterhorn.

Despite Tolkien's implicit localizing of this hut near Zermatt, it could be that Tolkien was describing the ascent to the Bertol Hut near Arolla since his presence there is documented by his signature. Also, the phrase "high hut" fits the Bertol Hut (10,863 feet; 3,311 meters) even better than the Monte Rosa Hut (9,455 feet; 2,882 meters), and from there, the Matterhorn can also be seen above a "tumbled snow-desert." Besides, Arolla is with regard to Tolkien's quote, unlike Zermatt, French-speaking, but this does not exclude French-speaking women in Zermatt, of course. While it is conceivable that the group (or at least Tolkien) reached the Bertol Hut from Zermatt via the

53 The Matterhorn above the Gorner Glacier; photo: Robert Fuchs, *Switzerland Ski Tour in the Monte Rosa Massif*, slightly edited, CC-BY 3.0.

---

342   See www.section-monte-rosa.ch/fr/cabanes/monte-rosa.

Col d'Hérens through the glacier world, Brookes-Smith described the ascent from Arolla.[343] Conversely, Brookes-Smith did not mention Zermatt in his route description, but I find it hard to believe that Tolkien later thought he had been in Zermatt if he had not. So even if he misplaced this event, I would still think that Tolkien was in Zermatt before or after Arolla.

II.   Mordor in the Valais

Does Mordor lie in the Valais? It would hardly be surprising, and one of Tolkien's letters to his son Christopher of August 1944 seems to indicate it.[344] The Allied Forces were just reconquering France from the Nazis, and Christopher was in military pilot training in South Africa. Meanwhile, Tolkien was in Oxford working on Mordor passages of *The Lord of the Rings*, which he sent to his son for review.[345] The South African desert landscape, which his son apparently did not like much, seemed to remind Tolkien of his trip to Switzerland, for he wrote:

> Much though I love and admire little lanes and hedges and rustling trees and the soft rolling contours of a rich champaign, the thing that stirs me most and comes nearest to heart's satisfaction for me is space, and I would be willing to barter barrenness for it; indeed I think I like barrenness itself, whenever I have seen it. My heart still lingers among the high stony wastes among the moraines and mountain-wreckage, silent in spite of the sound of thin chill water. Intellectually and aesthetically, of course; man cannot live on stone and sand, but I at any rate cannot live on bread alone; and if there was not bare rock and pathless sand and the unharvested sea, I should grow to hate all green things as a fungoid growth.[346]

Although Tolkien did not say it explicitly, he almost certainly referred to both Mordor and his Switzerland trip in this passage. It is unlikely that the "high stony wastes among the moraines and mountain-wreckage" lie in his native South Africa. Tolkien did not travel much, and only in one other letter did he mention moraines; it is his second Switzerland letter.[347] And before

---

[343]   Brookes-Smith (1982), 3; cf. Morton and Hayes (2008), 71.

[344]   *Letters of Tolkien*, no. 78.

[345]   *Letters of Tolkien*, no. 72.

[346]   *Letters of Tolkien*, no. 78.

[347]   *Letters of Tolkien*, no. 306; similarly, three years later he wrote to Sir Stanley Unwin, who was about to travel to Switzerland: *"How I long to see the snows and the great heights again!"* (*Letters of Tolkien*, no. 109).

and after this passage, he spoke of *The Lord of the Rings*: the Uruks, of whom there are many, especially—but not only—in Germany and Japan, and of the longing for the completion of the book. With the book, *The Lord of the Rings* of course, he was just about at the threshold of Mordor, on the pass of Cirith Ungol, where Frodo is captured by Uruks.[348] If Tolkien's heart, more than thirty years later, was still lingering in the high and stony alpine wasteland, it probably inspired Mordor and especially the mountain pass leading into it.

With the Monte Moro and the Monte Moro Pass, there are also place names in the Valais that may have co-inspired the name *Mordor*. According to Tolkien, Mordor means "Black Land" and the word part **mor* means "black" or "dark," just like *moro* in Italian.[349] This might seem somewhat questionable today, but the Italian word *moro* is simply derived either from the Latin word for black mulberry (*mōrus*) or from the name for the Moors (*Maurus*).[350] And Tolkien did vaguely suggest that the Moors co-inspired Mordor when he contrasted the Middle English word *Westernesse*—which gave the large island in the west of Middle-earth its name—with the Saracens living in the east.[351] The Monte Moro Pass could thus etymologically testify to a threat in these mountains that is similar to that in *The Lord of the Rings*, and some authors have indeed suggested that the Saracens may have settled in the valley beneath Monte Moro in the early Middle Ages.[352] This does not exclude other sources of inspiration for Mordor, such as the Old English word *morðor* (for "murder") or the character Mordred of the Arthurian legend and its mention in Dante's *Inferno*, but these words do not explain the meaning of the word that Tolkien had in mind, nor do they tell of a Saracen threat in the mountains.[353]

Blending creatures from fairy tales with elements of real peoples or ethnic groups perhaps really brings the creatures to life and creates credibility through detail.[354] However, from a present-day perspective, such blending is a delicate topic, especially in view of the pseudo-scientific racial theories prevalent in the early twentieth century. I do not think that Tolkien in any

---

348   Cf. *Letters of Tolkien*, nos. 70 and 72 and the fact that he writes in no. 78 that he is still in the same place as in spring.

349   *Letters of Tolkien*, nos. 144, 297.

350   Cf. "moro," Wiktionary, https://en.wiktionary.org/wiki/moro#Italian.

351   *Letters of Tolkien*, no. 276.

352   Below, pp. 187 ff.

353   Regarding *morðor* and Mordred cf. Garth (2020), 35, 184.

354   See John Howe's remark in the foreword regarding the suspension of disbelief through details.

way intended a judgmental division of people based on physical features or their origin. But the fact that Tolkien's *The Lord of the Rings* is strongly inspired by a Christian-European perspective of the Middle Ages, in which the inhabitants of Middle-earth are pressed from the east and south by foreign peoples who are not favorably portrayed, has understandably already led to criticism. And, moreover, certain comparisons are somewhat problematic with regard to stereotypes; Tolkien, for example, compared the Dwarves to the Jews and gave them a Semitic language.[355] However, it must be emphasized that Tolkien spoke out against racism and anti-Semitism more than once and at a time when this was by no means self-evident.[356] When he was asked by a German publisher in 1938 whether he was of "Aryan descent," for example, he was infuriated and described the "race-doctrine" in a letter to his English publisher as "wholly pernicious and unscientific."[357] And in an enclosed draft letter to the German publisher, he expressed regret that he was not aware of any Jewish ancestors (he concealed the fact that *The Hobbit* was, it seems, strongly influenced by a Zionist Jewish perspective of the recovery of the Temple Mount).[358] Moreover, in a later letter to his son Christopher in 1944, Tolkien expressed his displeasure at the treatment of people on account of their skin color.[359] And because of his Catholic faith, Tolkien himself suffered religious intolerance in England in his younger years; in a letter to his son Michael, he once described this experience of "persecution" as something that darkened his childhood.[360] Tolkien, in other words, was certainly a man who was full of empathy for all those who were persecuted because of their skin color or their faith; and the development of a friendship between Gimli and Legolas is certainly intended to encourage the casting aside of prejudices. All the different peoples or cultural groups simply fascinated and inspired Tolkien without any malicious ulterior motives. And the Orcs, of course, are not simply modeled on a people or cultural group; first and foremost, they are demons that slumber inside everyone of us.[361]

---

[355]   See e.g. *Letters of Tolkien*, no. 176; BBC interview with J.R.R. Tolkien first broadcast in January 1971, available under https://geocities.restorativland.org/Area51/Shire/5014/interview.html.

[356]   See e.g. *Letters of Tolkien*, no. 29, 30, 61, 71, 81.

[357]   *Letters of Tolkien*, no.

[358]   *Letters of Tolkien*, no. 30; cf. no. 176.

[359]   *Letters of Tolkien*, no. 61.

[360]   *Letters of Tolkien*, no. 306.

[361]   Cf. *Letters of Tolkien*, no. 81.

III. Mount Doom

Mount Doom is the destination of Frodo and Sam's journey. In its fire, they are to throw the One Ring to destroy it and with it the power of Sauron. Although there is no volcano in Switzerland, there is a quite good potential source of inspiration for Mount Doom: the Matterhorn.

1. The Matterhorn as Mount Doom

Some authors have already suggested that the Matterhorn might have served as a source of inspiration for the Lonely Mountain (Erebor).[362] This may be so, for the Matterhorn was, like the Erebor in *The Hobbit* and Mount Doom in *The Lord of the Rings*, Tolkien's destination on his journey through Switzerland—at least it seems so since Tolkien ends his travelogue with a glance at it.[363] However, the area around the Matterhorn lacks a long lake, and given it is located in a barren landscape, an inspiration for Mount Doom seems more probable. This does not exclude an influence on the Erebor, of course, but there is, I believe, a more convincing source of inspiration for the Lonely Mountain.[364]

Apart from the Matterhorn's location and destination function, Tolkien's own statements vaguely suggest a connection to Mount Doom. With "the tumbled snow-desert" and "the black horn some miles away," Tolkien named two elements that are characteristic of Mount Doom and its surroundings. Although Mount Doom is not surrounded by a snow desert, it is also a desert that looks much more passable from a distance than it actually is.[365] In *The Lord of the Rings*, Tolkien wrote from Sam's perspective, "As the light grew little he saw to his surprise that what from distance had seemed wide and featureless flats were in fact all broken and tumbled."[366] This is a typical glacier experience; Tolkien had to experience this first hand, for it was only thanks to his rope team that he did not fall into a snow-crevasse. Certainly, the Gorgoroth plain, with its impact holes, was also strongly influenced by

---

362   See for example Frías Sánchez (2009), 12; Howe (2018), 4.

363   *Letters of Tolkien*, no. 306.

364   Below, pp. 222 ff.

365   *Letters of Tolkien*, no. 306; *The Return of the King*, Book 6, chap. III: *"in the midst of a terrible desert."*

366   *The Return of the King*, Book 6, chap. III.

Tolkien's impressions from the Battle of the Somme,[367] but he probably mixed two frightening and life-threatening experiences and landscapes here.

From Zermatt, Tolkien may have climbed up to the Hörnli Hut, which sits on a crest quite high up on the Hörnli Ridge and serves as a starting point for ascents of the Matterhorn. The way up to the hut leads through a stony landscape and might have inspired Tolkien for Frodo and Sam's half ascent of Mount Doom. It would explain why they do not have to climb the summit of the volcano to throw the ring into its fire—for this would be what you would expect.

54 The Matterhorn from the path to the Hörnli Hut (tiny white spot on the quite level part of the ridge)—on Frodo and Sam's tracks up to Mount Doom?

2.   Edward Whymper's Report of the First Ascent

There has already been talk of a first ascent. Lord Byron's *Manfred* and Hans Christian Andersen's *The Ice-Maiden* were probably co-inspired by the first ascent of the Jungfrau in 1811. Through Byron's *Manfred*, this first ascent also found its way into *The Lord of the Rings* with the battle between Gandalf

---

367   *Letters of Tolkien*, no. 226.

and the Balrog on the summit of the Silvertine.[368] Could it be that the first ascent of the Matterhorn also influenced *The Lord of the Rings*?

The first ascent of the Matterhorn was carried out in 1865 by a rope team consisting of the Englishmen Edward Whymper, Reverend Charles Hudson, Lord Francis Douglas, and D. Robert Hadow, the renowned French mountaineer Michel Croz, and the Zermatt mountain guides Peter Taugwalder and his son, also called Peter Taugwalder. Tragedy struck on the descent. The inexperienced Hadow slipped and fell onto Michel Croz; together they plunged off the sheer-faced mountain, pulling Reverend Hudson and Lord Douglas, with them into the void.[369] Only Edward Whymper and the Taugwalders survived, for the rope connecting them to their falling companions ripped.[370] After the descent, Peter Taugwalder (the father) was accused of having cut the rope to save himself, his son, and Edward Whymper.[371] Whether this is true could never be clarified—for me, it would have been understandable if lives could have been saved that way.

Later, in 1880, Edward Whymper published the bestseller *The Ascent of the Matterhorn*, in which he reported in detail on the first climbing attempts and the first ascent. And he also wrote a travel guide for the Zermatt area, published in 1897. As an Oxford professor of language and literature and as Whymper's compatriot, Tolkien probably knew of the first of these two books, at least, and the following passage from *The Ascent of the Matterhorn* could indicate an inspiration for Mount Doom:

> [The readers] will know too that it was the last great Alpine peak which remained unscaled,—less on account of the difficulty of doing so, than from the terror inspired by its invincible appearance. There seemed to be a cordon drawn around it, up to which one might go, but no farther. Within that invisible line gins and effreets[372] were supposed to exist—the Wandering Jew[373] and the spirits of the damned. The superstitious natives in the surrounding valleys [...] spoke of a ruined city on its summit wherein the spirits dwelt; and if you laughed, they gravely shook their heads; told you to look yourself to see the

---

368 Above, pp. 55.

369 Whymper (1880), 285 ff.

370 Whymper (1880), 286.

371 See for example H. Kreitling, "Die dramatische Erstbesteigung des Matterhorns," *Welt*, last modified on July 12, 2015, www.welt.de/geschichte/article143832008/Die-dramatische-Erstbesteigung-des-Matterhorns.html.

372 Arab demon of the underworld.

373 This unfortunately does not seem to be the compassionate, supernatural figure we have seen before. But this figure, cursed for denying Christ, could potentially be an element that links the two maiar Sauron and Gandalf.

> castles and the walls, and warned you against a rash approach, lest the infuriate demons from their impregnable heights might hurl down vengeance for one's derision. Such were the traditions of the natives. Stronger minds felt the influence of the wonderful form, and men who ordinarily spoke or wrote like rational beings, when they came under its power seemed to quit their senses, and ranted, and rhapsodised, losing for a time all common forms of speech.[374]

A mountain that radiates terror and is inhabited by demons, a cordon that surrounds it and robs you of your senses when you cross it, castles and walls on the mountain flanks: all this fits Mount Doom. The loss of the senses in particular evokes memories of Frodo, who almost breaks in front of Mount Doom under the weight of the Ring.

It is also noteworthy that Whymper referred to a place on the way to the top as the Great Tower and mentioned it many times. The Great Tower, he said, is one of the most striking features of the ridge; it stands out like a turret at the angle of a castle, and behind it, a "battlemented wall" leads upward to the citadel.[375] During an attempt to climb the Matterhorn, Whymper was caught in a thunderstorm there at the Great Tower, a frightening experience that he described in much detail.[376] However, when they reached the summit, there was no demon city there, but they celebrated the myth, nevertheless, by rolling down stones to the south, where there was a group of climbers with whom Whymper had competed for the first ascent.[377] The act may be described as childishly high-spirited, stupid, arrogant, or grossly negligent. Here, the passage is of interest since the myth of the demon city collapses when the group reaches the summit—for in *The Lord of the Rings*, the myth of Sauron crumbles in a similar way. From Sam's perspective, it looks like this:

> A brief vision he had of swirling cloud, and in the midst of it towers and battlements, tall as hills, founded upon a mighty mountain-throne above immeasurable pits; great courts and dungeons, eyeless prisons sheer as cliffs, and gaping gates of steel and adamant: and then all passed. Towers fell and mountains slid; walls crumbled and melted, crashing down; vast pires of smoke and spouting steams went billowing up, up, until they toppled like an overwhelming wave, and its wild crest curled and came foaming down upon the land.[378]

---

[374]   Whymper (1880), 44.

[375]   Whymper (1880), 73 f.

[376]   Whymper (1880), 116 ff.

[377]   Whymper (1880), 281.

[378]   *The Return of the King*, Book 6, chap. III.

This passage fits extremely well with Whymper's account of the first ascent of the Matterhorn. Especially, it seems like there was also a kind of demon city with battlements and towers on Mount Doom.

3.   A. F. Mummerys: The Dead Marshes Part 2

Albert F. Mummery was another famous British climber. He and his companions were the first to reach the Matterhorn's summit over the Zmutt Ridge and later over the Furggen Ridge. He reported on this in his book *My Climbs in the Alps and the Caucasus* from 1895—the same year in which he disappeared in the Himalayas and was never seen again. Similar to Whymper, Mummery mentioned old legends according to which spirits populated the stone swept slopes of the Matterhorn. And not only that: according to his local mountain guide Alexander Burgener, there were not only ghosts in the Val Anzasca south of the Monte Moro Pass, there were also goblins.[379]

Of particular interest is his description of the ascent over the Furggen Ridge because when they reached the boggy ground under the Schwarzsee during the night, the following happened there:

> A few minutes later we were surrounded by the weird, unearthly flicker of innumerable will-o'-the-wisps. At every step they floated away on either hand, yet, seemingly, no sooner had we passed, than they crept up stealthily behind, dogging our footsteps with a cruel vindictiveness from which there appeared no hope of escape or flight.
>
> The men were horror-struck. Burgener gripped my arm and hoarsely whispered — "Sehen Sie, Herr, die todten Leute!"[380]
>
> We were marked out for the vengeance of the immortal gods. The fiends who haunt the crags of the Matterhorn were already gloating over their prey! Such was the purport of the agonised whispers of the men. I am fain to confess, the crawling, bluish flames, the utter silence, and the contagion of my companions' superstitious fear, thrilled me with instinctive horror.[381]

Mummery then realized, however, that in order to continue the ascension attempt, the "delights of a spiritualistic *séance*" had to be given up in favor of a matter-of-fact explanation:

---

[379]   Mummery (1895), 1 f., 13.

[380]   "Look, Sir, the dead people!"

[381]   Mummery (1895), 30 f.; Garth (2020), 89, pointed out this passage and a possible connection to the Dead Marshes.

> My efforts in this direction led Burgener and Venetz to the somewhat erroneous belief that every square yard of England, Scotland, and Wales is illuminated, nightly, by similar, but far more brilliant and nerve-shattering, displays. Despite the unfortunate way in which my German would give out just as I was making a really effective point, the men were evidently inclined to think that these "Geister" [ghosts or spirits] were, perhaps, impostors.[382]

But his companions did not let themselves be put off so quickly: "Ach lieber Herr [dear Sir], did you not see the wandering light on the Gorner glacier? There is no boggy ground there. That was a Geist." Their situation was serious enough, for to the best of their knowledge, it was a "well-known fact"— confirmed by all the ecclesiastical authorities of the valleys of Saas, Zermatt, and Anzasca—that anyone seeing a *Geist* was certain to be killed within twenty-four hours. In vain, Mummery pointed out to his companions that under these circumstances, there was no advantage in turning back, for either they were ghosts, in which case they would be killed anyway, or they were not, in which case they might as well continue. The men did admit the dilemma but did not find it a pure and unalloyed joy to climb a peak just to be chucked off it by mischievous *Geister*, a point to which even Mummery readily had to consent. But by pointing out to Burgener that the people of Zermatt could mock him as a Saas Valley man—if he were, in front of their eyes, grabbed by giant claws on his flight and taken to the underworld by black wings—Mummery was finally able to convince him and his companions to move on. Being the most skeptical of the party, he recalled, he was allotted the post of leader.

Thus, pursued by a ghost, let us call him Gollum, and flying Nazgûl, they went on, but they did not get far when two lights appeared again:

> "The other parties!" I exclaimed, thinking the men's fears would be somewhat allayed by company. But Burgener and Venetz had "Geister" on the brain, and vowed that these also were undoubted specimens of that genus. I urged them to force the pace and find out. "What!" cried they, "do you know so little of Geister as to attempt such a thing as that?" Burgener, after much persuasion, consented to jodel, a proceeding attended with very grave danger—"Geister" don't like being jodelled at—and only to be effected in doubtful and tremulous sort. To our delight, however, back came a cheery yell, that the men recognised as belonging to Peter Taugwalder.

The mood improved as a result, but on the remaining way to the summit and also on the descent, they were still haunted by ghosts from time to time. Only

---

[382]   Cf. Mummery (1895), 31 ff.

148

after Mummery, under pressure from the locals, threw a few francs into the glacier to settle their debt, did they finally make it back to Zermatt unharmed.

The boggy ground, the will-o'-the-wisp, the dead: together, these elements strongly recall the Dead Marshes in *The Lord of the Rings*. There, Sam observes the lights for some time before he asks Gollum about the nature of the lights. To this, Gollum replies, "The tricksy lights. Candles of corpses, yes, yes. Don't you heed them! Don't look! Don't follow them! Where's the master?"[383] The location near the Matterhorn, a likely source of inspiration for Mount Doom, speaks all the more for an influence on Tolkien. The ghost that haunts them, perhaps Gollum, and the big black wings—that take you to the underworld similar to the flying Nazgûl—are just an encore. Thus, when creating the Dead Marshes, Tolkien may have linked Mummery's account with stories from the Totensee on the Grimsel Pass and impressions from the Battle of the Somme.[384]

55 The Schwarzsee (Black Lake) with black mountains in the background—or the way through the Dead Marshes to Mordor?

---

383   *The Two Towers*, Book 4, chap. II.
384   See above, pp. 96 ff.

IV.   Arolla, the Bertol Hut, and the Pass into Mordor

According to Colin Brookes-Smith, Arolla seems to have been the last base on the journey.[385] Tolkien himself did not mention the place, but his presence in the Bertol Hut near Arolla is documented as August 25.[386] If Brookes-Smith is accurate, the group reached Arolla from St. Niklaus over three passes, probably the Augstbord Pass, the Forcletta Pass, and the Col de Torrent.[387] As seen, several forest fires and thunderstorms might have forced the group to choose another route. In any case, the sky was overcast, and the air was warm and probably stuffy: a Mordor atmosphere came up.[388]

So on August 25, Tolkien climbed from Arolla to the Bertol Hut to an altitude of 10,863 feet (3,311 meters). The weather was better than before, but there was also rain that day, at least in Sion. Colin Brookes-Smith reported that they had climbed over long scree slopes and finally over glaciers and rock, crossing crevasses connected by ropes to a high hut at an altitude of

56 The view up to the Bertol Hut; Tolkien climbed up here in 1911 over what was then a much larger glacier. It is a probable source of inspiration for the Cirith Ungol Pass to Mordor.

---

[385]   Cf. Brookes-Smith (1982), 3.

[386]   Above, p. XIV; Denis Bridoux was probably the first to suggest that the group climbed up to the Bertol Hut; he did so back in 2014.

[387]   Above, pp. 101 ff.

[388]   For the forest fires see above, pp. 124 ff.

11,000 feet.[389] This climb was a daring undertaking for a group of people with hardly any mountain experience, especially since the Bertol Glacier was much larger then than now.[390] It is unclear whether this is the same ascent that Tolkien described and (implicitly) located in Zermatt, but it seems likely.

This climb to the Bertol Hut brings back memories of the Cirith Ungol pass, the pass over which Frodo and Sam reach Mordor in *The Lord of the Rings*. It is a real crescendo: at first, the path leads comfortably along the valley on a gravel road before turning left and steeply up the mountain to a flatter place called *Plans de Bertol*: perhaps the Stairs of Cirith Ungol. At the top, the valley opens up, and you can see the hut sitting on a rocky peak

57 The adventurous ladders up to the Bertol Hut, where Tolkien signed the guest book—perhaps a source of inspiration for the hut to which Frodo is taken by Uruks.

above the scree slopes and the remains of the glacier: *all ways to Mordor are watched, yes, of course, they are.*

The view up to the hut resembles a sketch that Tolkien made of the pass.[391] If you look closely at the drawing, it seems as if the caves of the giant spider Shelob (Shelob's Lair) was inspired by the (at that time much bigger) Bertol Glacier, or at least by another glacier; for above her lair, medial moraines can be seen on the sketch. As Tolkien told us himself, he would have fallen into a snow-crevasse on the way up to the hut if he had not been roped. So it seems as if he processed this frightening experience, at least in part, with the giant spider's cave in *The Lord of the Rings*, especially since glaciers are sometimes compared to spiders and their webs.[392]

---

[389]   Brookes-Smith (1982), 3; cf. Morton and Hayes (2008), 71.

[390]   Morton and Hayes (2008), 71, who already suspected that the adventurous events here had served Tolkien as a source of inspiration for his later works.

[391]   See also *Artist & Illustrator*, 175.

[392]   See for example the book *Die Weisse Spinne (The White Spider)* by Heinrich Harrer.

From the waypoint Glacier de Bertol, the path leads up to the hut as a blue, alpine route over scree, snowfields, and finally dizzying ladders. The trail is classified as T5 on the Swiss Alpine Club (SAC) scale (see page 274) and, according to the SAC, requires mountain boots, safe terrain assessment and very good orientation skills, good alpine experience in high alpine terrain, as well as elementary knowledge of how to use an ice ax and rope. Crampons and poles are definitely highly recommended on the steep snowfields—and a guide if you are not used to this kind of alpine trail. Under the hut, the view opens up to the other side, a fantastic sight onto a glacier landscape like from another planet, and behind it, a few miles away, the black cone of the Matterhorn rises: perhaps the plain of Gorgoroth and Mount Doom.

58 The glacier world on the other side with the Matterhorn a few miles away as a possible source of inspiration for the plain of Mordor with Mount Doom.

Of the spectacular hut perched on a rocky outcrop, Colin Brookes-Smith recalled that it was sparsely furnished and yet had a toilet that was "highly" hygienic: a simple gap between two rocks with a drop of 1,000 feet (about 300 meters).[393] Even more dangerous than the ascent was the descent back to Arolla. According to Brookes-Smith, stones and even larger chunks had come loose due to the heat of the midday sun and "came on in leaps and bounds making an unpleasant buzzing sound from rapid rotation." The members of their group, especially Dorothy Le Couteur, barely escaped "these venomous and unwelcome visitors."[394] The incident is strongly reminiscent of the one Tolkien himself located in the region of the Aletsch Glac-

---

[393]   Brookes-Smith (1982), 3; Morton and Hayes (2008), 71.

[394]   Ibid.

ier.[395] It is, therefore, likely that either Tolkien or Colin Brookes-Smith was mistaken about the location.

V. Mont Miné as Mount Doom or Minas Morgul

In addition to the Matterhorn, there is surprisingly enough another candidate for Mount Doom in the valley behind the Bertol Hut: Mont Miné. Like Mount Doom and the Matterhorn, the sloping black cone of Mont Miné is located in the center of a mountain arena with only one easy access, and the shape looks very similar to Tolkien's sketch of the mountain—much more so actually than the Matterhorn.[396] The same applies to the description; in *The Lord of the Rings,* Tolkien reported a "huge mass of ash and slag and burned stone, out of which a sheer-sided cone was raised into the clouds."[397] However, it should be added that the glaciers were still enclosing the cone of Mont Miné at the time of Tolkien's trek. So, there was less black scree as a base, but rather an extensive snow desert with crevasses as the plain of Mordor around the mountain.

Tolkien must have first seen Mont Miné when he crossed the Col de Torrent from the Val d'Anniviers into the Val d'Hérens. Murray's guide described the view from the top of the pass as follows:

> The view from this point with the dark mountains to the West, bold in their forms, delicately marked with lacework of snow, and with long sweeping glaciers winding amongst them, is most striking and beautiful. The black Mont Miné separates the glaciers of Ferpècle and Mont Miné [...].[398]

By the way, Murray's travel guide reported that the Col de Torrent was on July 23, 1868, the scene of the murder of a Mr. Quensell, a respected lawyer from Hanover:

> The assassin was a well-known *mauvais sujet*, a Swiss Valaisan, who had once served in the Neapolitan army, and having escaped for an imprisonment for forgery, had taken to the hills. The murderer was ultimately captured; but while being transferred to Berne, in charge of two old gendarmes, he made a

---

395   Above, pp. 118 ff.

396   For the sketch see "J. R. R. Tolkien - Orodruin," Tolkien Gateway, http://tolkien gateway.net/wiki/File:J.R.R._Tolkien_-_Orodruin.jpg.

397   *The Return of the King*, Book 6, chap. III.

398   Murray (1904), 176.

59 The black cone of Mont Miné as another likely source of inspiration for Mount Doom (or Minas Morgul).

sudden dash and wholly escaped. [...] The gendarmes were imprisoned for their carelessness.[399]

A harsh regime was thus applied to the law enforcement officers, but what is more interesting here is that the mountains served as a place of refuge for all kinds of riffraff: so you never knew who was roaming around. And this seems to still be the case today. When we reached the secluded town Arolla, on what appeared to be the worst road in Switzerland, a local instructed us: *"Il n'y a pas de police ici* (There are no police here)." It was clear that we were on our own.

By the way, the Col de Torrent murderer is also reminiscent of *Alpöhi* (Alp-uncle or grandfather) in Johanna Spyri's Heidi novels. For, according to rumors, Alpöhi had served in the army of Naples for many years and then fled back into the Swiss mountains after killing a man in a brawl—good old grandpa.

Enough rambling. So, at least on the way to Arolla, Tolkien must have seen the black cone of Mont Miné, and maybe, later on, he got even closer to the mountain: from Les Haudères to the Alp Bricola.

Perhaps, there is yet another indication that Mont Miné inspired Tolkien. In *The Lord of the Rings*, the main gate to Mordor is guarded by the so-called

---

[399]   Ibid.

154

Teeth of Mordor, two towers sitting on either site of the Black Gate. Frodo and Sam cannot pass through that gate because of the orcs stationed there, and therefore, they choose the pass of Cirith Ungol. In the French-speaking Alps, mountains are often compared to teeth (*dents*) or other objects or people, such as needles (*aiguilles*) and guards (*guards*). Consequently, the access to Mont Miné—similar to the access to Mordor—is guarded by teeth: the Dents de Veisivi (Teeth of Veisivi) and the Dent Blanche (White Tooth). Tolkien's detour then led up to Arolla and the Bertol Hut, similar to Sam and Frodo's detour to the Pass of Cirith Ungol.

One might argue that the name *Mont Miné* instead recalls Minas Morgul, the sister city of Minas Tirith controlled by Sauron during the War of the

60 Tolkien's presumed path to Arolla (blue) with possible variants (dashed) as well as the likely sources of inspiration for places in Middle-earth (red). The map is based on: Bergfex OSM, © OpenStreetMap.org-Contributors, CC-BY-SA, see p. 286, no. 2.

Ring. This is possible, especially if Tolkien reached Zermatt from Les Haudères via the glaciers since on this route, Mont Miné stands like a guard in the way. Thus, like Frodo and Sam in *The Lord of the Rings*, Tolkien would have had to sneak past it to reach the Col d'Hérens and the other Mount Doom, the Matterhorn.

Nevertheless, I believe that Mont Miné served Tolkien, with its shape and location, primarily as a volcano model for Mount Doom, which, of course, does not exclude additional inspirations from the Matterhorn and real volcanoes. It thus seems that Tolkien was to a substantial extent inspired not by the very famous mountain, the Matterhorn, but by a less famous one, Mont Miné. This corresponds to the fact that the Silberhorn, not the Jungfrau, inspired the shape of Celebdil (Silvertine). And if you compare the two mountains, the black cone of Mont Miné does indeed look like the fictional counterpart, the antithesis, to the shining white Silberhorn.

Gondor

The lands of Rohan and Mordor were thus probably at least co-inspired by landscapes in Switzerland, which raises the question of whether this is also true for Gondor.

I.   The Roman Empire

In his letters, Tolkien himself gave some hints about his sources of inspiration for Gondor. A glance at them shows how strongly historical models inspired him: once he compared Gondor with Byzantium, once with the Holy Roman Empire (HRE), once with Ancient Egypt, and, in terms of religion, once even with the Hebrews.[400] Furthermore, he noted that Minas Tirith was located at about the latitude of Florence or Ravenna (but near Belgrade), and that the Mouths of Anduin and the ancient city of Pelargir were at about the latitude

---

[400]   *Letters of Tolkien*, no. 131 for Byzantium, no. 211 for the Egyptians and the Hebrews, and no. 294 for the HRE.

of ancient Troy.[401] And once, he compared the coastal city of Pelargir with Venice.[402]

The Byzantine Empire emerged directly from the Eastern Roman Empire and thus had a great imperial past; but like Gondor, it experienced a slow decline in the Middle Ages. The empire's borders gradually but steadily receded until they finally reached just outside the gates of Constantinople before the twenty-one-year-old Ottoman Sultan Mehmed II conquered the city in 1453. At that time, the western part of the empire, Western Rome, had not existed anymore for almost a thousand years, just as Arnor, the northwestern sister kingdom of Gondor, had not existed anymore for a long time when the War of the Ring broke out.[403] Moreover, both Ravenna and Belgrade were for some time in the early Middle Ages on the edge of the Byzantine Empire, just as Minas Tirith is on the edge of Gondor during the War of the Ring.

However, Ravenna was also the residence city of the late Western Roman emperors; and the Western Roman Empire—and not Byzantium—fought on the side of the Visigoths against the Huns in the Battle of the Catalaunian Plains—a battle that most probably was a source of inspiration for the decisive battle in *The Lord of the Rings*.[404] In other words, the late Western Roman Empire, too, makes a good candidate for Gondor. However, whether it is more Byzantium or the late Western Roman Empire is not that important, for at the time of the War of the Ring, Gondor is essentially a shadow of the great Roman Empire.

After the dissolution of the Western Roman Empire, various efforts were made to restore it, for example by the Ostrogoth King Theodoric[405], the Eastern Roman Emperor Justinian, the Lombard king Alboin, and the East Frankish King Otto I. The latter is usually considered the founder of the Holy Roman Empire (HRE), which from the tenth century onward encompassed—apart from present-day Germany and adjacent lands—at least during some periods, large parts of Italy.[406]

These later empires, too, are good candidates for Gondor. As discussed, both Alboin, the elf-friend, and Theodoric, the omnipresent Dietrich von Bern, almost certainly inspired Aragorn, the returned king of Gondor. And

---

[401]   *Letters of Tolkien*, no. 294; regarding Ravenna see www.tolkiensociety.org/wp-content/uploads/2015/11/transcribed-map.jpg; see also Snyder (2013), 39 ff.

[402]   Letter to Jennifer Paxman of July 28, 1955; Scull and Hammond (2017b), 580 f.

[403]   Cf. Snyder (2013), 41.

[404]   See below, pp. 169 ff.

[405]   Formally as the deputy of the Eastern Roman Emperor Zeno.

[406]   Charlemagne is sometimes also mentioned.

probably, so did Otto I, for Tolkien explicitly referred to the HRE and not just the Roman Empire in his letter. Besides, Arnor's location and empire division recall the Frankish Empire, which was divided into different parts in the ninth century after Charlemagne's death. And this supports a setting of the War of the Ring in the tenth century around the time of Otto I, who became first East Frankish King and later Holy Roman Emperor.

Unlike in European history, the restoration of the Roman Empire is successful in *The Lord of the Rings*. More precisely, Tolkien said, "The progress of the tale ends in what is far more like the re-establishment of an effective Holy Roman Empire with its seat in Rome than anything that would be devised by a 'Nordic'."[407] So, while Tolkien explicitly referred to the Holy Roman Empire, he did not want to see a Nordic-Germanic empire in it, understandably so in the context of the world wars.

It should be noted, though, that the historical HRE was not intended as a German nation-state. Otto I and his successors may well have aspired to an effective Holy Roman Empire based in Rome. Some evidence suggest this: the name of the empire, the papal coronation in Rome, the Byzantine insignia used, and the fact that Otto I married his son and heir to the throne Otto II to a Byzantine princess. Otto I was certainly not a German nationalist; he only became one in the writings of the historians of the nineteenth century. So, Tolkien did not necessarily deviate from history in this respect.

II.   The Romance Lower Valais

With this background in mind, the French-speaking Lower Valais is the only potential source of inspiration for Gondor in Switzerland. There, the Romance language still bears witness to the great Roman Empire, and the Romance-speaking area only slightly reaches over the southern ridge of the Alps, just as Gondor only slightly reaches over the White Mountains to Minas Tirith during the War of the Ring. Rohan, just like the Upper Valais, had already been Germanized by immigrants from the north. The linguistic situation in the Valais, therefore, fits very well with Rohan and Gondor in *The Lord of the Rings*.

Tolkien's route through the Bernese Oberland and the Valais also speaks for a Gondorian Lower Valais. Just as the protagonists in *The Lord of the Rings* reach Gondor last, Tolkien last reached the Lower Valais on his trip. On his way to Arolla, he crossed the language border either on a mountain

---

[407]   *Letters of Tolkien*, no. 294.

pass or in the Rhône Valley between Leuk and Sierre. For the language enthusiast Tolkien, this step across a language border must have been an extraordinary experience. And the fact that there is a perfect candidate for Minas Tirith in the Lower Valais also speaks for such an inspiration.[408]

In the Lower Valais, there is even a legend in which Egyptians with a Hebrew religion are found. According to this legend, the Theban legion, which had been raised by the Romans in Egypt, set up camp in Octodurum (today's Martigny) under the leadership of Mauritius.[409] All members of the legion were Christians and therefore refused to sacrifice to the Roman gods and to fight against Christian brothers in faith. Because of that, the Roman Emperor Maximian had, allegedly twice, a part of them killed before he finally gave the order to execute the entire legion; and the Egyptians are said to have submitted to this fate without offering any resistance. In the context at hand, I do not want to give too much importance to this dreadful legend, but I found the tragic picture of these Christian Egyptians and the Roman Emperor in the middle of the mountains in the Gallo-Roman Valais noteworthy given that Tolkien once compared Gondor to Ancient Egypt, and in terms of religion also with the Hebrews.

III. The Name Gondor

The name *Gondor* means "Stone-land" or "Stone-using people's land."[410] When Tolkien was almost eighty years old, he remembered how he had read in a little book at the age of about eight that nothing of the language of the peoples (who lived in Europe) before the Celtic and Germanic invaders was known, except perhaps that *ond* means "stone." And from this, Tolkien said, he had derived the word element **gon(o)* or **gond(o)*.[411]

Tolkien did not mention a connection to Switzerland, but in the Valais, on the south side of the Simplon Pass, there is a village with the same name—Gondo—and near Sion, there are two mountains called Mont Gond. Did Tolkien suspect that these names might derive from a pre-Indo-European word for *stone*?

The origin of the name Gondo is unclear, but, in 1906, the researcher Henri Jaccard believed that the term was related to the Rhaeto-Romanic word

---

408   Below, pp. 161 ff.

409   For the legend and its historicity and historical classification see Speidel (2003).

410   *Letters of Tolkien*, no. 324.

411   *Letters of Tolkien*, no. 324.

ganda, which, he said, meant "scree," "piles of stone," or "landslide."[412] Tolkien need not necessarily have known Jaccard's explanations; perhaps he himself conjectured that the place name was of pre-Indo-European origin and connected with the word *ond*. However, regardless of this, it seems doubtful that this connection between Gondor, Gondo, and "stone" is coincidental. Furthermore, the location of the places would be appropriate, because Gondo lies on the southern side of the Simplon and thus south of the White Mountains; and the two mountains named Mont Gond form (at least on the map) something like a gate to the Roman world, similar to the pillars of Argonath.

An influence by these place names may be speculative, but, as seen, Tolkien was inspired by other place names in Switzerland, too, such as the Silberhorn (for the Silvertine, Celebdil), Lauterbrunnen (for the river Loudwater, Bruinen), and possibly also the Rhône (for Rohan), the Weisshorn (for the White Mountains), and Monte Moro (for Mordor).

IV. Warning Beacons of Gondor on August 1st

A feature of Gondor is its warning beacons. With them, Gondor calls Rohan and other allies for help. When Pippin and Gandalf ride together on Shadowfax to Gondor at the beginning of Book Five, they see the beacons glowing on the hills. This method might first bring to mind the signal transmission on the Great Wall. However, it is also familiar to Swiss people, for even today, large bonfires are kindled on the mountains on August 1, the National Holiday.

There are different theories about the origin of these bonfires, but it is believed that they originate from the tradition of the so-called *Hochwachten* (high guards or high watch-men).[413] From the fifteenth century on, these high guards were placed on hills and mountains like lighthouses to transmit information and, especially, to mobilize villagers in case of war.[414] They were still in use in 1870 at the outbreak of the Franco-Prussian War, only about forty years before Tolkien visited Switzerland.[415]

The first of August has been celebrated as Swiss National Day since 1891, so Tolkien probably witnessed the celebrations during his trip in 1911. For

---

[412] Jaccard (1906), 193; see also the entry "Zwischbergen" at https://search.ortsna men.ch according to which this interpretation is rejected today.

[413] See, e.g., www.luzernerzeitung.ch/schweiz/1-august-hoehenfeuer-einst-bei-gefahr-heute-fuers-gemuet-ld.79275.

[414] Ibid.

[415] Ibid.

on Saturday, August 5, 1911, he signed the guestbook in the Obersteinberg mountain inn in the rearmost Lauterbrunnen Valley, and at that time, he must have been already on the road for a few days.[416] So maybe he had just arrived in Interlaken when he saw the bonfires above the lakes of Thun and Brienz. And if he saw them with his own eyes, it seems highly likely that they at least co-inspired the warning beacons of Gondor.

When Tolkien arrived in the Gondor area of the Valais, there were no more first of August bonfires, but there were plenty of forests ablaze.[417] I doubt that signal fires were ignited because of that—this would seem somewhat counterproductive—but the forest fires may have looked a bit like signal fires. Notably, the first of August bonfire on the Grammont had started a forest fire that burned for almost a whole month.[418]

V.   Sion as Minas Tirith

This brings us to Minas Tirith, the magnificent capital of Gondor and the scene of the decisive battle in *The Lord of the Rings*. If Gondor was inspired by Byzantium, then Constantinople is a natural candidate for Minas Tirith. However, apart from the Theodosian Walls and a few defensive battles against Arabs and Ottomans, Constantinople bears little resemblance to Gondor's capital. If you look for Constantinople in the literary world, you are much more likely to find it (along with London) in George Martin's *King's Landing*.

As mentioned above, Tolkien connected Minas Tirith with Florence, Ravenna, and Belgrade.[419] Florence probably served primarily as a reference point for Ravenna; but Tolkien may also have thought a bit of Dante, who was cast out of that city. Ravenna was government seat of the late Western Roman Empire around the time of the wars against the Huns as well as during the time of Theodoric the Great, the you-know-who.[420] Taking this into account, Gondor's former capital, Osgiliath, recalls Rome or, perhaps even more and due to its location, Mediolanum (Milan), which served as the gov-

---

416   Above, p. XIV.

417   Above, pp. 124 ff.

418   Above, pp. 124 f.

419   Above, pp. 156 ff.

420   Dietrich von Bern, of course; however, it was precisely during Attila's Italian campaign that the emperor was in Rome, see for example Maenchen-Helfen (1973), 137; for Theodoric see, for example, Heinzle (1999), 5; in Ravenna, there is also his mausoleum.

ernment seat for the Western Roman rulers directly before Ravenna. Tolkien's comparison of Pelargir with Venice fits this link; the Anduin seems to be the Rhine, Danube, and Po united. The seat of government was moved to Ravenna since the city was easier to defend; and Mediolanum was indeed conquered by Attila on his Italian campaign, just as the Orcs occupy Osgiliath during the War of the Ring.[421] Ravenna, therefore, quite obviously helped shape Minas Tirith.

With Belgrade, however, Tolkien mentioned another source of inspiration. The name *Belgrade* means "White City" and thus fits well to Minas Tirith with its white walls;[422] and the old German name *Griechisch Weißenburg* (Greek White Castle) assigns the city to Greek Byzantium, on which Gondor is based, among others. The location of Belgrade west of the so-called Iron Gates (access to Mordor) and southeast of the Pannonian Plain (the Plains of Rohan) also speaks for a source of inspiration for Minas Tirith. Furthermore, the siege of Belgrade in 1456 by the Ottoman Sultan Mehmed II—who had just conquered Constantinople—bears similarities to the decisive battle in *The Lord of the Rings*.[423] And according to Tolkien's son Christopher Tolkien, himself a researcher and university lecturer, the Battle of the Goths and Huns, from the poem "Hlöðskviða" of the *Hervarar saga ok Heiðreks*, was also set in this area.[424] Thus, Belgrade, along with Ravenna, was most probably a source of inspiration for Minas Tirith.

Ravenna and Belgrade do show some similarities to Minas Tirith in historical pictures,[425] especially Belgrade, which in one painting is depicted with three white walls and many towers on a hill (Figure 69, page 183). But today, the cities hardly show any features that could be reminiscent of Minas Tirith—Belgrade is said to have been destroyed more than forty times in its history—and the city hill is not nearly as high as the hill of Minas Tirith. If Tolkien traveled from Rohan to Gondor in the Valais, an additional autobiographical source of inspiration might have to be sought there, and there is only one city in the Lower Valais that seems suitable: Sion.[426]

---

[421]   Maenchen-Helfen (1973), 137 f.

[422]   See for example *The Fellowship of the Ring*, Book 2, chap. X, for the white walls; see also *The Return of the King*, Book 5, chap. I for a more detailed description; however, Rome is also called a white city, and Virgil's *Aeneid* comes to mind.

[423]   See below, pp. 182 ff.

[424]   Tolkien (1953), 142; above, pp. 104 ff.

[425]   Ravenna, however, only on the view of Hartmann Schedel and only somewhat.

[426]   Also Lewis and Currie (2019), 150 ff.; Minas Morgul can perhaps rather be found in Mont d'Orge, but there are paintings that support their hypothesis.

Sion, the capital of the Canton of Valais, is located in the French-speaking Lower Valais. The Romance language (Gondor) and its location next to the Germanized Upper Valais (Rohan) would fit Minas Tirith well; and Tolkien probably reached Sion after Arolla at the end of his trip to Switzerland, just as Minas Tirith is the destination of the protagonists in *The Lord of the Rings*. Moreover, the name Sion inevitably recalls the Temple Mount in Jerusalem, Mount Zion,[427] so that the place seems predestined for a decisive battle of humankind against dark powers—the Wachowskis send their greetings. And Tolkien did once compare the Numenóreans' religion (and thus the Gondorians') with that of the Hebrews. Above all, however, it is the city of Sion itself which, at least in its historical form, recalls Minas Tirith, as the paintings here and the one on the cover show. Like Minas Tirith, Sion is built around a hill (two to be precise) and was apparently, at least if you believe the painters, once entirely white. To reach the Valère Basilica on the lower of the two castle hills, still today, four gates must be passed, but there were probably more once, which fits the seven walls of Gondor's capital. And when you arrive at the top of the platform in front of the basilica, you can still imagine yourself in Minas Tirith, at least if you think Sion's newer districts and agglomeration away.

One important source of inspiration for Minas Tirith, I only mentioned once briefly, about a hundred pages above: Mount Purgatorio in Dante's *Divine Comedy*. On it, Dante experiences the seven levels of spiritual growth,

61 View from Sion's castle hill Tourbillon down the Rhône Valley with the Valère on the left and Mont d'Orge on the right; for an old perspective see the cover image.

---

[427]   For the actual etymology see Hamon (1996).

which is recalled by the seven walls of Minas Tirith. But Mount Purgatorio and Sion are not mutually exclusive as sources of inspiration for Minas Tirith. On the contrary, I think Tolkien understood his hiking journey through Switzerland to Sion somewhat as a pilgrimage to Zion, and this became—consciously or unconsciously—a central theme in both *The Hobbit* and *The Lord of the Rings*. *The Hobbit*, as indicated, follows a Zionist perspective of the recovery of the Temple Mount, and *The Lord of the Rings* was regarded by Tolkien—at least retrospectively—as a very Catholic work, as evidenced by parallels to Dante's Hell (Inferno) in Moria and the purification mountains of Minas Tirith and on Mount Doom. Tolkien thus seems to have overlaid his pilgrimage in Switzerland with Dante's *Divine Comedy* when creating *The Lord of the Rings*.

This does not mean that Tolkien intended to give emphasis to Dante's views. While he did consider Dante a superior poet, he regarded his pettiness a "sad blemish in places."[428] Indeed, the importance of compassion and mercy is perhaps the most central message of *The Lord of the Rings*, even if it is somewhat difficult to see in light of Gollum's fall into the fires of Mount Doom.[429] Tolkien expressed this as follows: "In this case the cause (not the 'hero') was triumphant, because by the exercise of pity, mercy, and forgiveness of injury, a situation was produced in which all was redressed and disaster averted."[430]

Let us turn back to Sion: It is even possible that the name Minas Tirith is related to Sion. Minas Tirith means Tower of Guard and could therefore come from the higher of the two castle hills of Sion, the Tourbillon. Although *tourbillon* in French means "whirl" or "whirlwind," I suspect that the philologist Tolkien did not consider this to be the word's probable origin. Now, I am not a linguist, but a separation into *tour-billon* seems conceivable to me, and *tour* would be intuitively translated as "tower." In *billon*, one might—from the layman's point of view who speaks a little French—first see a connection to wood or coins,[431] or to Gallic *bilia*, which denotes trees, especially large, sacred ones.[432] On the other hand, *billon* could also mean "guard" or "watch," for the French word for "to guard" is *veiller* and comes from the

---

[428]   *Letters of Tolkien*, no. 294.

[429]   *Letters of Tolkien*, no. 191, 192, and 246.

[430]   *Letters of Tolkien*, no. 192.

[431]   See "billon," Wiktionary, https://fr.wiktionary.org/wiki/billon.

[432]   See "bille," Wiktionary, https://fr.wiktionary.org/wiki/bille#fr.

Latin *vigilo*, and a sound shift from *v* to *b* is frequent.[433] *Tourbillon* would then mean "tower of guard"—just like Minas Tirith.

Linguists may disagree, but I noticed after forming the hypothesis—which was admittedly formed a bit from the end—that Tolkien translated Minas Tirith not only with "Tower of Guard" but also with "Tower of Vigilance;"[434] and this seems to support the hypothesis of a connection to the *Tourbillon*, even if you just look at the word picture. However, perhaps Tolkien was not so sure about the word origin himself and therefore planted the White Tree onto the platform of Minas Tirith. This may be somewhat speculative, but it could explain why Tolkien chose this somewhat surprising name for the city.

Moreover, Sion with its surrounding Mont Gonds is also a likely source of inspiration for Gondolin, the hidden city in Beleriand surrounded by mountains. Even Alan Lee's cover picture of the book published in 2018 bears some similarities with the historical paintings depicting Sion shown here and on the cover. And last but not least, the Sion of Celtic antiquity actually looked a lot like Edoras.

62 Sion as a likely source of inspiration for Minas Tirith and Gondolin, engraving entitled *Sitten* (Sion) by Kaspar Burkhardt from a painting by David Alois Schmid, 19th century (before 1860), digitized by the Swiss National Library, GS-GUGE-IS-ENRING-A-10, slightly edited.

---

433   See "veiller," Wiktionary, https://en.wiktionary.org/wiki/veiller.
434   *Letters of Tolkien*, no. 131.

The Battle of the Pelennor Fields

I.   In *The Lord of the Rings*

On the Pelennor Fields outside the gates of Minas Tirith, the decisive battle takes place in *The Lord of the Rings*. There, the peoples of Middle-earth face the overwhelming armies of Mordor. Sauron is supported by forces from the eastern and southern neighboring regions of Middle-earth, the lands of Rhûn, Harad, and Khand. Apart from trolls, this alliance also leads huge elephant-like creatures into battle, the mûmakil, who live in Harad's southern forest areas.

After an initial siege, Sauron's armies penetrate into the city's outer rings in the first phase of the battle. The situation seems hopeless, but at that very moment, the Riders of Rohan arrive, and with them, the real battle starts before the gates of Minas Tirith. There, Éowyn, disguised as a man, succeeds in killing the Witch-king of Angmar, and after that, believing her dead, her brother Éomer leads his horsemen in a daring attack against the enemy. But the attack soon falters due to the enemy's numerical superiority so that the horsemen have to entrench themselves on a hill by the river Anduin. As if the situation were not already desperate enough, ships of Mordor's ally, the Corsairs, appear on the Anduin. But it turns out to be Aragorn with his Rangers, Gimli, Legolas, and troops from South Gondor on the ships, and with the arrival of these reinforcements, the defenders finally gain the upper hand.

II.   Pyrrhos and Hannibal

In an annotated map of Middle-earth, Tolkien revealed a source of inspiration for the elephant-like Mûmakil: he wrote that they appear in the great battle outside Minas Tirith as they did in Italy under Pyrrhus.[435] Pyrrhus of Epirus was a Greek king and commander who crossed the sea from Greece to southern Italy around 280 BC and marched against Rome with twenty war elephants — which he had borrowed from Ptolemy II Philadelphus of Egypt.[436]

---

[435]   See www.tolkiensociety.org/wp-content/uploads/2015/11/transcribed-map.jpg.

[436]   Plutarch (ca. 100), 391 ff.; regarding the loan Hammond (1988), 406, 412, who interprets a passage of Justin, according to which 50 elephants were loaned.

63 *Hannibal traverse le Rhône* (Hannibal crosses the Rhône), Henri-Paul Motte, 1878.

After a costly victory against the Romans at Heraclea, he reached the gates of Rome with his elephants, but he did not dare to attack the city.[437] And after further battles against the Romans and the Carthaginians, he finally had to return to Greece, weakened by his proverbial Pyrrhic victories, while Rome rose to become a great power in Italy and the Mediterranean.

Pyrrhus' war elephants may be reminiscent of the Haradrim's Mûmakil — especially when enlarged to mammoths[438] — but the Carthaginian commander Hannibal Barca is an even more obvious source of inspiration for the advance of the Haradrim. Hannibal came, also with war elephants, through Spain and France, and across the Alps to the Italian peninsula, where he terrified Rome for years by moving almost freely around in Italy and defeating Rome's legions again and again. Like Pyrrhus, he almost reached the gates of Rome, *Hannibal ad portas*, but he, too, did not even try to conquer the city.

Hannibal's North African Carthaginians fit much better into the role of the Haradrim than Pyrrhus' Greeks, for like North Africa, Harad was filled

---

437   Plutarch (ca. 100), 401 ff.

438   Cf. *Letters of Tolkien*, no. 64, where Tolkien referred to the prehistoric size of the Mûmakil.

64 *Hannibals Übergang über die Alpen* (Hannibal's crossing of the Alps), colored woodcut by Heinrich Leutemann, 1866.

with deserts, and camels lived there, to name but two examples.[439] And with the crossing of the Alps, Hannibal's campaign also has a connection to Switzerland. Although it is still not completely clear today which route Hannibal chose when he crossed the Alps—and the most likely pass candidates lead directly from France to Italy—passes of the Valais were for a long time also considered. Besides, Colin Brookes-Smith mentioned in his memoirs that the boys enjoyed Tolkien's "quips and sayings" during the Swiss journey, and one of these was about Hannibal's crossing of the Alps (with one eye and a mackintosh).[440] So, we know that Tolkien remembered Hannibal while hiking through Switzerland, which makes a connection between the Swiss journey and the elephants outside Minas Tirith more probable.

The showdown between the Romans and Carthaginians took place in North Africa near Carthage in the Battle of Zama. The Romans benefited from the fact that the Numidian prince Massinissa changed sides—allegedly due to a broken promise of marriage—and arrived shortly before the battle with his Numidian cavalry to support the Romans. Similar to how Gondor was supported by reinforcements of the Riders of Rohan, the Roman Empire could thus benefit from cavalry reinforcements and win the battle. The interpretation by Henri-Paul Motte from 1890 (Figure 65) could also be used to visualize the Battle of the Pelennor Fields.

Were the Numidians right to choose the Roman side? Well, later, the Romans also conquered Numidia, of course.

---

439   See for example Tolkien's annotation at www.tolkiensociety.org/wp-content/up loads/2015/11/transcribed-map.jpg.

440   Brookes-Smith (1982), 2; cf. Morton and Hayes (2008), 71.

65 *La bataille de Zama* (The Battle of Zama), by Henri-Paul Motte, 1890.

III. The Huns

1.   The Battle of the Catalaunian Fields

Thus, the Battle of the Pelennor Fields may contain a Carthaginian element, but overall, Tolkien was more inspired by the events of late antiquity and the early Middle Ages.[441] While Gondor represents a remnant of the Roman Empire, the Rohirrim were especially inspired by the Goths (or another Germanic tribe) and the Orcs by the Huns.[442] In view of this, the epic Battle of the Catalaunian Fields (or Plains) seems to be an obvious source of inspiration for the decisive battle in *The Lord of the Rings*.[443]

In the middle of the fifth century, Rome trembled once again, this time before the Huns under their seemingly invincible leader Attila; defeat seemed tantamount to the apocalypse. After his ride through what is today southern Germany, Attila crossed the Rhine and stood with his countless horsemen in

---

[441]   Among other things, see above, pp. 83 ff., 156.

[442]   Cf. *Letters of Tolkien*, no. 226; see also 83 ff.

[443]   See also Shippey (2003), 18; Lee and Solopova (2015), 307 ff.

66 *The Huns at the Battle of Chalons* (the Battle of the Catalaunian Plains), by Alphonse de Neuville, 19ᵗʰ century.

the Gallic province of the Roman Empire. In the face of this, the Occident, embodied by Romans and Visigoths, came together to face the enemy united, at least that is what romantic historiography wanted.[444] The battle probably ended in a Pyrrhic victory for the Western Allies, which, however, did not prevent Attila from undertaking his Italian campaign the following year, against which Rome (or Ravenna) could not do much. Nevertheless, with the battle, the myth of the invincibility of the Huns around Attila fell.

The participants of the Battle of the Catalaunian Fields were essentially the same as those of the Battle of the Pelennor Fields. A Western Roman Gondor, supported by Visigothic Rohirrim, faced Hunnic Orcs and their subordinates. That the Huns in *The Lord of the Rings* additionally allied themselves with Hannibal's Carthaginians was simply an addition of terror. Apart from the participants, the death of the Visigoth king Theodoric I (Theodorid, not Theodoric the Great) also commemorates the death of Théoden in *The Lord of the Rings*.[445] According to Jordanes, Theodoric was thrown from his horse and trampled to death by his men, while Théoden is crushed by his horse after falling from it. Like Théoden, he had reached a proud age, sixty, and was then carried from the field by his knights with lamentation and song.[446]

Tolkien himself mentioned Attila in a letter to his son Christopher after the latter had pointed out in a lecture that many Germanic tribes had fought under Attila and that even the name Attila seems to be of Gothic origin and

---

[444]   Cf. Jordanes (ca. 550), nos. 191 ff.

[445]   Cf. Lee and Solopova (2015), 309; Shippey (2003), 18; Jordanes (ca. 550), no. 209.

[446]   Jordanes (ca. 550), nos. 209 and 214; *The Return of the King*, Book 5, chap. VI and Book 6, chap. VI.

means as much as "little father" (*atta*, *attila*).[447] Referring to this, Tolkien wrote to him:

> I suddenly realized that I am a pure philologist. I like history, and am moved by it, but its finest moments for me are those in which it throws light on words and names! Several people (and I agree) spoke to me of the an with which you made the beady-eyed Attila on his couch almost vividly present. Yet oddly, I find the thing that really thrills my nerves is the one you mentioned casually: *atta, attila*. Without those syllables the whole great drama both of history and legend loses savour for me — or would.[448]

By this, Tolkien probably meant that Attila was perhaps not perceived by his Germanic subjects as the scourge of God and enemy of the West — i.e., not as the person the church and romantic historians made him into — but as a thoroughly respected ruler.[449] The legend of Dietrich von Bern also conveys this image. History and the legends associated with it thus shed light on the name Attila, and conversely, the name also illuminates history: this was what fascinated Tolkien.

2. Attila's Italian Campaign

With the Battle of the Catalaunian Fields, the danger, as just mentioned, was not averted. On the contrary, Attila invaded Italy the following year, thus advancing right into the Roman heartland; and with regard to this Italian campaign, the perspective of Ravenna, the city that co-inspired Minas Tirith, is of particular interest. Edward Hutton wrote on this subject in 1913:

> All the Cisalpine plan north of the Po was in Attila's hands; Vicenza, Verona, Brescia, Bergamo, Pavia, even Milan opened their gates. No defence was offered, they saved themselves alive. And southward, over the Po, between the mountains and the sea, the gate which Ravenna held stood open wide. Italy without defence lay at the mercy of the Asiatic invader.
>
> Without defence! Valentinian and his court were in Rome; no one armed and ready waited in impregnable Ravenna to break the Hun as with a hammer when he should venture to take the road through the narrow pass between the

---

447   *Letters of Tolkien*, no. 205, end note 1.
448   *Letters of Tolkien*, no. 205.
449   Cf. Shippey (2003), 18.

mountains and the sea. The great defence was not to be held; the road, as once before, lay open and unguarded.[450]

It was not an emperor then who opposed Attila at the Minicio[451] in the Po Valley and saved Italy, Hutton continued, but an old and unarmed man, alone and defenseless—it was Pope Leo the Great. And so Hutton concluded: "The new emperor, the true head and champion of the new civilisation […]. It was the pope."[452]

The scenery is reminiscent of *The Lord of the Rings*, for Hutton described Ravenna here as the city that holds the gate to Italy. He implies that with Ravenna, Italy stands and falls, after the former imperial residence city of Milan had already fallen, similar to Osgiliath. Moreover, according to the legend (which is to be doubted), it is not the Emperor Valentinian who saved Rome, but the unarmed pope with his persuasive power, similar to how Frodo and Sam defeat Sauron virtually unarmed. It would be a second papal legend that inspired the figure of Frodo (or Sam), since the throw into a volcano is, as mentioned above, probably based on the legend according to which the late Pope John I plunged the soul of Theodoric the Great into the Liparian volcano.[453]

The inspiration by papal legends should not surprise, for Tolkien was a devout Catholic. With respect to *The Lord of the Rings*, he once stated in a letter:

> *The Lord of the Rings* is of course a fundamentally religious and Catholic work; unconsciously so at first, but consciously in the revision. That is why I have not put in, or have cut out, practically all references to anything like 're-ligion', to cults or practices, in the imaginary world. For the religious element is absorbed into the story and the symbolism.[454]

In view of the mentioned parallels to Dante's *Divine Comedy*, this should now not be surprising.

---

[450]   Hutton (1913), chap. V.

[451]   River in Northern Italy.

[452]   Hutton (1913), chap. V.

[453]   Pope Gregory I (ca. 590), chap. 30; see Heinzle (1999), 8 f.

[454]   *Letters of Tolkien*, no. 142.

3.   The Battle of Nedao

After Attila's retreat and his legendary death on his wedding night,[455] there was another remarkable battle, this time probably near Belgrade, the city that Tolkien mentioned in the same breath as Minas Tirith.[456] According to Jordanes, in this battle, Attila's former vassals inflicted a heavy defeat on the Huns, from which they should never again recover decisively.[457] The battle was probably the legendary Battle of the Goths and Huns, which the Hervararar saga tells of and from which Tolkien drew various inspirations. Although Rome, that is, Gondor, was not involved in this battle, the battles against the Huns in Morris' *The Roots of the Mountains* were probably at least co-inspired by this saga, and it was precisely this work by Morris that had a great influence on Tolkien.[458]

4.   A Possible Link to Switzerland

On their campaigns, the Huns seem to have passed Switzerland first to the north and then to the south; they did not find Gondolin. Thus, there is at least no historically secured connection to Switzerland, and yet there are good reasons why Tolkien linked the Huns with his trip to Switzerland. The conflict between the Huns and the Goths in William Morris' *The Roots of the Mountains,* for example, takes place in a mountain range that is more reminiscent of the Alps than of the Carpathians. Morris' description of the Dale valley, which is endangered by Huns, for example, recalls the Lauterbrunnen Valley; and in the Lauterbrunnen Valley, there is also a rock face called Hunnenfluh (Mountain of the Huns), which may have been an inspiration trigger for Tolkien or even for Morris. As in *The Lord of the Rings*, the protagonists of the *The Roots of the Mountains* set out from this place (Burgdale or Rivendell) to fight the Huns in another valley, a story that Tolkien probably linked to his journey from Lauterbrunnen across the mountains into and through the Valais. Apart from that, there are—as will be shown later—legends about Huns in the Valais, and the course of the Battle of the Pelennor Fields is strongly reminiscent of a battle that took place at the gates of Sion.[459]

---

455   See Jordanes (ca. 550), nos. 254 ff.

456   www.tolkiensociety.org/wp-content/uploads/2015/11/transcribed-map.jpg.

457   Jordanes (ca. 550), nos. 260 ff.

458   *Letters of Tolkien*, no. 226; above, p. 83 ff.

459   Below, pp. 185 ff.

IV. The Hungarians

The battles against the Huns were certainly an important source of inspiration for the decisive battle in *The Lord of the Rings*, but they did hardly inspire it alone; the Hungarians in particular probably played an important role as well.

1.   Threats from All Sides

After the victory over the Huns and the fall of the Western Roman Empire, Christian Western Europe continued to be threatened from all sides. In the eighth century, Arabs occupied a large part of Spain and advanced from the south as far as France and Constantinople, and in the ninth century, it was mainly the still pagan Vikings who spread fear and terror from the north. In the tenth century, the situation became even worse, at least in continental Europe: Viking longships still threatened mainly from the north (and Danes and Normans overland); Muslim Saracens plundered and pillaged from the south and from the Alps; and from the east, apart from still pagan Slavs, Hungarian horsemen invaded from Central Asia. And it was precisely these Hungarian horsemen who caused Western Europe a great deal of trouble; from 899 onwards, they roamed Western Europe, plundering for over fifty years, without the Christian kingdoms able to prevent it.

2.   The Hungarians as a Source of Inspiration for the Orcs and the Riders of Rohan

The threat situation with the Hungarians coming from the east is similar to that in Middle-earth during the War of the Ring. This should not be surprising, for the Hungarians were long considered to be descendants of the Huns, a mistake that likely found its way into the English word *Hungary*.[460] In *The Lord of the Rings*, however, the Hungarians have a double role, for with their Christianization they became defenders of the West. They took on the role of the Riders of Rohan against the Mongols and Ottomans.[461]

For a connection between the Hungarians and the Orcs also speaks that Tolkien compared the story of *The Lord of the Rings* with the creation of the Holy Roman Empire, for which the victory over the Hungarians played an

---

[460]   Maenchen-Helfen (1973), 386.

[461]   Below, pp. 181 ff.

important role.[462] And Tolkien even considered giving the Orcs a language based on Hungarian, the language Mágo or Mágol, which he had developed himself.[463] Later he wrote "Ork, Orkish" on the Mágo manuscript but then changed his mind, crossed out the words, and placed a "no" next to them.[464]

Furthermore, there is possibly even a philological connection between the Hungarians and the Orcs, one that is independent of the link via the country name *Hungary*. As mentioned earlier, the word *orc* comes from the Old English word *orc*, which Tolkien translated with the New English word *ogre*.[465] This new word *ogre* is interesting, for there are different theories about its origin. While one believes the Roman underworld, the *orcus*, to be behind it, another suggests that the word could come from the *Ugri*, an old name for the Hungarians; the term of the Finno-Ugric language family still contains it today.[466] This could also explain even better the presence of Orcs in the Mountains of Moria, for the Eiger is often associated with an ogre.[467]

Just this Finno-Ugric or Uralic language family is also of interest for the connection between the Orcs and the Elves. According to the Silmarillion, Morgoth (the predecessor of Sauron) created Orcs by enslaving, torturing, and breeding Elves.[468] Tolkien may have derived this connection from the—today again challenged—relationship between Finnish and Hungarian, for the Elven language Quenya is co-inspired by Finnish.[469] It seems like he thus linguistically separated the Elves and Orcs from the Indo-European people. However, as shown, the Elves also have connections to the Celts, who spoke an Indo-European language.

The origin myth of the Huns from Jordanes' *Getica* might also have inspired Tolkien, but this myth would instead speak for kinship with humans, as it reads as follows:

> Filimer, king of the Goths, son of Gadaric the Great, who was the fifth in succession to hold the rule of the Getae after their departure from the island of Scandza,—and who, as we have said, entered the land of Scythia with his tribe,—found among his people certain witches, whom he called in his native tongue Haliurunnae. Suspecting these women, he expelled them from the

---

462   *Letters of Tolkien*, no. 294; below, pp. 178 ff.

463   Fisher (2012), 109.

464   Ibid.

465   Tolkien and Tolkien (1975), 9.

466   See Partridge (1966), 450.

467   Above, p. 45.

468   *The Silmarillion*, 47.

469   *Letters of Tolkien*, nos. 144, 163.

midst of his race and compelled them to wander in solitary exile afar from his army. There the unclean spirits, who beheld them as they wandered through the wilderness, bestowed their embraces upon them and begat this savage race, which dwelt at first in the swamps,—a stunted, foul and puny tribe, scarcely human, and having no language save one which bore but slight resemblance to human speech. Such was the descent of the Huns who came to the country of the Goths.[470]

And so the goblins became Orcs or even Uruk-hai—and Shrek.

Finally, it is also remarkable that Tolkien gave one of the tribes of Elves the name Avari, which recalls the equestrian people of the Avars, who inhabited the Hungarian plain in the period between the Huns and the Magyars (Hungarians).

3.   The Hungarian Invasions

The Hungarian invasions of the tenth century were described in at least one work from which it is known that Tolkien owned it, the six-volume monumental work *The History of the Decline and Fall of the Roman Empire* by Edward Gibbon.[471] It is a classic, which, through Isaac Asimov and his *Foundation* series, also shaped *Star Wars* and inspired (also via Asimov) people like Paul Krugman, Elon Musk, and Demis Hassabis (founder of the AI company DeepMind); thus some of the most innovative minds of our time.[472]

The following passage in Gibbon's work is striking:

> When the black swarm of Hungarians first hung over Europe, above nine hundred years after the Christian era, they were mistaken by fear and superstition for the Gog and Magog of the Scriptures, the signs and forerunners of the end of the world.[473]

Orcs! Clearly—and this should also explain why Tolkien called the language he created based on Hungarian *Mágol* and considered using it for the language of the Orcs. Why Gibbon talked about a black swarm, I do not know, but I imagine that he meant the Hungarians' clothes and perhaps the dark color of their horses.

---

[470]   Jordanes (ca. 550), nos. 121 ff.

[471]   Cilli (2019), nos. 763 ff.; Gibbon (1776/89).

[472]   For the influence on Asimov see for example Hassler (1988), 41.

[473]   Gibbon (1776/89), 5. Band, 548.

Switzerland was also affected by this Hungarian invasion: In 917, the Hungarians plundered Basel, and in 925, St. Gallen and the rest of Alemannia.[474] Although the territory of present-day Switzerland was not affected more than the surrounding countries, the (almost) contemporary chronicler Ekkehard IV from the Abbey of Saint Gall provides us with a particularly vivid picture of these Hungarians:

> The enemies [...] did not come all at once; rather, for lack of resistance they attacked towns and villages in droves and burned them after the plundering had been done, and so they came over the unarmed, unexpectedly, on whichever side they wanted. They also hid in forests in hundreds or in lesser numbers, to launch surprise attacks, but the smoke and the sky reddened by fire revealed where the individual heaps were. At last, those quiver-bearers stormed [into the monastery], staring and with threatening javelins and [other] missiles. They carefully searched the whole place; it was certain that there was no mercy for any gender or age. There they found [Heribald], who stood alone in the middle, undaunted. Astonished at what he wanted and why he had not fled, the captains asked him about it through interpreters, and they instructed the murderers to spare him for the time being; and when they realized that he was a monster of folly, they all left him untouched with laughter.[475]

Ekkehard knew a few more things about these Hungarians, such as that two of them fell to their deaths from the church roof, one of them after he crouched to insult the God of the sanctuary by emptying his stomach over the golden rooster on the rooftop. And Heribald, according to Ekkehard, asked a Hungarian to spare two barrels of wine with the question of what he thinks they should drink after the departure of the Hungarians. This made the Hungarian laugh, and he did spare the barrels. Later, the Hungarians made themselves comfortable on the square within the monastery and drank a lot of wine in a merry and cheerful atmosphere. But Heribald soon got on their nerves, and so they beheaded him. The Hungarians had not come to stay; before long, they moved on toward Constance.[476]

Despite the plundering of the monastery and the killing of Heribald, Ekkehard conveyed an almost cheerful and barbarian picture of these Hungarians. However, this should not hide the fact that they spread fear and terror in Western Europe for many years. Given the popular historical equation

---

[474]   See Hermann of Reichenau (ca. 1054), entries for the years 917 and 925; Ekkehard IV. (ca. 1035), nos. 52 ff.; the plundering of Rheinau and Chur are also reported, but I did not find any primary sources that support this.

[475]   Ekkehard IV. (ca. 1035), nos. 52 f.

[476]   Ekkehard IV. (ca. 1035), no. 55.

of the Hungarians with the Huns, one could even say that the Hun king Attila rose again, similar to how the evil reawakened with Sauron in the Third Age of Middle-earth.

4.   The Battle of Lechfeld

For more than fifty years, the Hungarians roamed Western Europe almost every year, but this was about to change. In 955, they tried to exploit a period of internal unrest in East Francia and invaded Bavaria with a large army.[477] They tried to take Augsburg, and since an immediate capture failed, they began a siege of the city. Abbot Berno of Reichenau described the besiegers as more cruel than any monster, as a city of the devil, and as wolves, which the holy high priest of God had never seen in such numbers before.[478] But when the Hungarians became aware of the approaching East Frankish army under Otto I, they gave up the siege to face the battle.

The battle began while the East Frankish army was moving through the bushes in rugged terrain to counter the Hungarian mounted archers' hit-and-run strategy. The Hungarians had managed to bypass the East Frankish train with a part of their cavalry and attacked from behind. Thereby, they captured or killed many of the defenders and seized the entire army's baggage. Pressed from front and behind, Otto I supposedly ordered the fourth legion, under the once

67 The Battle of Lechfeld, untitled illustration from the Sigmund Meisterlin Codex, 1457.

---

[477]   Cf. Berno of Reichenau (ca. 1001), XX for the Augsburg perspective; Widukind of Corvey (ca. 973), Book 3, nos. 44 ff. for the course of the battle; see also Gibbon (1776/89), vol. 5, 557 ff.

[478]   See Berno of Reichenau (ca. 1001), XX.

178

renegade Conrad the Red, to the rear, and the latter succeeded in recovering the booty and captives and stirring up the Hungarians. Nevertheless, the king and the army were worried, for apart from the upcoming main battle against the Hungarians, the news of a victory of Slavic tribes over the margrave Thiadrich spread. Legend has it that Otto then gave a rousing speech and rode into the battle ahead of his army, carrying a shield and a holy lance. Little is known about the events that followed. Conrad the Red was supposedly hit in the neck by an arrow and killed after the heat made him loosen his ruff. But the Hungarians were defeated, and many of them were swallowed by the river Lech as they fled.

This battle thus shows similarities to the Battle of the Pelennor Fields. The Hungarians, the dreaded enemy who inspired the Orcish threat, could be decisively repulsed; and apart from the image of the besiegers, which the Abbot Berno of Reichenau gave us, the course of the battle somewhat recalls the Battle of the Pelennor Fields, with the siege at the beginning, the arriving army, and the subsequent main battle. Besides, Otto's ride into the battle is somewhat reminiscent of how Théoden or Éomer lead their riders into battle, and perhaps even the history of Conrad the Red shows certain parallels with Théoden. But above all, it is the parallels between Otto and Aragorn that suggest that the Battle of Lechfeld inspired Tolkien.

5.   Aragorn Otto

In the aftermath of the battle, in 962, Otto I had himself crowned emperor by the pope.[479] He had attained the Italian claim to power by—probably not entirely unselfishly—rescuing and marrying Adelaide of Italy, the twenty-year-old widow of the former Italian King Lothair II. After he was able to assert his claim in Italy without much opposition, this made him eligible for the imperial crown, and so he obtained the coronation by the pope. According to Widukind of Corvey, Otto was already welcomed as emperor by his army after the battle of Lechfeld, but historians doubt that.[480] Regardless of this, Otto became emperor after the battle against the Hungarians, thus entering into the tradition of the Roman emperors.

This revival of the imperial tradition with the Holy Roman Empire (HRE) is one of the sources of inspiration for the return of the King of Gondor, Aragorn.[481] However, the result was not a true Holy Roman Empire based in

---

[479]   See for example Becher (2012), 214 ff.

[480]   Widukind of Corvey (ca. 973), Book 3, no. 49.

[481]   Cf. *Letters of Tolkien*, no. 294.

Rome, which distinguishes the template from the story in *The Lord of the Rings.* Still, Otto's daughter-in-law, the Byzantine princess Theophanu, ruled over the HRE after her husband Otto II died early, and their son Otto III was only three years old—imagine this, a Byzantine ruler in early medieval Germany; this is almost like King's Landing ruling the North. However, there would be no union with Byzantium or even a permanent seat of government in Rome. Otto III, who was half Byzantine and actually made Rome the seat of government of the Empire, was unceremoniously barred from the city by the Romans.[482] Although reconciliation is said to have taken place and the Romans accepted Otto's claim to power, he died shortly afterward under suspicious circumstances at the age of only twenty-one.[483] His death possibly prevented a union with Byzantium, as the Byzantine emperor's daughter Zoë had supposedly just docked in Bari to marry him. But when she learned of the death of her betrothed, she immediately returned to Constantinople. Later, she ruled the Byzantine Empire for more than twenty years.

68 Otto I after becoming King of Italy, illustration *Otto I. Thevconicor Rex* from Otto of Freising's *Chronica sive Historia de duabus civitatibus* (*Chronicle or History of the Two Cities*), Milan manuscript, ca. 1200.

Otto I most probably had a significant impact on the figure of Aragorn, but he is of course, not the only source of inspiration. King Arthur, Alfred the Great, Dietrich von Bern (or Theodoric the Great), and the Lombard king Alboin have already been mentioned.[484] Frederick II and Charlemagne might have exerted a certain influence as well. According to legend, Frederick grew up as an orphan in the streets of Palermo, and in adulthood he had to assert his claim by travelling across the Alps. Charlemagne started the tradition of being crowned emperor by the pope in 800, he went east over the Vosges and south over the Alps (so, in a way, over the Misty Mountains and the White Mountains), and he fought the Avars, who lived in the Hungarian lowlands

---

[482]   Bernward of Hildesheim (ca. 1019), nos. 24 f.

[483]   Bernward of Hildesheim (ca. 1019), no. 37 just mentioned that he died of a disease.

[484]   Above, pp. 74 ff.

180

at that time. But unlike Otto I, Charlemagne was not primarily a defender but a conqueror, which is why he is less suited to the figure of Aragorn than Otto I.

By the way, George R. R. Martin once stated in an interview:

> I was in Germany last fall and looked everywhere for good reference books about the medieval Holy Roman Empire, which would be a treasure trove, I suspect. There are a ton of them that looked likely... but all in German.[485]

Well, Tolkien did not have this problem, for he spoke German, but he seems to have been strongly inspired by Edward Gibbon's monumental English work *The History of the Decline and Fall of the Roman Empire*.

V.   Mongols and Ottomans

So, the battles against the Carthaginians, Huns, and Hungarians—are these Tolkien's sources of inspiration for the Battle of the Pelennor Fields? With Tolkien, it is often a bit more complex than it might seem at first glance. Referring to the plot in *The Lord of the Rings*, he once remarked that the enemies of the West mostly came from the endless lands to the East.[486] Apart from the Huns of late antiquity and the Hungarian Magyars of the early Middle Ages, these enemies included the Mongols and Ottomans of the later Middle Ages. Tolkien once compared the appearance of the Orcs to the Mongolian type[487] and the scimitars used by the Orcs create associations above all with the Turkish Ottomans and Arab Saracens. Although neither the Ottomans nor the Mongols have a direct connection to Switzerland, they are too important for understanding Tolkien's sources of inspiration to be left out here; for yes, it seems that Tolkien united and blended all the historical enemies of Christian Western Europe in *The Lord of the Rings*.

The comparison between the Orcs and the Mongolian type understandably led to some criticism. At least on a conscious level, however, Tolkien always spoke out strongly against racism and anti-Semitism.[488]

---

485   See www.westeros.org/Citadel/SSM/Entry/Historical_Influences.

486   *Letters of Tolkien*, no. 163.

487   *Letters of Tolkien*, no. 210; Tolkien, however, probably referred primarily to ancient depictions of the Huns; above, pp. 83 ff.

488   See e.g. *Letters of Tolkien*, no. 29, 30, 61, 71, 81.

1.   The Mongolian Invasion

The first Mongolian invasions in Europe occurred in 1240 and 1241.[489] Under Genghis Khan's son Ögedei, the Mongolian Empire stretched from Ukraine to China, after Batu Khan, a grandson of Genghis Khan, had defeated the Russian lords between 1237 and 1240. The gate to the West stood wide open—and the West was not prepared.

In the spring of 1241, the Mongols first reached Poland, where they plundered various cities, such as Kraków, and finally defeated a large Polish-German army in the Battle of Liegnitz on April 9. Meanwhile, the Mongols' southern main force advanced into Hungary and destroyed the army of the Hungarian king Béla IV only two days later, on April 11, 1241. Fear spread all over Europe—only Emperor Frederick II and Pope Gregory IX were busy with themselves or rather with the power struggle between them. Therefore, there was hardly any resistance; at Liegnitz, local German lords had fought without their (excommunicated) emperor. Also, the Mongols used a fearsome new weapon: black powder. They are said to have used it, among other things, to make bombs that they fired at their enemies with catapults. Bombs against swords, and the Europeans in the role of the indigenous peoples of America—the West held its breath.

Again, as had occurred with Attila's Huns, it was not an army that seriously repulsed the Mongols but a turn of events fortunate for the West. When Great Khan Ögedei died in December 1241, Batu Khan and his troops left to participate in the election of the new Great Khan at the other end of the Eurasian continent. The West was able to breathe a sigh of relief (without a Battle of the Pelennor Fields), and the King of Hungary could return to his kingdom. Although there were further Mongol advances, especially to Hungary and Poland, the danger was never as great as in 1241.

2.   The Ottoman Siege of Belgrade

In the middle of the fifteenth century, Western Europe trembled again, this time before the Ottomans. In 1453, the young Ottoman sultan Mehmed II bombarded the thousand-year-old Theodosian Walls of Constantinople with gigantic cannons and captured the city.[490] In doing so, he sealed the end of the Byzantine Empire and, to a certain extent, the Roman Empire and the Euro-

---

[489]   For example Jackson (2018), The Mongol invasions of 1241-4.

[490]   See (critically) Gibbon (1776/89), vol. 6, chaps. LXVIII f., for Tolkien owned this work.

pean Middle Ages. It was a trauma for the West, for Constantinople was not only the seat of the Eastern Roman Byzantine emperors and (at least in the Middle Ages) the center of Greek cultural tradition, it was also the seat of the Orthodox Church and, during the previous thousand years, almost always the largest city of Christianity. Byzantium, that is, Gondor, was largely abandoned by its western fellow Christians and was no more.

And Mehmed advanced further. In July 1456, he arrived at Belgrade, which was then held by the Hungarians; at this point in time at the latest, he threatened Western Europe.[491] The West was again ill-prepared, for when Mehmed started the siege with his cannons, the Hungarian commander János Hunyadi was still gathering troops. Late, Hunyadi arrived in Belgrade from the Pannonian lowlands (Rohan), together with the Franciscan friar John of Capistrano, who was raising a crusader army in Hungary on behalf of the pope. Just like Aragorn reached the battlefield upstream in *The Lord of the Rings*, Hunyadi and Capistrano reached Belgrade downstream on the Danube, where they reinforced the hopelessly outnumbered garrison. Not too early, for Mehmed launched a night attack through the crumbling walls of the city; but with the reinforcements, the defenders managed to repel the attack.

The next day, an unplanned battle took place outside the city gates when the over-motivated and inexperienced peasants raised by John of Capistrano began to harass the besiegers. Under the peasants' influence, John is said to

69 Ottoman miniature of the Ottoman siege of Belgrade of 1456—a possible source of inspiration for the Battle of the Pelennor Fields in *The Lord of the Rings*.

---

491   E.g. Kovach (1996); see also Gibbon (1776/89), vol. 6, chap. LXVII.

have then spontaneously led a daring attack against the Ottomans so that Hunyadi, too, was forced to a seemingly desperate sally. But this surprised the Ottomans so much that panic broke out among the besiegers, many fled, and the sultan felt compelled to fight himself. Thereby, he was hit by an arrow, which is probably one reason why the Ottomans hastily left the following night.

Hunyadi and John of Capistrano became heroes, but the victory did not bring them luck; both died the same year from an epidemic, while Mehmed II continued to rule for many years. Yet the Ottoman advance into Central Europe was halted for quite some time, and Pope Calixt III ordered that church bells should always be rung at noon to commemorate this victory—a custom that continues in many places today. John, on the other hand, actually an ill-natured inquisitor and persecutor of Jews, was later canonized and declared a patron saint of lawyers.[492]

The fact that Tolkien located Minas Tirith in the area of Belgrade is reason enough to consider the siege of Belgrade in 1456 as a source of inspiration for the Battle of the Pelennor Fields. And there are also similarities in the battle's course: the siege with the subsequent onslaught on the city and the shifting of the battle to outside its gates; the reinforcements arrive late from the Pannonian Plain, the European Rohan, and they join the battle from the river just like Aragorn in *The Lord of the Rings*; and the desperate attack of John of Capistrano with his peasants is somewhat reminiscent of Éomer's daring attack. Moreover, the Corsairs, Sauron's allies, also fit in. The Barbary corsairs (or Ottoman corsairs) were Muslim caperers who, mainly for the Ottoman slave market, captured people on Europe's southern coast in the early modern period. All in all, an inspiration from the Ottoman siege of Belgrade thus seems likely.

3. The Ottoman Sieges of Vienna

Sixty-five years later, in 1521, Belgrade was finally conquered by the Ottomans, and the Hungarians suffered a crushing defeat in the Battle of Mohács in 1526. So in 1529, the Ottomans, led by Süleyman "the Magnificent," reached Vienna and besieged the city, another possible source of inspiration for the Battle of the Pelennor Fields.[493]

---

[492] Concerning the persecution of Jews see for example Levy (2005), 96 f.; Mühlbauer (2009); Cohn (1926); I do not assume, however, that Tolkien knew this.

[493] For example Weiß (1872), 24 ff.

In a sense, Vienna was the second gate to the West after Belgrade, so that this gate would have been wide open if Vienna were conquered. Apart from the city garrison and militia, the city was defended by German and Spanish mercenaries. Shortly before the siege ring closed, these were reinforced by armored riders under the command of Count Palatine Philip "the Contentious." But after weeks of siege and several attacks on the city, the attackers gave up and withdrew. In 1683, the Ottomans made another attempt and failed again, also thanks to the Polish support of the defenders.

These sieges would be another potential source of inspiration for the decisive battle in *The Lord of the Rings*, and yet I doubt that Tolkien was decisively inspired by them, for both sieges exhibit a characteristic that Tolkien would hardly have left out: underground warfare. The Ottomans dug tunnels to undermine, literally, Vienna's city walls and bring them down, and the defenders, in turn, could do nothing but dig tunnels themselves to track down the underground attackers. This kind of warfare with an invisible underground attacker would fit the light-shy Orcs too well for Tolkien to omit this detail if these battles had inspired him. Indeed, I would almost say that this detail would have added something to the siege of Minas Tirith.

VI. Possible Sources of Inspiration in Switzerland

The readers may wonder what all these peoples and battles have to do with Switzerland. Well, during my research, I came across legends of Huns, Hungarians, and Saracens in the Valais, which fit suspiciously well with the plot in *The Lord of the Rings*. So well that I finally concluded that Tolkien, in this respect as well, probably mixed elements of European history with elements of his journey in Switzerland and local legends when creating *The Lord of the Rings*. And with the Hannibal joke he told while hiking through the Swiss mountains, there is at least one direct clue to this. Apart from that, I came across a battle that was fought at the gates of Sion in the fifteenth century, which I believe fits the course of the Battle of the Pelennor Fields better than any of the previously mentioned battles. But, of course, only knowledge of these other battles allows a proper appreciation of this potential source of inspiration.

1.   The Val d'Anniviers as Valley of the Huns and Hungarians

Legend has it that Huns settled in the Val d'Anniviers (Anniviers Valley). According to the pastor and early alpinist Marc-Théodore Bourrit (1781), they rose from the underworld and founded a colony in this valley.[494] They found refuge there when they were persecuted after Attila's death, and thus, according to Bourrit, the Huns are the ancestors of the present inhabitants of the valley, whose way of life still reminds us of their origins (according to Bourrit).[495] And he even believed that perhaps they are the only remnant of those terrible Huns who once carried the terror from the borders of China to the Gallic and Italian regions.[496] Similarly, the pastor, author, and local history explorer Philippe-Sirice Bridel (1820) noted that the first inhabitants of the Val d'Anniviers were, according to tradition, Hun soldiers fleeing Italy in search of a safe place to settle.[497] The bishops of Sion had difficulty spreading Christianity among this multiplying horde as the name of the village Mission would still testify.[498]

Later, the legend was more connected to the Hungarians. In his *History of the Valais (Geschichte vom Wallis)* of 1850, Furrer wrote that the terrible Magyars—whom he still equated with the Huns—had occupied both the Simplon and the Great St. Bernard Pass as well as the gap at Saint-Maurice from the year 924 onwards, and that they had severely afflicted both Henry the Fowler and Otto I.[499] In 1896, the author Anton Karl Fischer even published a whole book titled *The Huns in the Swiss Eifischtal Valley and Their Descendants up to the Present Day (Die Hunnen im schweizerischen Eifischtale und ihre Nachkommen bis auf die heutige Zeit)*. In this book, he dealt with family and place names in the Val d'Anniviers and their analogies in Hungary. And finally, in 1912, one year after Tolkien's trip to Switzerland,

---

[494]   Bourrit (1781), 189 ff.; see also Tamassy (2018).

[495]   Bourrit (1781), 190 f.

[496]   Bourrit (1781), 192.

[497]   Bridel (1820), 133.

[498]   Bridel (1820), 133.

[499]   Who, he said, had built the cathedral in Sion; Furrer (1850), 28, 48 f.; it is not clear where he took this information from; perhaps he confused the Magyars with the Saracens; Otto does not seem to have built the cathedral in Sion, but Furrer created a connection between the Aragorn figure and Sion.

an academic still spoke of Huns not only in the Val d'Anniviers but also in the Val d'Hérens.[500]

Could Tolkien have been inspired by these legends? At least the following evidence speaks for that. First, we now know that Tolkien connected the Orcs with the Huns and Hungarians. Second, the Val d'Anniviers (Eifischtal) and the Val d'Hérens (Eringertal) are located in the region that probably served Tolkien as a source of inspiration for Mordor (Mont Miné and the Bertol Hut are even in the Val d'Hérens). Third, the Val d'Anniviers, seen from Sion, is situated in the mountains on the other side of the Rhône, similar to Mordor viewed from Minas Tirith. Fourth, Tolkien himself was in the Val d'Hérens and, according to Colin Brookes-Smith's route description, also in the Val d'Anniviers. Fifth, Anton Karl Fischer's book was published only 15 years before Tolkien's trip to Switzerland so that the legend was probably present in people's minds. Sixth, this book suggests etymological connections of local place names and local family names with the Hungarian language, which is a topic that would have been of particular interest to Tolkien.[501] And, notably, he also wanted to base the language of Mordor on Hungarian, as mentioned above.

Although the historical authencity of the legends is more than doubtful, it may be imagined how the Huns found refuge in these Alpine valleys and, similarly to Morris' *The Roots of the Mountains*, secretly multiplied there and regained strength. One may also imagine the situation in Sion at a time when Huns—or Hungarians as reincarnated Huns—occupied not only the mountains to the south but also the gate at Saint-Maurice to the west—the Gap of Rohan—and thus threatened the city from multiple sides. As allies of the Gallo-Roman Gondorians, only the newcomers from the north, the Germanic Rohirrim in the Upper Valais, would have been available in the tenth century, and the only way to and from Sion was via the Bernese Oberland Alps and thus the Misty Mountains. This situation is indeed very reminiscent of *The Lord of the Rings*.

2.   The Saracens in the Valais

While the presence or even settlement of Huns or Hungarians in valleys of the Valais belongs to the realm of legend, the same is not equally true for the

---

500   Wacker (1912), 441; he quoted Furrer; however, this does not result from Furrer (1850), 28, 48 f. or Furrer (1852), 49; see also Lewis and Currie (2019), 158 for Evolène.

501   See for example *Letters of Tolkien*, nos. 190 and 294.

Saracens. According to the contemporary chronicler Flodoard of Reims, the Saracens increasingly occupied Alpine passes from their base in Fraxinetum near Saint-Tropez from the 920s onwards.[502] On these passes, they ambushed Rome pilgrims and other travelers, and in his account of the year 936, Flodoard also mentioned raids in Alemannia north of the Alps.[503] From 940 on at the latest and until at least 972, Saracens were also active in the Valais. For in 940, they attacked and occupied the Abbey of Saint-Maurice[504] in what likely inspired the Gap of Rohan, and in 972, they captured the powerful Abbot of Cluny near Orsière north of the Great St. Bernard Pass and extorted one thousand pounds of silver for the Abbot's release.[505] Also, King Otto I justified two of his donations to the bishop of Chur, one in the spring of 940 and one in 954, with destructions by Saracens, which indicates their presence even in the eastern Alps as early as the 930s;[506] and according to the monk Ekkehard IV, the Saracens eventually even reached St. Gallen.[507]

It is unclear whether Saracen groups settled permanently in the Alps or were merely active on raids or as blackmailing seasonal kidnappers. While archaeological evidence is missing, the written sources indicate a relatively strong presence. An old inscription near the church of Bourg-St-Pierre on the Great St. Bernard Pass reports that the Saracens covered the area of the Rhône with fire, hunger, and sword for a long time.[508] Ekkehard IV of St. Gallen mentioned that the Saracens had occupied their alps and threatened the monastery from the south—and he also spoke of the predisposition of the Saracens to show their strength in the mountains.[509] Finally, the historian, diplomat, and bishop Liutprand of Cremona even reported that Hugh of Arles, King of (Upper) Italy, had made an agreement with the Saracens in 942 to protect himself from his rival, Berengar II, who had fled to the court of

---

[502] Flodoard of Reims (ca. 966), years 921, 923, 929, 931, 933, 940, and 951.

[503] Alemannia contained roughly the present-day German-speaking Switzerland and the southern part of Baden-Württemberg; Keller (1856), 8 assumed that it was the area around Chur and the Rhine Valley; whether the passes to the German speaking Upper Valais were covered by the treaty is not clear.

[504] Flodoard of Reims (ca. 966), year 940.

[505] Keller (1856), 14 ff.

[506] See von Moor (1865), nos. 44, 52, and 64; according to Sprecher (1672), 73, donations to the Disentis Abbey were also made because of devastation by Saracens, but he did not mention his source; cf. Keller (1856), 9 ff.

[507] For Chur see von Moor (1865), nos. 44, 52, and 64; Keller (1856), 8 ff.; for St. Gallen see Ekkehard IV. (ca. 1035), no. 126.

[508] See Pfaff (1977), 125.

[509] Ekkehard IV. (ca. 1035), no. 126.

Otto I.[510] The treaty provided that the Saracens would position themselves in the mountains "that separate Swabia from Italy" to prevent Berengar from returning to Italy.[511] The blood of countless Christians was shed because of this evil pact, Liutprand lamented, and therefore he compared Hugh to King Herod "the Great," who, according to the Bible, had countless children killed to secure his earthly kingdom.[512]

The passes that separate what was at that time Swabia and Italy were, in the strict sense, the Lukmanier, San Bernardino (Bird's Mountain), Septimer, Maloja, and Bernina Pass (or Pontresina, which goes back to Ponte Sarraceno[513]). But the agreement may also have included the passes of the Valais, in particular, the Great St. Bernard (Jupiter Mountain) and the Simplon Pass (and perhaps the Antrona, Monte Moro, and Albrun Passes), provided that Liutrand's tradition is correct and the Saracens fulfilled their obligation. However, Saracen units were already in these areas earlier anyway, as the raids in Saint-Maurice and the donations to the Diocese of Chur show; and Liutprand complained that Berengar II did not fall into the hands of the Moors when he crossed the Jupiter Mountain in 940.[514] At least the occupation of the San Bernardino Pass can be expected from 942 onwards since, according to Liutprand, Berengar's pregnant wife had fled over it on her way to the north.[515] However, the pact did not have the desired effect; Berengar crossed the Alps further east in 945 and gained de facto power in northern Italy. Though not for long, as the young widow of the official king (Lothair), Adelaide of Burgundy, refused to marry Berengar or his son and instead married her liberator, Otto.

Of particular interest to Tolkien must have been the widespread assumption at the time that certain topographical designations indicate the Saracens' presence in the Saas Valley. The Monte Moro Pass, Almagell, the Allalinhorn, Mischabel, Eien, and Balfrin were mentioned by different authors.[516] The Monte Moro was said to be the Mountain of the Moors, and concerning the

---

[510]   Liutprand of Cremona (ca. 962), Book 5, no. 17 (p. 78).

[511]   Ibid.

[512]   Ibid.

[513]   However, the name is supposed to go back to the personal name Saracenus, see the entry for Pontresina at www.ortsnamen.ch; even if there is no direct reference to a Saracen occupation, the personal name does at least create a link.

[514]   Liutprand of Cremona (ca. 962), Book 4, no. 11 (p. 74).

[515]   Ibid.

[516]   Engelhardt (1840), 130 ff.; see also Keller (1856), 19 ff.; Furrer (1850), 51; Imseng (2017), 295 ff.

other names, reference was made to Arabic words such as [dʒabal] (mountain), [maˈḥall] (settlement, camp), [ʕain] (source), [maːʔ] (water) and [ʕaːlin] (high).[517] In view of the treaty with Hugh, a presence of Saracens in the Saas Valley with its two alpine passes would not be astonishing, but there is still no archaeological evidence.[518] And therefore, historians disapprove of such etymological speculations; but Tolkien would have certainly been interested in them. It is striking that he used the word syllable *mor* as *black* in place names such as Mordor and Moria and that he once contrasted the Middle English word *Westernesse* with the East inhabited by the Paynim and Saracens.[519] Moreover, this theory of an Arabic origin of place names in the Saas Valley was mentioned in Murray's 1904 guidebook;[520] and finally, the Barbarian corsairs, whom Tolkien made allies of Mordor, were also called Saracens in Europe.

Independently of these speculations, the presence of the Saracens in the Valais from the 940s onwards is thus relatively well documented, and this (actual) situation—like the legendary setting of the preceding section—is also strongly reminiscent of *The Lord of the Rings*. The Roman world was still found in the Lower Valais, namely in Sion (Minas Tirith), while the Upper Valais (Rohan) had been settled by Germanic newcomers from the north. And the Alpine passes in the south (Mordor) and the gate at Saint-Maurice (Gate of Rohan) in the west were occupied by Saracens. Whether or not the Saracens were also in the Saas Valley and on the Simplon is not so important, for at least in the Entremont, their presence is documented. The setting described by Furrer might thus have existed, yet probably not with the Huns or Hungarians but with the Saracens as enemies. Unfortunately, sources on the situation in Sion at this time seem to be almost entirely missing. Only the already mentioned church inscription, according to which the Saracens covered the area of the Rhône for a long time with fire, hunger, and sword, gives us a rudimentary picture.

3. The Battle against Hungarians and Saracens

According to another legend, a battle between three peoples followed: the Burgundians, the Saracens, and the Hungarians (or Huns).[521] The Burgundian

---

[517] Essentially already Engelhardt (1840), 130 ff.
[518] Already Keller (1856), 19 f.
[519] *Letters of Tolkien*, no. 276.
[520] Murray (1904), 148.
[521] Furrer (1850), 51.

190

king Conrad I is said to have used a trick: he asked both the Hungarians and Saracens for support against the other, only to attack both of them from ambush after the battle had broken out. After Conrad's victory, the surviving Saracens supposedly settled in the Entremont and Saas Valley, while the Huns took refuge in the Val d'Anniviers.[522] And this context suggests an encounter in the Valais. The battle is said to have taken place in 954, thus only one year before the Battle of Lechfeld.[523]

However, it is unclear whether this battle occurred like this. The almost contemporary author Ekkehard IV did indeed mention a battle in which the Burgundian king Conrad incited the Saracens and Hungarians against each other, only to attack them both after the outbreak of the battle.[524] However, this does not necessarily mean that this is a historical fact. And more importantly, he localized the battlefield "in valle Fraxnith," and this is probably *Fraxinetum*, the main base of the Saracens close to St. Tropez. Although the jurist Raoul Imseng, in his book *Halbmond über der Rhone* (Crescent over the Rhône), recently put forward again the hypothesis that this battle took place near Gondo at the Simplon Pass, there is so far no archaeological evidence that would support this.[525]

Ekkehard did not mention the year of the battle, so it is unclear how the authors of the nineteenth century assumed the year 954. A possible point of reference would be Flodoard of Reims' chronicle, according to which Conrad "the Peaceful" ravaged northern France in 954 with the help of Hungarians, for many Hungarians, he said, died during the battles or of diseases, and the rest returned to their homeland via Italy.[526] Perhaps the nineteenth century authors suspected that the battle against the Saracens took place on this return journey. However, this way could have led via the South of France or via the Simplon. And the subsequent settlement of these peoples in the side valleys of the Valais, according to the present state of knowledge, is certainly to be consigned to the realm of legend.

Regardless of the historicity, a battle against Hungarians (or Huns) and Saracens in the Valais would fit the plot in *The Lord of the Rings* perfectly. For the Huns and Hungarians seem to have inspired the Orcs, and the Saracens both the Orcs and the Haradrim. Furthermore, this battle is said to have

---

[522] Ibid.; see also Ruppen (1851), 13 f.

[523] Ruppen (1851), 13; Keller (1856), 14, who, however, assumes a location outside Switzerland; see also Imseng (2017), 291.

[524] Ekkehard IV. (ca. 1035), Nr. 65.

[525] Imseng (2017), 272 ff.

[526] Flodoard of Reims (ca. 966), year 954.

taken place during the lifetime of Aragorn Otto and only one year before the Battle of Lechfeld—which might explain why Aragorn appears so late on the battlefield. Imagine this alleged battle with Hungarian horsemen attacking a valley fortified by Saracens in the Valais mountains and the subsequent chaotic battle between the Christian Burgundians, the Muslim Saracens, and the still pagan Hungarians.

The Burgundians also fit the subject, for they are Isildur's heirs. Their ancestors succumbed to the temptation of the Ring; the destruction of their empire on the Rhine by the Romans and Huns in 435 and 436 forms the historical core of the Nibelung saga.[527] Settled in the Lake Geneva region by the Roman commander Aëtius in 443—there could be worse places—they fought on the Roman side against the Huns in the Battle of the Catalaunian Fields in 451. And in the chaotic years that followed, during the disintegration of the Western Roman Empire, they were able to build themselves a medium-sized kingdom on the Rhône between the Ostrogoths, Visigoths, and Franks be-

70 The situation in the Valais in the tenth century, a likely source of inspiration for *The Lord of the Rings*; the Alemanni had not been long in the Valais, similar to the Rohirrim they were newcomers from the north. It is even conceivable that in some isolated places the Celtic language was still present; this would fit to the Elvish cells in Middle-earth. And in view of the Nibelungen saga, the Burgundians would fit to Isildur's heirs. Map data: © OpenStreetMap.org-Contributors, see p. 286, no. 1.

---

527   For example Ehrismann (2002), 29 f.; see above, pp. 61 f.

forc their realm (at first temporarily and later permanently) was absorbed by that of the Franks. The most dazzling figure of this early Burgundian kingdom on the Rhône was King Gundobad, whom Tolkien erected a monument to with Mount Gundabad in the Misty Mountains.

4.   The Battle of the Planta

All the battles mentioned so far have one thing in common: they are only to a limited extent reminiscent of the decisive battle in *The Lord of the Rings*. The reason may be that Tolkien combined elements of different battles—or that another battle primarily inspired him. And somewhat surprisingly, another candidate for this battle suddenly caught my eye during my research: the Battle on the Planta. During the so-called Burgundian Wars, it was fought in 1475 between the (Upper) Valaisans and the Savoyards, at the gates of Sion, the gates of Minas Tirith.

On the morning of November 13, 1475, the inhabitants of Sion faced a superior Savoy force. The main Savoy army had crossed the border river Morge and quickly advanced against Sion with about ten thousand men, while only about three hundred men were supposedly available to defend the city.[528] Soon the Savoy, therefore, succeeded in penetrating the western parts of the city, but it was precisely at this time that the forces from the Upper Valais arrived as reinforcements of about three to four thousand men; and with their help, the defenders could beat the Savoy attackers out of the city. But on the Planta, the plain outside the western gate, the attackers regrouped and quickly gained the upper hand over the outnumbered and outgunned Valaisan troops.[529] The battle seemed lost, but then, when the Valaisans were already withdrawing, another three thousand men from Bern, Fribourg, and Solothurn arrived to support them. They had risked their lives before even reaching the Valais by traversing the 7,388-feet-high (2,252-meter-high) Sanetsch Pass so late in the year. And with their support, the defenders put the Savoy forces finally to flight.[530] Furrer stated that these three thousand Bernese had thrown themselves upon (according to him) eighteen thousand Savoy: "The Swiss, who were not used to reckoning, put their fear aside with

---

[528]   Cf. Grand (1913), 73 ff., who quotes different numbers by different authors; von Tillier (1838), 263, for example, speaks of more than 10,000 and Furrer (1850), 218 ff. even of 18,000.

[529]   Cf. Grand (1913), 74, 76 f.; Dübi (1931), 70.

[530]   Grand (1913), 77 ff.; Furrer (1850), 318 f.

the attack."[531] It is probably an example of how exaggerated legends are created, but this is irrelevant for this book's purposes.

Do you think that this battle inspired Tolkien for the Battle of the Pelennor Fields? There is no direct evidence, but since the battle was fought at the gates of Sion, it should be considered; and the battle's course also shows remarkable parallels. While the attackers come from Minas Morgul in *The Lord of the Rings*, they cross the river Morge and pass by the valley hill Mont d'Orge in the Battle on the Planta. And in *The Lord of the Rings*, too, the attackers penetrate the outer areas of the fortified city of Minas Tirith in a first battle phase before the defenders can drive them out of the city with the help of reinforcement troops from Rohan. It is particularly noteworthy that these reinforcements in the Battle on the Planta came from the German-speaking upper Rhône Valley, that is, precisely the area that had previously been identified as a probable source of inspiration for Rohan. And like the counterattack by the Riders of Rohan, the counterattack by the Upper Valais forces quickly came to a halt due to the superiority of the enemy. But then, in both *The Lord of the Rings* and the Battle on the Planta, it is a second

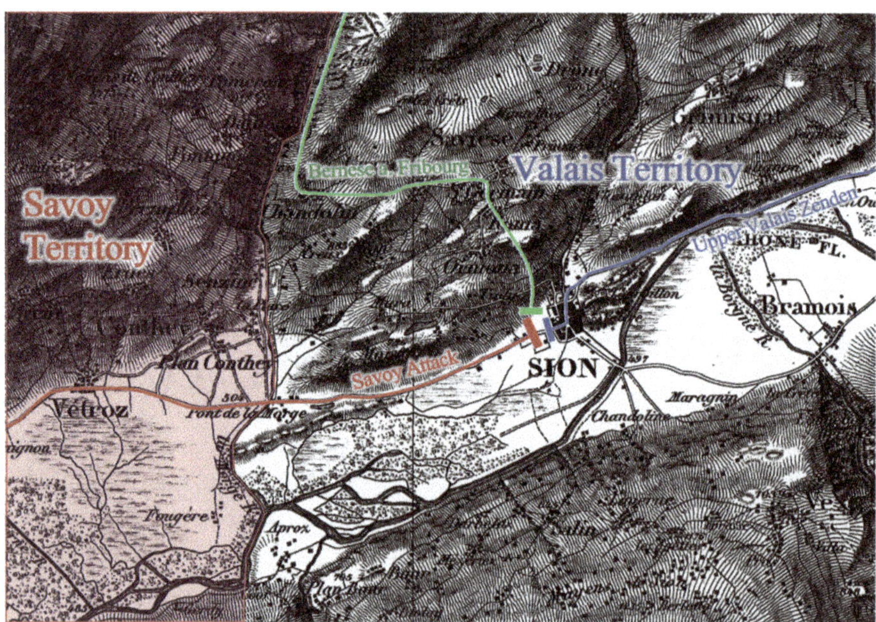

71 The Battle on the Planta, phase 2: Reinforcement by the Bernese (green). Based on the Dufour map of 1865; source: Swiss Federal Office of Topography.

---

531   Furrer (1850), 219.

reinforcement force that overpowers the attackers and puts them to flight: In the Battle on the Planta, it is the Bernese; in *The Lord of the Rings*, it is troops around Aragorn or rather Dietrich von Bern. And in both the Battle on the Planta and the battle in *The Lord of the Rings*, this second reinforcement reaches the battle via a high mountain pass.

These are already quite some remarkable parallels, and yet another legend is worth mentioning. Before the battle, a woman dressed as a man is said to have ridden to meet the Savoy lord to investigate him, a story that recalls Éowyn riding into battle dressed as a man in *The Lord of the Rings*.[532]

Three Basic Theses

With the Battle on the Planta, the journey through the Valais ends, and I hope you were able to enjoy it at least a little bit as I did during my research. I may have been wrong in one place or another—I am aware of that—but overall, I have little doubt that Tolkien's journey through the Valais had a huge impact on the landscapes of Middle-earth as well as on the plot in *The Lord of the Rings*. On closer inspection, three more fundamental theses have increasingly emerged in this second part.

Thesis 1: In *The Lord of the Rings*, Tolkien autobiographically followed the Valais part of his Swiss journey fairly closely when the protagonists reach Rohan, Gondor, and Mordor; and these autobiographical elements with their images and details made a significant contribution to the credibility and vividness of the story.

Thesis 2: The Lord of the Rings is co-inspired by the legendary and actual threat situation in the Valais of the tenth century with the Gondorians in the Romanic Lower Valais, the Rohirrim in the Germanic Upper Valais, last Celtic cells as Elves, and Saracens, Huns, and Magyars as Orcs (and Haradrim) in the mountains as well as at the Gate to the Valais near Saint-Maurice.

---

[532]   Dübi (1931), 59 f.

Thesis 3: The Lord of the Rings is a battle of languages, which is decisively influenced by the (actual or alleged) history of the origin of place and field names in the Valais, of Latin, Germanic, and Celtic names, but also of names with alleged Arabic, Hungarian, or pre-Indo-European origin; and the tale tries to explain these names to a certain extent and to reconstruct a historical situation (see Figure 72).

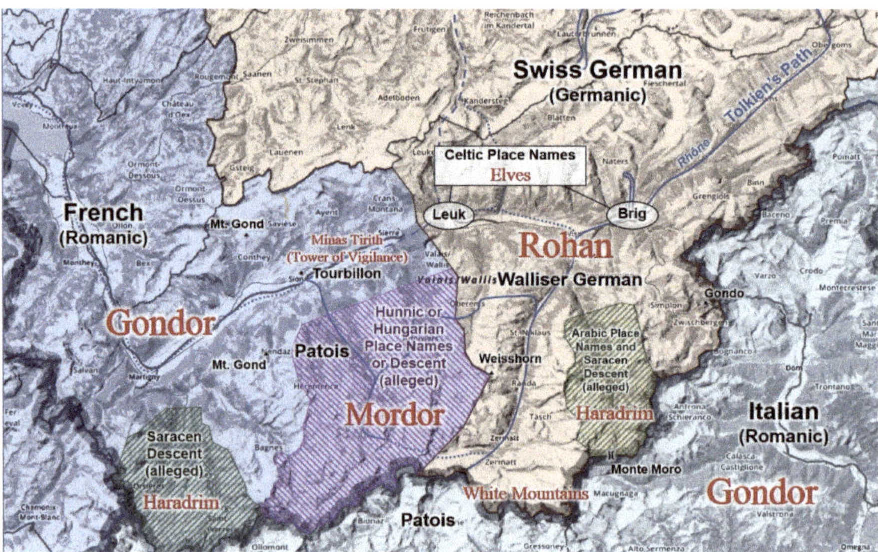

72 *The Lord of the Rings* – a battle of languages: the Valais from the perspective of a philologist one hundred years ago as a likely source of inspiration for Middle-earth. Tolkien's path is shown in blue, Middle-earth place names in red, and languages, place names, and descent legends in black, purple, and dark green. It is noteworthy that for a long time, there was no strong break between the French and Italian language areas, for traditionally a Franco-Provençal patois was spoken in both the Valais and the Aosta Valley, and partly still is today. This might also have distinguished the region marked as Mordor in Tolkien's time from the probably already French-speaking Sion (see also Tolkien's letter no. 306, in which he commented on the language of an uneducated French-speaking member of the party). Map data: © OpenStreetMap.org-Contributors, see p. 286, no. 1.

Part 3: Back to Lake Thun
The Finale of *The Hobbit*

73 Mount Niesen on Lake Thun.

From the Misty Mountains
to the Long Lake

I.   Over Hill or Under Hill

Mount Doom, Minas Tirith, the Battle of the Pelennor Fields: that would be a great ending, would it not? Peter Jackson at least quite saw it that way when making the film adaptations, but not Tolkien, who added almost another hundred pages. Well, I am probably just too young: George R. R. Martin once said in an interview that "the brilliance and the necessity of the scouring of the Shire [had become] clearer and clearer to [him]" as he grew older.[533] Entirely to his taste, it is a bittersweet ending: with the victory over Sauron, yes, but at the great cost of the destruction of the Shire and Frodo's never-healing war wound. Autobiographical elements they are; there is hardly any doubt; but this is not what this third part is about, for when Tolkien was in Switzerland in 1911, the world still seemed to be in order. This part will be mainly about the second half of *The Hobbit*.

First, there is the question, though, of Tolkien's exact route back to England. While he himself did not mention it anywhere in his letters, his companion Brookes-Smith figured that they had probably taken the train from Sion down the Rhône Valley, that is, through the Gap of Rohan and then—more or less—directly to England. However, he no longer actively remembered this, for he wrote:

> We must have gone down the Rhône Valley by train to Lake Geneva and then to Lausanne. From our return trip to England, I remember an impressively long railroad tunnel, but nothing else.[534]

Wait, an impressively long tunnel? Was there an impressively long tunnel between Sion and Lausanne or Lausanne and England in 1911? Of course, there

---

[533]   See the interview available at www.youtube.com/watch?v=3mPkqEqx3Gg.

[534]   Memoirs of Colin Brookes-Smith as quoted by Frías Sánchez (2009), 4 and thus translated back from Spanish, so the wording is unlikely to be exactly correct; also, in the version of the memoris I have seen, Brookes-Smith only mentioned that they returned to England from Sion by train, but nothing else; perhaps, there are thus different versions of these memoirs.

was no Channel Tunnel between England and France yet, and the other possibilities were either too short to fit Brookes-Smith's description or did not open until a number of years after 1911.[535] There was an impressive tunnel to the south, the 12.4-miles (20-kilometers) Simplon Tunnel between the Valais and Italy. But in the absence of any explicit reference, it seems unlikely that Tolkien's group hiked to Italy, especially since the foot-and-mouth disease was raging there.[536] And therefore, it remains a mystery at this point to which tunnel Brookes-Smith could have referred.

Frías Sánchez put forward the hypothesis that the way back did not lead down the Rhône Valley, but to Interlaken, where the journey began, as this circular route was very popular with English tourists at the time.[537] It should be added that Murray's contemporary guide recommended the railroad route from England to Switzerland via Laon and Basel since changing trains in Paris was cumbersome and involved an additional customs inspection.[538] A return trip to Lake Thun was thus a logical choice, and besides—there is no evidence that Tolkien was in Paris in 1911.

The most famous and, apart from the Sanetsch Pass, the shortest way from Sion back to Lake Thun was on foot over the legendary Gemmi Pass. It is no path for people with a fear of heights, as from the south the path climbs over 2,000 feet (610 meters) of altitude through the almost vertical Gemmiwand (Gemmi Wall). Many famous writers such as Goethe, Arthur Conan Doyle, and Mark Twain wrote about this path, and perhaps this is why the pass was so popular with the English.[539] There were no indications of Tolkien's presence in the guestbook of the only hut in the middle of the way, the Schwarenbach mountain inn.[540] However, the 12.5 miles (20 kilometers) from Leukerbad to Kandersteg can be hiked in one day, and signatures in the guestbook

---

[535] The Tunnel du Mont d'Or, which is 3.7 miles (6 kilometers) in length and cuts through the Jura between Lausanne and Paris, was only opened in 1915. The same applies to the over 5-mile (8-kilometer) Grenchenberg Tunnel between Delémont and Biel (1915) and the similarly long Hauenstein Base Tunnel between Olten and Basel (1916). The route via Lausanne and Paris still led through the Tunnel of Jougne, which was only about one mile (1,560 meters) long. And the route via Bern and Basel to the French East Railway (Chemins de fer de l'Est) was through the 1.55-mile (2,495-meter) Hauenstein Summit Tunnel.

[536] Briger Anzeiger of August 19, 1911.

[537] Frías Sánchez (2009), 13 ff., who referred to Elmer Wood (1910); similarly also Lewis and Currie (2019), 194 ff.

[538] Murray (1904), li f.

[539] See for example Bechtel (2004); Goethe (1830), 268 ff.

[540] Lewis and Currie (2019), 194.

are therefore not essential. But even this route still does not explain the ominous tunnel mentioned by Colin Brookes-Smith.

There would be another way back to Lake Thun, and this one does lead through a gigantic tunnel: the Lötschberg — *Moria*. A crossing of the Lötschberg Tunnel would have been theoretically possible in the summer of 1911, as mentioned at the beginning of this book, for the (literal) breakthrough occurred in the spring of that year.[541] However, since the tracks were not laid until 1912, the crossing would have had to be done on foot: 14.6 kilometers (9 miles) or at least four hours of darkness. This would explain why Colin Brookes-Smith remembered a gigantic tunnel from his return journey.

The numerous human sacrifices that the construction of the Lötschberg Tunnel entailed have al-

74 The Gemmi Wall; here, the path leads up. Photo: Wikimedia Commons user Photolovy, *Gemmi Daubenwand*, slightly edited, CC-BY-SA 3.0.

ready been mentioned; an uneasy feeling must have gripped someone who crossed the tunnel in 1911. In January 1910, an avalanche buried the southern entrance to the tunnel and temporarily trapped several workers.[542] This event must have still been very present in people's minds in 1911 and could explain why the entrance to the Mines of Moria gets buried in *The Lord of the Rings* after the companions step into the mines. But the way over the Gemmi Pass was dangerous as well. In her novel *An Oberland Châlet*, published in 1910, for example, Edith Elmer Wood reported little tablets and monuments along the path that commemorated those who had fallen to their deaths, and she also mentioned another tablet on the high plateau near Lake Dauben (Daubensee), where six people had died in a glacier collapse in 1895.[543] She felt the somber and menacing character of the scenery keenly when she passed

---

541   Above, pp. 31 f.

542   See Briger Anzeiger of 26 January 1910, 2; Le Nouvelliste of 25 January 1910, 3.

543   Elmer Wood (1910), 145 f.

this place under the glaciers herself.[544] Sir Arthur Conan-Doyle probably described the same place, autobiographically I suppose, in the famous Sherlock Holmes finale "The Final Problem."[545] As they walked along the melancholic lake, a large rock broke loose, he remembered, and crashed into the lake behind them. In vain, the mountain guide assured Holmes that a rockfall in spring was not unusual at this place; Holmes (or better Sir Arthur Conan-Doyle) was not reassured at all.[546] The episode recalls the rockfall that Tolkien himself located near the Aletsch Glacier and indicates that this passage near Lake Dauben must have been hazardous in the hot summer of 1911.

Colin Brookes-Smith mentioned a dangerous walk near the end of his trip report. The group had to negotiate protruding obstacles with towering rock on one side and an "apparently bottomless" valley on the other, he remembered,[547] and this may well have been at the Gemmi Pass. Were they maybe even forced to turn back, just like the companions in *The Lord of the Rings*, and to choose the path through the Lötschberg Tunnel? It is speculative but

75 Drainless Lake Dauben as a possible source of inspiration for Mirrormere; photo: Adrian Michael, *Daubensee1*, slightly edited, CC-BY-SA 3.0.

---

544   Elmer Wood (1910), 146.

545   *Arthur Conan Doyle*, The Final Problem, 1893, 14 f.

546   *Arthur Conan Doyle*, The Final Problem, 1893, 15.

547   Brookes-Smith (1982), 3; cf. Morton and Hayes (2008), 71; Frías Sánchez (2009), 16.

76 Johann Rudolf Bühlmann, *Le lac de la Daube, passage de la Gemmi*, 1837–1839, digitized by the Swiss National Library, GS-GRAF-ANSI-VS-24.

conceivable, and they would not have been the first who had to turn back at this very place. None less than Johann Wolfgang von Goethe had to turn around, too, he because of snowfall, as he told us in his report on his second trip to Switzerland.[548]

Apart from the Gemmi Pass and the Lötschberg Tunnel, there is a third conceivable way back to the Bernese Oberland, the Lötschen Pass. The Tolkien researchers Lewis and Currie convincingly suggested that the group might have chosen this higher, less common pass, just like in *The Hobbit*.[549] On this path, they would have not only passed by the so-called High Bridge (Hohe Brücke; Figure 77), the Gestelnburg castle Helm's Deep, and the Lötschen Valley with its orkish masks but also by both the south and the north portal of the Lötschberg Tunnel. And this could explain, too, why Brookes-Smith remembered an impressively large railway tunnel, for if you look closely, it does not necessarily follow from his statements that they passed

---

[548]   Goethe (1830), 268 ff.
[549]   Lewis and Currie (2019), 194.

77 The High Bridge near Leuk would also be a good Bridge of Khazad-dûm; photo: Björn Sothmann, *Hohe Brücke mit Kapelle Leuk 07 12 2014 01*, slightly edited, CC-BY-SA 3.0.

through the tunnel. The solution to the riddle perhaps: Tolkien would have crossed the tunnel only in his imagination.

However, the crossing of the Gemmi Pass has features that are more reminiscent of Tolkien's works. Lake Dauben, for example, is reminiscent of Mirrormere, the lake below the East-gate of Moria, for apart from its (somewhat) oval shape and position cut into the mountains, Lake Dauben, like Mirrormere, has no above-ground outlet.[550] Furthermore, in *The Lord of the Rings*, Mirrormere's dark water is repeatedly mentioned, which would etymologically fit Lake Dauben (dialect: Dubesee), since the Celtic word *dubo*, which means "black," is said to have given the lake its name.[551] If Lake Dauben inspired Mirrormere, then the spring of the Silverlode could be found in the crystal-clear Arveseeli or in the Spittelmatteseeli—small lakes which are located to the north of Lake Dauben. And the Dimrill Dale could perhaps be

---

[550]   In the case of Mirrormere, this seems to result from the following statement: *"About [the mere] lay a smooth sward, shelving down on all sides to its bare unbroken rim."* (*The Fellowship of the Ring*, Book 2, chap. IV); only a little below the lake, the fellowship reach the spring of the Celebrant.

[551]   Sommer (1957), 102 f.

found in the valley of the Schwarzbach (meaning "black stream") below. Further down, the Schwarzbach flows into the larger Kander, which etymologically fits the Silverlode, for the name *Kander* is derived from the Celtic word **kandarā*, which means "shining" or "white."[552] And finally, in Kandersteg, Tolkien and his friends would have reached at least the north portal of the

78 The three main options for a return journey to the Bernese Oberland in blue (and black): the Gemmi Pass, the Lötschen Pass, and the Lötschberg Tunnel (on foot), with possible sources of inspiration. The larger the font the more likely an inspiration seems to me. The map is based on: Bergfex OSM, © OpenStreetMap.org-Contributors, CC-BY-SA, see p. 286, no. 2.

---

552   See the entry for Kandersteg at www.ortsnamen.ch; however, the same applies to some other streams such as the Lütschine.

Lötschberg Tunnel and the workers' settlements there, which could still explain why Colin Brookes-Smith remembered an impressive tunnel.

The assumption of a return trip to the Bernese Oberland thus remains speculative, but there are a few indications that support it. Regardless of the exact route, such a return to Lake Thun would also fit the plot in *The Hobbit* exceptionally well, as will be shown in this third part. But even if the assumption of such a return journey is not correct, it could still be that Tolkien was inspired by Lake Thun and its myths, as he began his journey in Interlaken, which lies between Lake Thun and Lake Brienz.

II.   Into the Woodland Realm at Blausee

On the other side of the old Lötschberg Tunnel lies Kandersteg and, not far from there, on the right-hand side, is Lake Oeschinen. The lake is a possible source of inspiration for the lake at the West-gate of Moria, that is, the lake where the Watcher in the Water lurks for the companions in *The Lord of the Rings*. Apart from that, it is also conceivable that it inspired Mirromere, but Lake Dauben is, I would say, a more probable source of inspiration for that lake. Regardless of this, the sparkling dark lake under the high mountains offers a most beautiful picture and is definitely worth a visit—but better during the week and not in the main holiday season (Figure 79).

Further down the valley, you then reach a wooded area with another—somewhat too crowded—pearl: the Blausee (Blue Lake). Inspiration or not, whoever is looking for an inspiring place for Wood-elves should stop here. The clear light blue of the lake in the middle of the dark green of the forest is magical, and an Elven type of legend tells of how the lake got its blue color.[553]

A long time ago, a young woman who lived nearby fell in love with a shepherd. The two spent many joyful hours together on the lake, but one day, the shepherd fell over a cliff to his death. The young woman was inconsolable. At night, she would sneak to the lake, row to the middle, and abandon herself to her grief. Again and again, she would beg heaven to return her beloved to her, but to no avail; and so her senses gradually became confused. In vain, her parents tried to keep her from these nocturnal excursions; a mysterious force drew her back again and again to this place where she had once been so happy. So, she continued to sneak out at night until one morning she was seen lying at the bottom of the lake, the waters of which were suddenly deep blue. The

---

[553]   See www.blausee.ch/de/chronik.

79 Lake Blausee, a perfect place for Wood-elves.

tears of the blue-eyed young woman, the people speculated, must have given the lake this color.

The legend fits Tolkien's tales of love between immortal Elves and mortal men: between the mortal Beren and the Elven Lúthien, and between Aragorn and Arwen. Lúthien takes her own life after Beren dies in the fight against the giant wolf Carcharoth, while Arwen seeks out the hill Cerin Amroth in Lórien after Aragorn's death. Like the lake in the legend, this hill is a place where the two of them had once been very happy; Aragorn had proposed to her there. And like the young woman in the legend, Arwen also passes away in her grief at this place.

I do not want to give the impression that Lake Blausee and its legend necessarily inspired Tolkien; there is simply too little evidence, and there are probably many similar tales. But the place is worth a visit, and it fits the Woodland Realm between the Misty Mountains and the Long Lake in *The Hobbit* suspiciously well in terms of the picture, the location, and the legend.

By the way, the story of Beren and Lúthien was a very personal one for Tolkien. He and his wife Edith even had the names of the two figures engraved on their gravestone.

III. Esgaroth and the Alpine Lake Dwellings

From the palace of the Elvenking in the Woodland Realm, Bilbo and the dwarves get downstream in barrels to the Long Lake. Similarly, the Kander flows down the valley past the Blausee and then, along with the river Simme, through a channel built in the eighteenth century, into Lake Thun. Like the Rhône, the Kander was used for forestry in the nineteenth century, and probably still at the time of Tolkien's trip to Switzerland. Logs were driven, that is, loosely left in the creek and then collected further down; and there, maybe still before the lake, they were probably tied together into rafts.[554] It is the perfect place for the Raft-elves.

The Long Lake, the town in it, and the adjacent Lonely Mountain form the last scenery of *The Hobbit*. Could this scenery also have been inspired in Switzerland? In a letter to his son Michael, Tolkien stated, "The hobbit's (Bilbo's) journey from Rivendell to the other side of the Misty Mountains, including the glissade down the slithering stones into the pine woods, is based on my adventures in 1911."[555] Does that, conversely, mean that the rest is not? The opposite seems to be true.

As various authors have convincingly pointed out, Lake-town (Esgaroth) was most likely inspired by the Alpine lake dwellings from the Bronze Age (in German *Pfahlbauten*, "pile structures"), and this fact alone already shows a connection to Switzerland.[556] Tolkien hinted at such an inspiration quite clearly in *The Hobbit* when he mentioned the rotting piles of a larger city that would become visible during a drought.[557] This is precisely how the first lake dwellings were discovered. The so-called *Pfahlbaufieber* (pile-dwelling fever), which apparently also infected Tolkien, broke out in Switzerland in the nineteenth century after Ferdinand Keller had first scientifically investigated a pile-dwelling settlement in Lake Zurich in 1855 (cf. Figure 80).[558] Public interest was enormous. Even a national myth about the origins of the Swiss people quickly formed, which was gratefully received by politicians in the still young and both linguistically and denominationally heterogeneous Swiss federal state.[559]

The fascination for these lake dwellings quickly spilled over to other countries, and quite a few such settlements were discovered around the world. Nevertheless, the lake dwellings remained characteristic for Switzerland and were mentioned in detail in the Murray's handbooks for travelers (in 1886,

---

[554] Bütschi (2008), 34 f.

[555] *Letters of Tolkien*, no. 306.

[556] So already for example *Artist & Illustrator*, 132, 135; of the 111 sites in the UNESCO inventory, 56 are located in Switzerland.

[557] *The Hobbit*, chap. X.

[558] That there were piles in the lakes was known much earlier, see Ischer (1911).

[559] See for example Christian Harb et al. (2010), 127.

still with an illustration).[560] Although this idea of settlements in lakes was put into question after that, more recent research, as in Zurich, showed that there were settlements in the water indeed—there were settlements also on the shores, yes, but this was never in question.[561]

80 *Swiss prehistoric lake dwellings*, drawing by Adrien de Mortillet, 1903; Credit: Wellcome Library, London. This file comes from Science Museum Group, in the United Kingdom. Refer to Wellcome blog post (https://wellcome.org/press-release /thousands-years-visual-culture-made-free-through-wellcome-images), slightly edited, CC-BY 4.0.

IV. Lake Thun as the Long Lake

If Lake-town was inspired by the Alpine lake dwellings, the question arises whether the Long Lake was inspired by a specific lake. As already indicated, Lake Thun would be an obvious choice, as it formed the beginning and perhaps also the end of Tolkien's journey. At first glance, the location in the middle of the mountains does not seem to fit very well, but Tolkien's illustration of the Long Lake is reminiscent of Lake Thun,[562] and there is also a

---

560   Murray (1904), xcv; Murray (1886), lxxvii still with a special title.

561   See Harb et al. (2010), 130; Bleicher (2015), 30.

562   See *Artist & Illustrator*, 131; today, the view towards Lake Thun is somewhat disturbed by the ship canal and the freeway, but in 1911 none of these constructions existed yet, see Dubler (2012).

good candidate for the Lonely Mountain at its side.[563] Moreover, Lake Thun is the only large lake that we know for certain Tolkien saw during his journey in Switzerland, and there is even a legend there that suspiciously recalls the plot in *The Hobbit*. However, I was not entirely convinced until I learned of an event on Lake Thun that took place while Tolkien was still in Switzerland—but more on that later.

Another lake candidate is Lake Brienz, which is on the other side of Interlaken, but much speaks for Lake Thun. And whether Lake Thun or Lake Brienz is from a historical point of view—as we say in Switzerland—anyway *"Hans was Heiri"* ("John or Henry," meaning "it does not matter"), because at the time of the lake dwellers, there was only one long lake. The delta of the stream Lütschine at Interlaken did not completely divide the original lake until around the beginning of the Common Era.[564]

81 Lake Thun in the direction of the Niesen (*Der Thunersee nach dem Niesen*), by Johann Heinrich Bleuler Jr., 1837, digitized by the Swiss National Library, GS-GUGE-BLEULER-1-13.

---

[563] See below, p. 222; the mountain group with the Niederhorn and the Sigriswiler Rothorn could also be a candidate, for this mountain group rises on the opposite side of Lake Thun (and above the Beatus Caves) if you come from Kandersteg.

[564] See for example Welten (1976), 34; I would like to thank Gabriel Gertsch for pointing this out to me.

82 View near Goldweil on Lake Thun (*Aussicht bei Goldweil am Thunersee*), by Johann Heinrich Bleuler Jr.,1836, digitized by the Swiss National Library, GS-GUGE-BLEULER-1-14.

Until recently, Lake Thun had not been famous for its pile dwellings, but they became a subject of discussion there as early as 1897, when piles were discovered in a clay pit, and in 1924, there were clear findings.[565] Nevertheless, the fact that finds at Lake Thun were scarce indicates that Tolkien might have been inspired more by other lakes further away from the mountains, such as Lake Neuchâtel, Lake Zurich, Lake Geneva, or Lake Maggiore (in German *Langensee*, meaning "Long Lake"). However, Tolkien's itinerary, local legends, and the special event already hinted at allude to a primary influence by Lake Thun.

Tolkien made a very nice illustration entitled *Bilbo comes to the Huts of the Raft-elves*; it shows Bilbo reaching the Long Lake on a barrel.[566] The lake depicted is indeed somewhat reminiscent of Lake Thun, and even more so when one looks at the two paintings by Johann Heinrich Bleuler Jr. from the years 1836 and 1837 (Figures 81 and 82). The first one particularly caught my attention, as it shows Lake Thun with barrels. But the second one is also in-

---

565   See Schärer and Ramstein (2017), 20 f.

566   *Artist & Illustrator*, 131.

teresting, as it shows a raft on the river if you look closely. Looking at these pictures, it is easy to imagine that Tolkien witnessed barrels being driven down the streams from Lauterbrunnen and Kandersteg to Lake Thun, and that they were tied together to rafts before they reached the lake—as is the case in *The Hobbit*.

V.   Interlaken or Thun as Lake-Town

Since Lake-town is essentially a pile-dwelling settlement, a comparison with an existing town seems to make only limited sense. From a toponymic point of view, such a comparison with the towns in question—Thun, Interlaken, and Unterseen—is noteworthy nevertheless. Both Interlaken and the neighboring community of Unterseen mean "between the lakes."[567] Thun, on the

83 Unterseen, a possible source of inspiration for Lake-town, with the Lauterbrunnen Valley and the Jungfrau in the background. Tolkien's journey began here, but this bridge no longer existed even then. Painting: Gabriel Lory the Younger, *Unterseen mit Blick auf die Jungfrau*, 1845, digitized by the Swiss National Library, GS-GUGE-LORY-A-4.

---

[567]   See the entry for Unterseen at www.ortsnamen.ch.

84 Lake-town Thun, aquatint by Gabriel Lory "père" and Johann Hürlimann, *Vue du Chateau et de la Ville de Thoune* (View of the castle and the town of Thun), early 19ᵗʰ century, digitized by the Swiss National Library, GS-GUGE-LORY-C-17.

other hand, is said to come from the Celtic word *dūnon* (Latinized *dūnum*), which means "palisade work," "castle," or "fortified place" and is said to be related to the English word *town*.[568] Thus, all the names are descriptive, just like Lake-town, which etymologically seems to carry both a part of Interlaken and a part of Thun.

This connection may be a coincidence, but as already mentioned several times, the origin of names was a topic that fascinated Tolkien and one he studied in his professional life. His reaction to his son's lecture about Attila,[569] along with a letter in which Tolkien wrote many lines about the Shire's toponymy, show his fascination particularly well.[570] And Tolkien also used other Swiss place names in Middle-earth such as *Lauterbrunnen* (for the river Loudwater or Bruinen), *Silberhorn* (for the Silvertine), and possibly *Rhône* (for Rohan), *Weisshorn* (for the Whitehorn Mountains), *Gondo* and *Mont*

---

[568] See the entry for Thun at www.ortsnamen.ch; see also Lewis and Currie (2019), 245 ff., 250, who already pointed this out.

[569] See above, pp. 171 f.

[570] *Letters of Tolkien*, no. 190.

Gond (for Gondor), *Tourbillon* (for Tower of Vigilance or Minas Tirith), and *Monte Moro* (for Mordor).

I prefer Thun with its old town and bridges to Interlaken as a possible source of inspiration for Lake-town, but this is ultimately more a personal preference, for unlike Interlaken, Tolkien did not mention Thun in his letters. A visualization of the Beatus legend might indicate that Thun is indeed the true Lake-town;[571] but today, to be completely honest, neither Interlaken nor Thun is tightly connected with the lake. In this respect, a better Lake-town is Spiez (see Figure 94, page 229), and this happens to be the place where Tolkien would have first arrived on his way back.[572] But looking at the word picture and the toponymy—taking that *Thun* means "town"—it is actually the lake itself that fits best to Lake-town. Yes, that might be it indeed: Lake Thun=Lake-town—it is the sort of thing you just notice if you translate your book into English.

85 View of Lake Thun from Thun with the Niesen and the Alps in the background, colored outline etching by Jakob Samuel Weibel, *Vue des Environs de Thoune* (View of the surroundings of Thun), 1796, digitized by the Swiss National Library, GS-GU GE-WEIBEL-E-1.

---

[571]   See below, p. 219.
[572]   Or at the castle Weissenau near Interlaken, see Lewis and Currie (2019), 29.

Inspiration in the Local World of Legend

As in the Misty Mountains, it is also worthwhile to look at Lake Thun's local legends. However, I would first like to go to the cozy Emmental valley to meet the priest Albert Bitzius with his wild imagination.

I.   Gotthelf's *The Black Spider*

Albert Bitzius, better known under his pseudonym Jeremias Gotthelf, is one of the most well-known Swiss writers of the nineteenth century, and his novella *The Black Spider*, from 1842, is his most famous work. The novella is set in an idyllic, quite Shire-like village in the Emmental, where a baptismal ceremony is taking place: there is plenty of food—Bitzius spared no details—chatting, and, of course, pipe smoking. As some of the members of the baptismal celebration stretch their legs with full bellies, the cousin, under a flowering tree, thinks that this would be an excellent place for a pipe; and while they are sitting there looking at the surroundings, a woman notices an old black window post at the new house of her grandfather below. Asked about it, the grandfather first takes a deep puff from his pipe, then he comes out with the story: the story of the black spider.

The grandfather recounts that centuries ago, the village inhabitants had been driven into poverty by their feudal lord and, therefore, made a pact with the devil: for his help, they promised him a newborn, unbaptized child. But while the devil fulfilled his part of the pact, the villagers kept baptizing their newborns as quickly as possible and thus angered the devil. Soon, a black spider grew out of a villager's cheek that the devil had kissed. The spider spread fear and terror, but this was just the beginning. Before long, spiders were swarming all around: They multiplied rapidly, infesting first the animals and then the people, and they settled in the vicinity of the village so that any attempt to escape was futile. Then it dawned on even the last of them that this was a plague of evil: a means of coercion to enforce the pact. But after a period of great suffering, a mother finally managed to seal the spider—suddenly it was just a spider again—with invocations to God into a post hole with a peg—the window post.

Tolkien's novels share remarkable similarities to Gotthelf's *The Black Spider*, but one should not jump to conclusions. Mirkwood's spiders, like Gotthelf's black spider, are indeed a sign of evil, a shadow of the resurgent devil Sauron stretching over Mirkwood.[573] The spiders are also associated with a spreading disease in the movies. However, the latter does not seem to be the case in the books, and the former alone is hardly enough. This connection between the strengthening of the devil and the appearance of spiders can therefore be seen, if at all, only as a weak indication of an influence.

Another common feature is the framework of the plot. Similar to Tolkien's *The Hobbit* and *The Lord of the Rings*, Gotthelf's *The Black Spider* begins in a country idyll with its simple but generally good-natured and content inhabitants before the story drifts off into a legendary world and finally leads back to the country idyll. However, this similarity should not be overestimated either, for it may be just because both Gotthelf and Tolkien combined elements of the literary trends of the Romantic and Biedermeier periods in their works. While the turning to the past and the world of legends as well as the travel element are typical characteristics of Romanticism, the Biedermeier period is characterized above all by domesticity, closeness to nature, folklore elements, and a need for harmony, as we find them in Gotthelf's Emmental but also in Tolkien's Shire. The plot frames are thus remarkably similar, but one cannot necessarily derive Tolkien's inspiration from this either.

Finally, similarities can also be found in Gotthelf's other novellas, above all *Sintram und Bertram* and *Die Rotentaler Herren*. In the novella *Sintram und Bertram,* two brothers first fight their way through the dense woods of the Swiss midlands in the early Middle Ages before they meet an elven-like lady of the river and finally fight a dragon near Burgdorf. And in the story *Die Rotentaler Herren (The Lords of the Red Valley),* an older man with silver hair tells his neighbor on a bench on a hill the story of these lords of the Red Valley: on the slopes of the Jungfrau they had once lived as giants in a golden city, he explains, but when they started assaulting humans, a superhuman old man appeared and took revenge so that the descendants now roam the land cursed.

However, in these stories, the similarities are probably due to Tolkien and Gotthelf being inspired by the same legends. Gotthelf's *Sintram and Bertram* is linked to the *Thidrekssaga* with its stories about Dietrich von Bern[574] and Gotthelf's *The Lords of the Red Valley* to the legend of the same name. Both sources seem to have inspired Tolkien directly. In fact, Gotthelf's version of

---

573   Cf. *The Silmarillion*, chap. "Of the Rings of Power and the Third Age."

574   Above, pp. 67 ff., 79.

The Lords of the Red Valley could not have inspired Tolkien—at least not for *The Hobbit*—since it was posthumously published in 1941 and thus after *The Hobbit*. Gotthelf did not publish the story during his lifetime because his wife thought it was a complete failure—poor guy. The lords should not be giants but, rather, more ordinary people, she supposedly told him.[575] Well, Tolkien would probably agree that they should be smaller—maybe even smaller than humans in the shadow of these mountains that make everyone a dwarf.

It is remarkable, though, that a mountain spirit appears in the figure of an old man in Gotthelf's version of *The Lords of the Red Valley*, for this allows a new reading of Tolkien's works. In that case, Gandalf would be responsible for the appearance of the dragon in the Lonely Mountain and the Balrog in Moria. His purpose would be to teach the greedy Dwarves a lesson, as an educational measure, so to speak.

There are some quite remarkable parallels between Tolkien's and Gotthelf's works, but at least at this point, they are not sufficient to conclude that Tolkien was inspired by the Swiss pastor.

II.   The Dragon and the Dwarfs

Smaug and his conversations with Bilbo in *The Hobbit* are in debt to the dragon Fafnir in the late Norse versions of the Sigurd-story. Tolkien once admitted this himself.[576] And *Beowulf* probably had an influence as well, even though Tolkien said in this respect that the poem was not actively present in his mind when he wrote *The Hobbit*.[577] Is there perhaps room for another legend as a source of inspiration?

1.   Beatus and the Dragon

At Lake Thun, there is also a dragon myth, the Beatus legend. It has already been considered by different authors as a possible source of inspiration of Tolkien.[578] The legend takes place in a time when the inhabitants of the Bernese Oberland still lived in paganism and the long lake, called Wendelsee, was not yet entirely divided into two parts by the Interlaken plain delta. Dur-

---

86 The dragon Fafnir from the Saga of the Nibelungs: the left image bears similarities to Tolkien's own illustration of Smaug, the right is perhaps somewhat reminiscent of the elevated cave entrance. Illustrations by Arthur Rackham from Richard Wagner's *The Rhinegold and the Valkyrie*, 1910 (right image) and *Siegfried and the Twilight of the Gods*, 1911 (left image); Tolkien mentioned Rackham in Letters nos. 202 and 235.

ing this time, two strangers with coats and pilgrim's staff crossed the Brünig Pass to this still inhospitable plain and then on to the ancient village of Sundlauenen on what is now Lake Thun.

There, the two, the monk Beatus and his companion Achates, were welcomed by friendly shepherds. But the idyllic atmosphere was deceptive, for the shepherds told the strangers about a large, cruel dragon that was hidden in a nearby cave and caused mischief in the surrounding area. So Beatus asked a shipman to take him to the mountain where the dragon lived, and since Beatus could not pay for it, the shipman took him there for free. Once there, he climbed up to the cave and subdued the dragon by holding up the cross — a bit boring, I know, but, unfortunately, holding up the cross is something like the Death Star of Christian mythology.

With a faint howling, the dragon left the flames-wrapped cave and fell into the lake; a thunderous crash could be heard with an echo from the Evening Mountain on the lake's other side, and the lake is said to have boiled and bubbled. The danger was thus averted, for which the inhabitants of the area were extremely grateful to Beatus. And he himself then moved into the cave and lived there as a hermit until he passed away at an old age.

2.   Beatus and the Dwarfs

Part of the same story is the legend of Beatus and the dwarfs.[579] According to this legend, dwarfs were living in the cave when the dragon settled there, and they, too, were extremely grateful to Beatus when he subdued the dragon. They quickly established friendly relations with him and helped him however they could: they brought him chamois milk, cheese, water, and dry wood for the fire, and they supported him in planting and caring for fruit trees and herbs below the entrance to the

87 Beatus fights the dragon, in the background Thun, from Heinrich Murer's *Helvetia Sancta*, 1648, p. 6.

cave. Most of the harvested fruits and healing herbs, Beatus did not use for himself; he brought them to the many suffering people in the region.

3.   Appreciation: Beatus Bilbo

There are some reasons to believe that the Beatus legend inspired Tolkien. The story of a dragon that wreaks havoc on a long lake fits the plot of *The Hobbit* very well, especially if the dragon drives away or at least disturbs dwarfs living in the cave. But this is not all: just like in *The Hobbit*, there is also a waterfall at the cave entrance, a stranger helps the dwarfs, and the dragon finally plunges into the lake. Furthermore, all this happens at Lake Thun, a probable source of inspiration for the Long Lake, and the city of Thun indeed resembles Lake-town a bit in an old visualization of the Beatus legend (Figure 87). Moreover, quite late during my research, I finally found out that a "settlement site of prehistoric times" was discovered in the Beatus

---

[579]   Hartmann (1910), 53; Dummermuth (1889), summarized by Ueli Häsler, "Beatus, der Thunersee Heilige," jakobsweg.ch, https://jakobsweg.ch/de/eu/ch/spiritualitaet /impulse-fuer-unterwegs/geschichten-reflexionen/beatuslegende.

Caves while Tolkien was probably still in Switzerland, thus a mountain-dwelling supplement, so to speak, to the lake dwellings.[580]

The origin of the monk Beatus is also remarkable, for he is said to have come from England or at least the British Isles.[581] Very similarly, the hobbit Bilbo comes from the England-inspired Shire and makes an adventurous journey over the Switzerland-inspired Misty Mountains before he finally faces a dragon at a long lake to help the humans and dwarves living there. And unlike ordinary dragon fighters, both Beatus and Bilbo do not excel in fighting power but instead in wit and courage. Since Bilbo's tale and Tolkien's journey to Switzerland are firmly linked, it even seems likely that Tolkien could identify himself a bit with Beatus.

88 The entrance to the Beatus Caves with the small waterfall.

An inspiration for Bilbo's story in *The Hobbit* by Saint Beatus should come as no surprise since Frodo's story in *The Lord of the Rings* appears to be inspired by at least two papal legends.[582] Tolkien was a devout Catholic, and he confessed on his vacations in Switzerland.[583] So he probably also attended church services, and perhaps he heard about Saint Beatus there. But the legend was also mentioned in Murray's guidebook from 1904; and maybe Tolkien visited the caves himself at the beginning or end of his journey, as it is located not far from Interlaken and was accessible to tourists in 1911—and even already equipped with electric light.[584] Yet perhaps

---

580   *Tagblatt der Stadt Thun*, September 1, 1911, p. 3.

581   Gelpke (1862), 1; Lütolf (1871), 1 speaks of a handsome and rich young man from the nation of the Britons; other sources refer to Scotland or Ireland, see for example Murray (1904), 221.

582   Above, pp. 171 f.

583   See e.g. *Letters of Tolkien*, nos. 195, 213, 306.

584   Cf. Thomas Cook & Son (1908), 153; Murray (1904), 221; *Thuner Tagblatt*, August 19, 1911, p. 2, according to which there was a forest fire there too.

more than the caves, the cave entrance with the waterfall flowing out of it and the magnificent view over Lake Thun to the Niesen on the other side is worth a visit.

III. Gold Caves in the Rothorn and near Lauterbrunnen

Various legends tell of gold caves in the Bernese Oberland. One mentions caves with rich gold treasures in the ridge flanks near the Eisee lake on the east side of the Brienzer Rothorn, that is, next to Lake Brienz. However, in order to be able to dig for gold, one has to know a magic spell, and a time came in which no one remembered it. Searchers still found gold-diggers' old tools at the site, but gold was no longer shown to anyone.[585]

A second legend, which is part of Hermann Hartmann's collection, tells of a little old man who, from time to time, descended to the hamlet of Lauterbrunnen from the Steinenberg (Stone Mountain) and the Hohenalp (High Alp) with a large carrying basket on his back. One day he told the villagers that he was leaving; whoever climbed up to the Dürlocherhorn would find steps carved into the rock and a pickaxe marking a spot on the rock face. If the visitor were to knock on the wall with the pickaxe, he said, it would open to a great treasure of gold. No sooner had he uttered these words than the little man disappeared. Three men then set out to look for the gold, but while they found the place with the steps in the rock face, there was no trace of the pickaxe. And, oh horror, instead, a huge lizard was lying across the path and gazed at them with rolling eyes (see Figure 89).[586]

89 *The Little Gold Digger of Lauterbrunnen,* pen and ink drawing by Paul Kammüller, from Hartmann (1910), 33.

---

[585]   Streich (1978), 76.

[586]   Hartmann (1910), 56 and *Tafel IV.*

There are many more such legends. Goldswil near Interlaken, for example, is said to have once been a gold-digger village, and the inhabitants of Roll at Lake Thun were also allegedly once known for their gold-digging skills. However, when they insulted dwarfs, their luck came to an abrupt end, for their village was buried by a rockfall.[587]

Especially the first two legends strongly recall *The Hobbit*. A secret entrance to a treasure chamber with a dragon, steps carved into the rock, and a gate opening spell: all this can also be found in *The Hobbit*. Furthermore, the first of these stories is set at a mountain called Rothorn (Redhorn) on Lake Brienz and thus on the Wendelsee, the former Long Lake. And the second one is set just next to the very mountains that inspired Tolkien for the Mountains of Moria.[588] Nevertheless, as long as it is not established that Tolkien knew these legends, or at least Hermann Hartmann's collection, such an influence is speculative since there are probably many similar mining legends.

The City of Dale
and the Lonely Mountain

I.   The Niesen as the Lonely Mountain

If the Long Lake was inspired by Lake Thun or perhaps even the former Wendelsee, the question arises whether the Lonely Mountain Erebor also has a model in Switzerland. The Matterhorn and the Temple Mount have already been mentioned as a possible source of inspiration, but there is probably a more convincing one at Lake Thun, the Niesen. With its extraordinary pyramid shape, this mountain has always inspired artists. Seen from the Beatus Caves, it rises majestically above the water on the opposite side of the lake. And from the villages of Gunten and Sigriswil, the pyramid shape can be seen even better (Figure 90).

Three anecdotes about the Niesen are worth mentioning. First, one peak of the Niesen chain is called Drunengalm, and according to the operator of the Niesen Funicular (the cable car leading up to the mountain), *Drunen*

---

[587]   Hartmann (1910), 56.
[588]   Above, pp. 26 ff.

222

means "dragon."[589] A dragon on the Lonely Mountain seems appropriate, but the alleged word origin is doubtful. Second, the Niesen Funicular leading up to the summit was completed in 1910, the year before Tolkien visited Switzerland, and there were not many such funiculars in existence at that time. And third, according to the *Guinness World Records*, the cable car is accompanied by the world's longest staircase: 11,674 steps lead up to the summit over a height difference of 5,390 feet (1,643 meters). In *The Lord of the Rings*, there is also an endless staircase that leads from the deepest halls of Khazaddûm up to Durin's Tower on the Silvertine. While it is conceivable that the endless Niesen staircase was the source of inspiration, it seems more likely to me that the Jungfrau Railway was the primary source.

Perhaps, if you will allow me, there is a fourth, final anecdote: The painter Paul Klee gave the name *Ad Parnassum* to one of his paintings, which most likely shows the Niesen. In Greek mythology, the Muses, the goddesses of the arts, lived on Mount Parnassus above Delphi. The mountain was thus the home of poetry, music, and learning: a truly fitting place for the Lonely Mountain in *The Hobbit*.

90 The Niesen from Gunten as a possible source of inspiration for the Erebor.

---

589   See www.niesen.ch/de/info/geschichte/?oid=1856&lang=de.

I have to admit, Tolkien's sketches of the Lonely Mountain do not necessarily support the hypothesis of an inspiration by the Niesen.[590] But when I found out about a special event in August 1911, I was nevertheless finally convinced. At the very end of this book, I will come back to it.

II.   Mount Pilatus as the Lonely Mountain

Mount Pilatus near Lucerne is a third candidate for the Loney Mountain in Switzerland following the Niesen and the Matterhorn (aside from Mount Zion). It is said that a dragon once lived on Mount Pilatus, too; the Museum of Nature in Lucerne even keeps a dragon stone as a relic.[591] Apparently, Switzerland, just like Bethesda's Skyrim, was once teeming with dragons. However, Tolkien was, as far as we know, not in Lucerne, and Lake Lucerne also does not fit too well to the Long Lake, which is why I believe that Tolkien's primary sources of inspiration were the Niesen and Lake Thun.

The legend about how the mountain got its name is nevertheless worth mentioning. Such ecclesiastical tales seem to have particularly interested Tolkien, and this famous legend was also mentioned in the contemporary travel guidebook of Murray.[592] It is a bit reminiscent of Tolkien's work, more so actually of *The Lord of the Rings* than of *The Hobbit*; yet first and foremost, I found the story too remarkable to leave it out here.

According to the legend, the Roman prefect Pontius Pilate, accused by the Roman Emperor of the crucifixion of Jesus, took his own life in a prison cell in Rome.[593] After his death, the Romans first threw his body into the Tiber River, but soon storms and epidemics of all kinds occurred. Therefore, they fished the body out of the river and brought it to Gaul, where they threw it again near Lyon into a river, this time the Rhône. But there, too, it was like hell afterward; so they fished the body out of the river once more and brought it to Lausanne, but the spirit did not find peace there either. Eventually, they decided to take the body to an isolated place, so they transported it to a mountain lake on the Frakmunt, today's Mount Pilatus near Lucerne. But the spirit simply would not rest. On this mountain, he only did worse: with heavy storms and avalanches, which he threw in the spring against his sparring partner King Herod. Only with horror did the inhabitants of the area

---

590   See for example *Artist & Illustrator*, 130, 142 ff.

591   See www.pilatus.ch/entdecken/drachenweg and www.naturmuseum.ch.

592   See Lienert (2006), 69 ff.; Murray (1904), 301 f.

593   This is doubted, though.

look up to the dark mountain, whose head was almost always in a black cap of fog.

Thus, the inhabitants lived in fear of Pilate's ghost until a traveling student from the underground school of Salamanca came to Lucerne and offered to banish the ghost forever into the lake. They gratefully accepted this offer, and so the student climbed the highest peak of Mount Pilatus and began the incantation. The rocks started to sway, the whole mountain threatened to collapse, but the spirit did not give way. On the Widderfeld (Ram Field), the disciple dared a new attempt: There too, a terrible battle raged, but the spirit finally found its master in the student and rode into the lake on a horse-like demon.

However, he is said to have since appeared in the lake once a year, on Good Friday, with bloody hands and fastened with an iron chain to a judge's seat; but whoever saw him there, had to die within a year. Moreover, the ghost still caused severe thunderstorms to break out when someone threw stones into the lake, which is why it was forbidden to climb the mountain for a long time.[594] And to some, the evil spirit still showed itself as a wild horse, a large

91 View of Lucerne with Mount Pilatus in the background (*Vue de Lucerne vers le Mont Pilate*), painted by Anton Winterlin, engraved by Friedrich Salathé, ca. 1840.

---

[594]   See also Businger (1811), 258 ff.

dog, or a ghostly calf, and as a dragon at night in the sky from Lucerne. In 1594, the superiors finally tried to put an end to this belief by draining the lake without further ado.[595] Yet the legend is still alive today.

You might say that in my search for the Lonely Mountain, I found another Mount Doom and old scripts from *The Elder Scrolls* instead. Fair enough: A cold mountainous region, which is teeming with dragons and visited by Imperials from the neighboring land to the south, is indeed somewhat reminiscent of Skyrim—especially if a foreign conjuring mage from an underground school also shows up. So much the better; maybe this trip through Switzerland can make you feel a bit like you have not only been transported to Middle-earth but to Skyrim, too.[596] Middl-earth and Skyrim are connected anyway, not least because Whiterun seems pretty obiously inspired by the depiction of Edoras in Peter Jackson's film adaptations.

III. Wimmis as Dale

At the foot of the Lonely Mountain, the city of Dale once lay in a river bend, but still before Bilbo's journey, it was destroyed and depopulated by the dragon Smaug. One of Tolkien's sources of inspiration for Dale was most probably William Morris' Burgdale, for Burgdale is located in a valley with the exact same name, Dale, in his novel *The Roots of the Mountains*[597], and it is also situated in a river loop and inhabited by a (North) Germanic tribe.[598] However, the cities are not identical in every respect: while Burgdale is located in a deep valley, Tolkien's Dale lies between two arms of the Lonely Mountain. But at least a loose connection seems likely.

Based on Morris' description, Burgdale and thus Tolkien's Dale may be searched for in the Lauterbrunnen Valley at first. However, this valley primarily inspired Rivendell. Although it cannot be ruled out that the same place inspired several locations in Middle-earth—this may even be the case for the fictitious place Burgdale—I rather see it as an indication against such an inspiration.

---

[595] See, e.g., www.luzernerzeitung.ch/zentralschweiz/luzern/timeline-pioniere-am-pilatus-ld.1045902.

[596] I am well aware that the inhabitants of this area, and especially the northern coast, were influenced by Scandinavian people and landscape.

[597] Cf. *Letters of Tolkien*, no. 226; above, pp. 83 ff.

[598] Cf. *Letters of Tolkien*, no. 144, where Tolkien compared the language of Dale and the Long Lake as more or less Scandinavian in character.

Another possible source of inspiration would be Brig, for Brig, like Burg-dale, lies in a deep east-west valley, and Tolkien may have seen a sea of flames above Brig during his journey.[599] An association with a dragon, such as the one from the Natterloch (Colubrid Snakes Hole) near Naters, would be quite natural. Other factors in favor of Brig are that Tolkien may have been inspired by the area around the palace of the Elvenking in the upper Rhône Valley and that Tolkien's path then led to the Matterhorn, a possible source of inspiration for the Lonely Mountain.[600] However, I see Brig more as a source of inspiration for Tolkien's Edoras, the capital of Rohan.

If we believe that the Niesen inspired the Lonely Mountain, we would have to look for a source of inspiration for the town of Dale around there; and there is only one town that would come into question: Wimmis. Wimmis once had a city wall that surrounded the small town attached to the castle, a massive wall that was 38 feet (11.5 meters) high.[601] In the eighteenth century, however, it was torn down after a fire, so Tolkien could not have seen it; and

92 Wimmis Castle with the Niesen in the background; colored outline etching by Johann Ludwig Aberli, *Vûe du Chateau de Wimmis et des environs*, 1783-1784, digitized by the Swiss National Library, GS-GRAF-ANSI-BE-408, slightly edited.

---

[599]   See above, pp. 125 ff.

[600]   See above, pp. 104 ff.

[601]   See Liechti (2006).

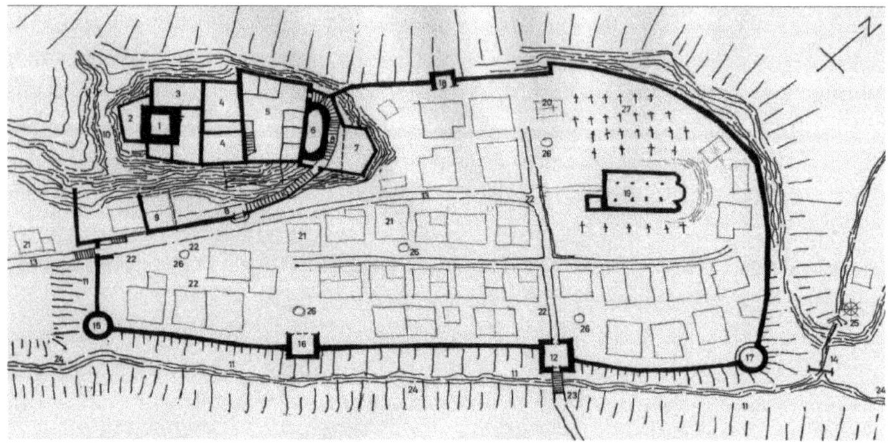

93 Old town map of Wimmis with city wall. From: Erich Liechti: "Die Mauern von Wimmis" (The Walls of Wimmis), 2006.

unfortunately, there is nothing left of the old town today—let us call the reason Smaug—but Wimmis Castle still towers above the village.

Figure 92 shows the area around Wimmis Castle in the late eighteenth century with the prominent Niesen in the background. In the picture, the old town with its city wall is on the left side of the castle, but it no longer existed even when the painting was drawn. Figure 93 shows the former city map.

IV. Dale and Esgaroth in Flames

1. The Great Fire of 1911

As in the Valais, it was also hot and dry in the Bernese Oberland. A contemporary in Grindelwald, for example, noted: "The valley resembled an embers pan. Again and again, temperatures of around 40°C (104°F) were measured, and that for weeks. The brooks dried up visibly and the worst thing: the wells too."[602] He probably exaggerated with the 40°C, but it was hot: in the Swiss Midlands in the first half of August, every day around 30°C (86°F), making August 1911 one of the hottest in recorded history.[603]

---

[602] *Peter Bernet* on the year 1911 in Grindelwald, available at www.grindelwaldgeschich ten.ch/jahresrueckblick/1911.

[603] Billwiller (1911), 4.

The heat was not without consequences: in the Bernese Oberland, forest fires occurred as well. The largest one broke out on a rocky mountain called Simmenfluh, and this mountain is located right next to the Niesen and above Wimmis. It was ignited, presumably by lightning, on August 20 and, from then on, raged for a whole month.[604] A whole month! It was thought to have been contained after some days, but then it suddenly spread very fast, and on August 29, a first fire avalanche thundered towards Wimmis.[605] The fire horn sounded; the church bells started ringing nonstop; a catastrophe was imminent.[606] In the nights to come, a gruesome-beautiful natural spectacle is said to have taken place: The whole Simmenfluh was ablaze with light. Burning logs thundered down to the valley and like torches lit up everything in their path, and the night sky over the Simmenfluh turned red.

94 Spiez and the Niesen; the mountain cut off to the right was the one that was on fire, and just to the left of it is Wimmis. Aquatint by Jakob Samuel Weibel, *Vue du Chateau de Spiez* (View of Spiez Castle), 1807, digitized by the Swiss National Library, GS-GRAF-ANSI-BE-309.

---

604   Erich Liechti, "Der Waldbrand an der Simmenfluh 1911," essai, available at www. wimmis.ch; Dal Farra (2011) speaks of August 22.

605   Ibid.

606   Ibid.

This spectacle attracted numerous onlookers: Wimmis is said to have been inundated with them. On Saturdays and Sundays, special trains were even run from Bern to transport them to Wimmis; and a hundred years later, the *Thuner Tagblatt* wrote: "The great fire on the Simmenfluh 100 years ago is still unparalleled today. The people were shocked but fascinated by this natural spectacle, which the authorities at the time criminally underestimated."[607]

The fire department was initially powerless, which is why the military was called up on September 5, and finally, over 800 military and civilian firefighters were deployed. But even so, they were barely able to contain the fire, and a windy situation caused the village of Wimmis to experience frequent showers of sparks. It was not until September 16 that the fire was gradually brought under control with the onset of rain.[608]

2. The Perspective From the Other Valleys

Tolkien was almost certainly in the Valais when the fire broke out, as he signed the guestbook in the Bertol Hut near Arolla on August 25.[609] Therefore, the perspective from other Alpine valleys is of particular interest. The situation in Grindelwald, for example, was described by one author as follows: "Then, on August 21, 1911, the news came from people above Wagisbach: a huge cloud of smoke could be seen down the valley, and in the evening the sky appeared blood-red. People believe that Thun is in flames."[610]

Thun, Lake-town—*in flames*! Those who knew the Beatus legend may well have thought of the dragon: the legend was brought to life. Soon it became known that it was not Thun that was burning, but the Simmenfluh. However, this is no less interesting since the Simmenfluh is located right next to the Niesen, the Lonely Mountain, and Wimmis, Dale.

3. A Likely Influence on Tolkien

How did Tolkien experience this natural phenomenon? From the Valais, perhaps he could see the cloud of smoke rising from behind the Misty Mountains, the red glow of the night sky, and the blood-red daylight broken by the smoke. So the fire might have helped to shape the scenery of Mordor, but

---

[607] Dal Farra (2011).

[608] Liechti (Fn. 604); Dal Farra (2011).

[609] See Lewis and Currie (2019), 166.

[610] Peter Bernet, "1911: Sind die Gletscher in Gefahr?" available at www.grindelwald geschichten.ch/jahresrueckblick/1911.

above all, a co-inspiration for *The Hobbit* finale seems likely. If he returned to Lake Thun as assumed here, he must have arrived there just when the mountain was ablaze. He would have witnessed the spectacle at close quarters and how the Beatus legend came to life; but even if he did not return to the Bernese Oberland, this event would still be a likely source of inspiration.

Indications of a return and and inspiration may be found in Thorin's words in *The Hobbit* itself: "[F]rom a good way off we saw the dragon settle on our mountain in a spout of flame. Then he came down the slopes and when he reached the woods they all went up in fire. By that time all the bells were ringing in Dale and the warriors were arming."[611] Did Tolkien here perhaps reproduce his perceptions from Wimmis? In any case, the description strongly recalls the reports about the forest fire on the Simmenfluh: the avalanches of flames, the ringing bells, and perhaps also the people, the warriors, who took part in the extinguishing work but were powerless. Although Tol-

95 *The Hobbit*'s finale at Lake Thun, Tolkien's presumed path (blue), and likely sources of inspiration (red), map based on: Bergfex OSM, © OpenStreetMap.org-Contributors, CC-BY-SA, see p. 286, no. 2.

---

[611] *The Hobbit*, chap. I.

kien may have witnessed similar scenes in Brig, this picture is even more reminiscent of Wimmis.

For me, this fire was the one decisive element that finally convinced me that Tolkien liekly found inspiration in Switzerland not only for the crossing of the Misty Mountains but also for the rest of *The Hobbit*. The whole way over the mountains, past the Lötschberg Tunnel, into the forests of the Kander Valley, to the elven-like Blausee (Blue Lake), and then along the Kander and its raftsmen to Lake Thun, to the pyramid of the Niesen, to the Beatus legend with its dragon, and to Wimmis, where the flames seized an entire mountain and threatened the village, the church bells, the fire avalanches, the rain of sparks, the red night sky: this is, it seems, the fund for *The Hobbit*, the autobiographical elements that brought alive the story of Bilbo, Bilbo the Hobbit.

One last insight remains: we owe *The Hobbit* and *The Lord of the Rings*, it seems, to a lightning bolt.

Bonus: John Howe's Inspirations for the Film Adaptations

This book concentrates on Tolkien's Middle-earth, not on the Middle-earth of the movie adaptations. As we all know, Peter Jackson's movies were shot in New Zealand, and this is certainly the right place, not least because the natural landscapes of Switzerland have suffered over the last one hundred years. Urban growth and sprawl, dams, roads, power lines, and skiing infrastructures have affected them. Nevertheless, there are still many beautiful spots in Switzerland worth visiting. But it was only when the book was already well advanced that I suddenly realized that the movies also have a rather strong connection to Switzerland. The reason for this lies primarily in the person of John Howe.

John Howe is one of the most famous illustrators of Tolkien's works. A Canadian national, he grew up in Vancouver, but after graduating from high school, he moved to Strasbourg to study art at the *École supérieure des arts décoratifs*. He then worked as an illustrator and on other art projects, and soon, in 1985, he moved to Neuchâtel, Switzerland with his wife and son.[612] Five years later, in 1990—it was a normal day—his life would undergo a profound change. The phone rang, a man he did not know was on the line—a certain Peter Jackson—and this man wanted to invite him to an adventure in New Zealand. He did not know what to expect, but he was just like Bilbo up for the adventure and would not regret it. For almost fourteen years, he commuted between Neuchâtel and New Zealand, producing a good two thousand sketches for the making of *The Lord of the Rings* and a good four thousand drawings for *The Hobbit*, an enormous number.[613]

How does he succeed with these expressive and convincing sketches? The answer is mostly his secret, but one reason might be that he intensively studied Tolkien's sources, both in the mythical world and in the real world; high bookshelves in his studio bear witness to this.[614] Anything less than a thorough understanding of Tolkien's way of thinking, he once said, would have led to a rather disappointing result.[615] He sees himself as a decoder: "Whatever myths and legends Tolkien wrapped up in a text, I open it up and make it accessible."[616] But this is not all: he draws even more inspiration from the real world,[617] and this is where Switzerland comes into play.

On the one hand, John Howe was well aware that Tolkien had been inspired in Switzerland.[618] But even more so, it seems, Howe drew inspiration from the nature he himself knew best, and this was the nature around Neuchâtel, among others, where he had been living since 1985. Some of his drawings of the Shire were directly inspired by landscapes near his home; Lake Neuchâtel helped him depict the Long Lake and Lake-town, and the forests of the Jura Mountains and extraordinary nearby trees helped him visualize Mirkwood and Fangorn.[619] He also drew inspiration from the rock formation of the Creux du Van, the Areuse Gorge, the Val-de-Travers, and the choir stalls of the Collégiale of Romont with their gargoyles.[620] However, the details he has so far kept for himself.

---

612   See www.john-howe.com/blog/biography/formations; Werlé (2019), 16 f.

613   Werlé (2019), 17.

614   Fahy (2015).

615   Fahy (2015).

616   Howe, quoted from Meyer (2014) (twice translated).

617   Meyer (2014).

618   Howe (2018), 4 f.; Howe (2019), 20; Fahy (2015).

619   Cf. Howe (2019), 99, 101, 110; Howe (2018), 156 f.; Meyer (2014).

620   Werlé (2019), 16.

So, to a certain extent, John Howe tried, as this book does, to get into Tolkien's perspective by looking at his sources of inspiration. But at the same time, he did not allow himself to be restricted by this; he went further; he had to go further, for otherwise, he would not have been able to fill in all the details in his illustrations in a convincing way. By doing so, however, he—and others like Peter Jackson and Adam Lee—did not simply recreate Middle-earth as decoders. No, they developed Middle-earth further; they filled the world with colors and details, and to a certain extent, they also created a new Middle-earth and a masterpiece themselves. John Howe once said that he considered pilgrimages to the places that inspired Tolkien to be of great value;[621] and the same is now true of John Howe's places of inspiration, which partly coincide with those of Tolkien, but only partly. So let us go not only to England, the Bernese Oberland, and the Valais, but also to New Zealand, Patagonia[622], Alsace, and the Neuchâtel Jura!

96 View from the Creux du Van rock formation in the Jura Mountains at sunrise. John Howe lives close to this place and finds inspiration in these less famous and much older mountains and forests of Switzerland. Photo: iStock.com/Marco Ca.

---

621   Fahy (2015).
622   Based on John Howe's remarks in the foreword; I previously wrote Canada.

Concluding Remarks

The journey thus comes to an end, and I hope it was as exciting for you as it was for me—and for the nineteen-year-old boy from Birmingham back in 1911, when he hiked over many high Alpine passes, heavily loaded and without any experience. What remains is the impression that this boy, John Ronald Reuel Tolkien, was far more inspired by this journey in creating Middle-earth and its stories than is commonly known. Not only Bilbo's journey across the Misty Mountains, no, his entire trek from Rivendell to the Lonely Mountain, and also the journeys in *The Lord of the Rings* to Mount Doom and Minas Tirith, seem to be based on this adventure.

The journey led Tolkien first to Lauterbrunnen, the Elven valley of Rivendell, and then over the Misty Mountains into the Upper Rhône Valley to Rohan, on to the Matterhorn, Mount Doom, then to Sion, Minas Tirith, and finally probably back to Lake Thun, the Long Lake from *The Hobbit*. Tolkien's hiking experience was particularly marked by the extraordinary heat and dryness of August 1911. Numerous fires broke out, and so Tolkien must have witnessed a special battle: a battle against the elements, against nature. High columns of smoke rose, the fire horn sounded, the church bells rang nonstop, avalanches of fire came down the mountains, and the night sky turned red. Both the Rohirrim and Gondorians of the Valais and the inhabitants of the long Lake Thun in the Bernese Oberland took up arms. With the village priest and the local councils at the head, they threw themselves heroically into the battle. These were probably models for the battles in *The Lord of the Rings* and *The Hobbit*. At the same time, industrialization was advancing in his homeland; Sarehole, where he had lived from the age of four to eight, his Hobbiton, was absorbed by the growing city of Birmingham in November of the same year.[623] These are autobiographical elements that brought Tolkien's fantasy world to life.

But not only that: stories, myths, and legends linked to Switzerland also seem to have greatly influenced Tolkien's novels. The mountain spirit, which helped to shape the figure of Gandalf, is one example; the Beatus legend of Lake Thun with its dragon and dwarfs another; and the legend of the shep-

---

[623] See Carpenter (1977), 27 ff.; Ezard (1991); https://billdargue.jimdofree.com/place names-gazetteer-a-to-y/places-s/sarehole; www.yardleyconservationsociety.co.uk /100-celebration-cake-of-yardey-in-birmingham-1911-2011.

herd of Lake Heli, who, possessed by an object, finds a dwarf kingdom in the interior of the Bernese Oberland mountains and there ages very slowly but starts to resemble a gaunt ghost, a third. And Tolkien also seems to have associated the legendary figure of Dietrich von Bern and Dante's *Divine Comedy* with his pilgrimage through the Bernese Oberland and to Sion — although "von Bern," according to the prevailing view, refers to the Italian city of Verona and not the Swiss capital. Apart from the legends, there were also historical sources of inspiration with a connection to the Alps, such as the lake dwellings of the Bronze Age and Hannibal's crossing of the Alps, and perhaps also artistic works such as William Turner's paintings of the Devil's Bridge and Emil Nolde's postcards. But perhaps above all, literary works exerted a great influence: While *The Hobbit* was influenced mainly by stories from George MacDonald and William Morris, the path in *The Lord of the Rings* to Rivendell and over the Misty Mountains seems to float poetically from Goethe's "Erlking" and his "Song of the Spirits over the Waters" to Schiller's "Berglied" ("Song of the Mountains"), Dante's *Inferno*, and Byron's *Manfred*. And the path through the Dead Marshes and to Mount Doom was likely influenced — apart from Tolkien's own mountain hiking and war experience — by Edward Whymper's *The Ascent of the Matterhorn* and Albert Mummery's *My Climbs in the Alps and the Caucasus*. Tolkien was probably already familiar with many of these tales while he journeyed through Switzerland, for his travel companion Colin Brookes-Smith mentioned in his memoirs that the young Tolkien told the other boys many stories during the trip, including one about Hannibal.[624]

One last important source of inspiration in Switzerland were place names. This should not be surprising since Tolkien was a philology professor and owned at least forty works on the interpretation of place names.[625] Names fascinated him exceedingly, and not only that; once he even wrote: "The 'stories' [like *The Hobbit* and *The Lord of the Rings*] were made rather to provide a world for the languages than the reverse. To me a name comes first and the story follows."[626] Names were, in a sense, the origin of everything, and at least in part, it is known that they were inspired by Swiss place names. In the case of the Silberhorn, for example, Tolkien himself stated that it inspired him for the Silvertine (Celebdil); and in the case of Lauterbrunnen, too, it is considered certain that the place gave its name to the stream Loudwater (Bruinen),

---

[624] Brookes-Smith (1982), 2; cf. Morton and Hayes (2008), 71.

[625] Cilli (2019), Foreword by Tom Shippey and nos. 175, 195, 634, 638, 699, 702, 819-823, 1462, 1532-1536, 2021, 2128, 2131-2137, 2281, 2423, 2580, and 2587 f.

[626] *Letters of Tolkien*, no. 165.

which flows through Rivendell. However, this is probably only the tip of the iceberg. Likely other sources of inspiration are: Rhône for Rohan; Weisshorn for White(horn) Mountains; Gondo and Mont Gond for Gondor; Tourbillon for Tower of Vigilance (Minas Tirith); Monte Moro for Mordor; Lake Thun for Lake-town; and considering the meaning of the names also: Brig for the hill town Edoras and Belalp for the war alp Dunharrow.

Although Tolkien was interested in history as such, it fascinated him most when historical events shed light on words and names.[627] Precisely in this respect, place names in the Bernese Oberland and Valais are a paradise, for there, Latin, Celtic, and pre-Celtic terms are mixed with Germanic and French names. And for certain names, at least in the past, some even suspected an Arabic-Saracenic or Hungarian-Hunnish origin: it is a veritable battle of languages that tells of past events. Based on this, Tolkien seems to have reawakened the history of the early Middle Ages, in which Germanic Rohirrim (in the Upper Valais) fought with Romanic Gondorians (in the Lower Valais) and Celtic Elves (as last language cells) against Hunnic-Hungarian Orcs and Arab-Saracenic Haradrim. It is roughly the situation in the Valais of the tenth century, the time when the Hungarians plundered Europe and Saracens occupied Alpine passes—perhaps also the one at Monte Moro, the Mountain of Moors—and the gate at Saint-Maurice. Legend has it that in 954, a battle was fought against both the Hungarians and the Saracens, and Tolkien seems to have chosen the city of Sion, which recalls the Temple Mount Zion in Jerusalem, as the site for this battle. It is the time of Aragorn Otto I, who decisively defeated the Hungarians in the battle of Lechfeld in the following year, and who, in 962, as the savior of Christendom, was crowned Roman Emperor by the pope, thus bringing the Western Roman Empire, Gondor, back to life.

Tolkien, of course, did not only make use of Swiss inspirations, and his novels are also not merely a conglomeration of different stories. Rather, Tolkien masterfully managed to combine his own experiences with tales, myths, and legends so that, despite the multitude of sources of inspiration, the product does not appear to be a conglomerate at all, but rather a coherent whole. I was perhaps a little irritated only once when I read *The Lord of the Rings* for the first time: it was when the self-doubting Manfred-Gandalf stood on the top of the Silvertine, for this did not seem to fit the down-to-earth Jane-Neave-Gandalf. But of course, you may be mistaken when judging a person from the outside. In any case, it certainly does not detract from the masterful work: *The Hobbit* and *The Lord of the Rings* are undoubtedly products of such a kind.

---

[627] *Letters of Tolkien*, no. 205; above, pp. 171 f.

With this book, I have pursued one main goal and five secondary goals, and I hope I have achieved them more or less. First and foremost, I wanted to find Tolkien's sources of inspiration for Middle-earth in Switzerland and shed light on them; some of my hypotheses might be somewhat daring, I know, but I hope that this will provide an incentive for further research. Also, I wanted to open a gate for the readers, a gate to Middle-earth, and thus give an opportunity to experience Middle-earth in the real world and to see it in the creator's eyes. Tolkien has forever changed the way I look at and experience the Bernese Oberland and the Valais, and perhaps you feel the same way. Second, it has increasingly become a goal of this book to show examples of what a creative process can look like, in the hope of perhaps inspiring readers. Third, I also increasingly pursued the goal of somewhat reviving all those stories and anecdotes that were an essential part of the English tourists' fascination with Switzerland in the nineteenth century and that was increasingly lost in the travel guides of the twentieth century. Fourth, I wanted to remind mainly the Swiss audience, at least occasionally, of a bit of their past—of the poverty of the rural population, the begging locals who emigrated in droves abroad, and the diseases caused by malnutrition—in the hope of perhaps provoking a little more empathy with the suffering of this world. And finally, I also wanted to show how beautiful and natural certain places once were, in the hope of raising awareness of the need for measures to preserve the remaining natural treasures.

Regardless of these goals and the influence on Tolkien's works, the trip to Switzerland was a life-shaping experience for Tolkien, for he rarely traveled—he was a hobbit in this respect also, he once said. And probably also because of this, the Swiss adventures remained firmly anchored in his heart forever. Tolkien's own words show this particularly nicely, and anyway, it does seem appropriate to leave the last words to the master himself—to J. R. R. Tolkien, the professor, writer, and hobbit:

> I am [...] delighted that you have made the acquaintance of Switzerland, and of the very part that I once knew best and which had the deepest effect on me. (1967)[628]

> I left the view of Jungfrau with deep regret: eternal snow, etched as it seemed against eternal sunshine, and the *Silberhorn* sharp against dark blue: the *Silvertine (Celebdil)* of my dreams. (1967)[629]

---

[628] *Letters of Tolkien*, no. 306.
[629] Ibid.

> I do not suppose all this is very interesting now. But it was a remarkable experience for me at 19, after a poor boy's childhood. (1967)[630]

> My heart still lingers among the high stony wastes among the morains and mountain-wreckage, silent in spite of the sound of thin chill water. (1944)[631]

> How I long to see the snows and the great heights again! (1947)[632]

And in Bilbo's words from *The Lord of the Rings:*

> 'I want to see mountains again, Gandalf—*mountains*; and then find somewhere where I can *rest*. In peace and quiet, without a lot of relatives prying around, and a string of confounded visitors hanging on the bell. I might find somewhere where I can finish my book. I have thought of a nice ending for it: *and he lived happily ever after to the end of his days.*'

> Gandalf laughed. 'I hope he will. But nobody will read the book, however it ends.'

> 'Oh, they may, in years to come.[633]

He should be right—*and how*!

---

[630]   Ibid.

[631]   *Letters of Tolkien*, no. 78.

[632]   *Letters of Tolkien*, no. 109.

[633]   *The Fellowship of the Ring*, Book 1, chap. I.

Appendix 1: Hiking Suggestions

I.   Important Note for All Adventurous Hobbits

The author to the adventurous reader greeting! As in *The Hobbit*, I would like to leave you a little note before you set out on Tolkien's, Bilbo's, and Frodo's tracks to Wilderland yourself. Please make sure that you are well equipped and informed, and know your limits. Mountain hiking still holds dangers, and there is one thing you must know: the English who came to Switzerland back in the days were sometimes quite foolhardy. In German, you would say that they were *tollkühn*—or perhaps *tolkien*. Queen Victoria supposedly even considered banning mountaineering altogether.

Hiking trails in Switzerland are officially divided according to their difficulty into yellow *hiking trails*, red *mountain hiking trails* (red-white-red marked), and blue *alpine hiking trails* (blue-white-blue if marked). On page 273, you can find an overview of the requirements of the different categories. Please do not underestimate this classification. On the red-white-red marked trails, you need hiking boots, and you must be surefooted since the hikes sometimes pass slopes where slipping can be fatal. Two hikes (7 and 8) are even categorized as blue-white-blue alpine hikes. For these, please also check the more refined classification of the Swiss Alpine Club (SAC), which you can find on page 274. On the SAC scale, the ascent to the Bertol hut is classified as a *demanding alpine hike* (T5); it includes long and daring ladders.

The yellow and red paths are usually in good condition, but not always and only in good weather and suitable snow conditions. Avalanches and landslides can destroy the trails and make rather harmless passages hazardous. And snow, especially in spring and autumn but also in summer, can make usually good trails slippery and dangerous. So please inform yourself well; consult local webcams before hiking; do not overdo it; and turn back if a passage is dangerous. And do not go on glaciers without a guide! Tolkien warned about this himself when he pointed out in his letter no. 306 that he would have fallen into a snow-crevasse if he had not been roped. So please, I do not want to see any hobbits disappear in the Swiss Misty Mountains.

By the way, unlike Thorin & Co. I assume neither travel nor burial expenses, nor any other liability. But I wish you, literally, a fantastic trip! Yours deeply, the author.

II.   A Journey through Middle-Earth

Now that this is settled, let us follow Tolkien's path through Switzerland! Perhaps it already dawns on you—there is a catch. If we wanted to follow Tolkien strictly and enjoy the ideal trip, we would probably need about five weeks, and for the ordinary mortals among us, this will hardly be possible. However, what we can do is concentrate on the highlights, and this also not too bad. But I do recommend at least one week; two would be better.

I did most of the following hikes with friends last summer within one week (no. 3–9 and 11). We spent two nights in Lauterbrunnen, two nights in Brig, one night in Zermatt, two nights in Arolla, one night in Sion, and finally one night in Kandersteg. This is about the minimum program I recommend. For a one-week trip, I would probably choose Hikes 1, 3, 4, 6, 7–9, and 11, but you can also skip the blue alpine hikes and the overnight in Sion and, for example, hike from Grindelwald to Meiringen. There are many other beautiful places to spend the nights, of course; the ones we chose just seemed the most practical to us (Brig, for instance, since the Great Aletsch Glacier is hard to reach from Belalp today).

If you have two weeks, apart from more hiking, you can visit, for example, John Howe's sources of inspiration in the Neuchâtel Jura, the Rhine Falls, and the Greisinger Museum in Jenins with its great and unique Middle-earth art collection. The latter is also a good conclusion to a one-week trip, but it takes about 2h45 by car from Lake Thun to get to Jenins, and you need to book in advance a three-hour tour, which is mainly designed for big fans (www.greisinger.museum). Apart from that, I would plan an overnight stay at Lake Thun, for example in Spiez, Thun, or—if you want to treat yourself— at the Parkhotel Gunten (the perfect place for a Hobbit wedding with Erebor view, by the way).

You should also always keep an eye on the driving and check-in times. Pure travel times with little traffic are: Lauterbrunnen to Brig 2h20; Brig to Zermatt about 1h10 (40 min. to Täsch and from there by train); Täsch to Arolla 2h; Arolla to Sion 55 min.; Sion to Kandersteg about 1h20 (car transport Lötschberg). Public transport is good, but we chose the car for greater flexibility.

The nearest major airports from Lauterbrunnen are Zurich (2h), Basel-Mulhouse-Freiburg (2h), and Geneva (2h30). Bern-Belp would be closer, but it is a small airport with few connections. Zurich is best if you are visiting the Greisinger Museum or the Rhine Falls at the end of the trip. By the way, from Geneva, you can be in Sion in 1h40 and from Milano-Malpensa in Brig in 2h15, but I recommend starting in Lauterbrunnen.

For our hikes, we used the maps from www.map.wanderland.ch and the Bergfex app. However, you can use the Swisstopo maps more conveniently with a Schweizmobil subscription (www.schweizmobilplus.ch). There is also the Swisstopo app now, and things may be looking up as the Swisstopo maps were made freely available (with source citation) on March 1, 2021. Please note that the time estimate of the apps for the hikes are rather low.

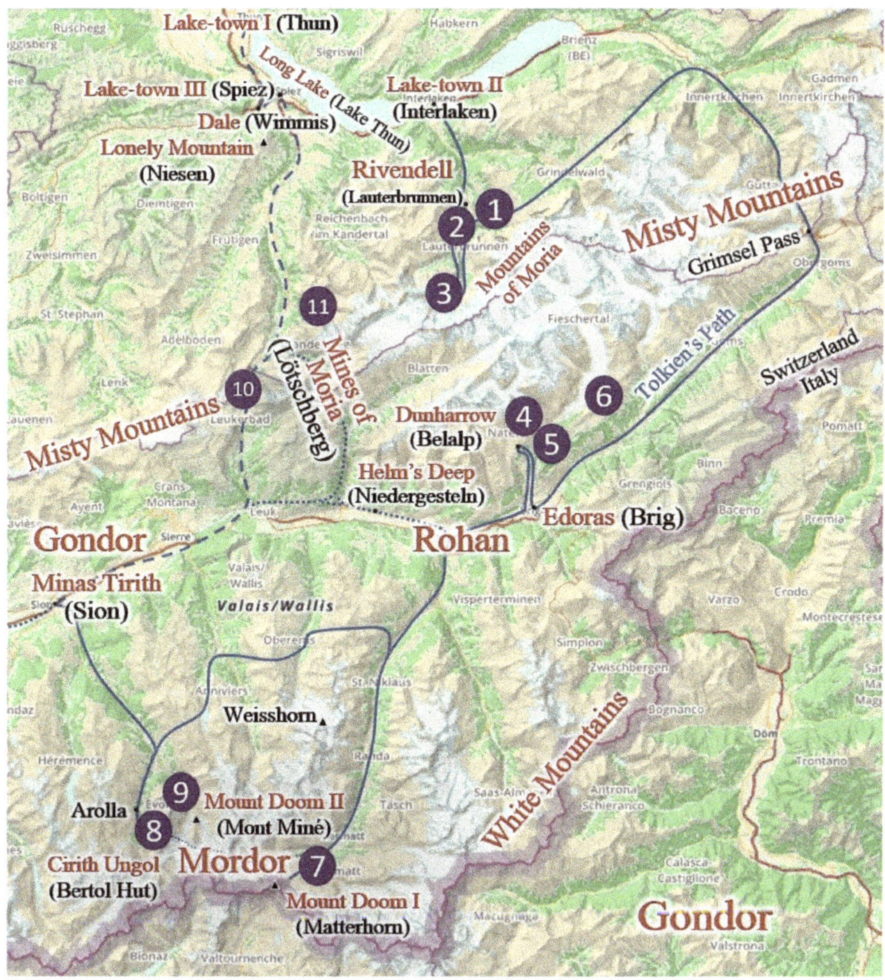

97 Overview map showing the places of the suggested walks (numbers), Tolkien's path (blue), and his probable sources of inspiration (red). Map data: © OpenStreetMap .org-Contributors, see p. 286, no. 1.

III.   The Hikes

Hike 1:   The Misty Mountains—Männlichen-Wengen

Enough talk, let us go on our first hike! While this one does not strictly follow Tolkien's path, I think it is the perfect way to start the trip—it is a breathtaking visual experience. From Lauterbrunnen, we took the train (12 min) to car-free Wengen, from where we walked (5 min) to the Wengen-Männlichen cable car. Already from the cabin and then also from the top, there is a magnificent view of the Bernese Oberland Alps, the Misty Mountains. In front of you rises the famous trinity of *Eiger, Mönch, and Jungfrau*, and to the right, deep down, you can see back into the Lauterbrunnen Valley, the Hidden Valley of the Elves.

From Männlichen, an easy hiking trail (yellow) leads towards Kleine Scheidegg. As you steadily approach the Misty Mountains, higher and higher the mountain giants rise in front of you, and smaller and smaller you feel—simply fantastic. The path is very easy, a bit too wide for my taste, and well frequented, but the mountain panorama compensates for that. After just under an hour, you reach the restaurant Grindelwaldblick, where I highly recommend a stop on the terrace, either for a snack or an early lunch. Below you is the Kleine Scheidegg, over which Tolkien hiked from Lauterbrunnen to

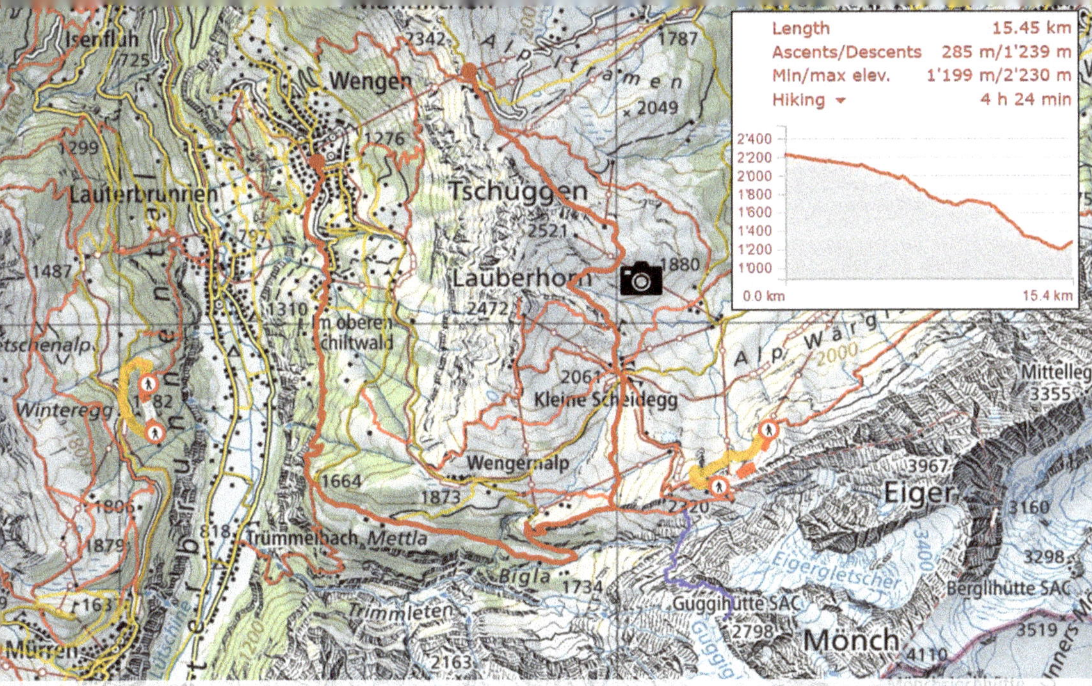

8 Route, source: Swiss Federal Office of Topography; tour/profile drawn with schweizmobilplus.ch.

Grindelwald, and further to the left, you can also see the Grosse Scheidegg, over which Tolkien then continued his journey. To the right, the Jungfrau rises majestically, and below it, the Silberhorn. From here, you have the view Tolkien alluded to in his letter, "I left the view of Jungfrau with deep regret: eternal snow, etched as it seemed against eternal sunshine, and the Silberhorn sharp against dark blue: the Silvertine (*Celebdil*) of my dreams."

From the restaurant, it is a quick 15-minute walk down to Kleine Scheidegg. It is a very touristy place, but it was the only place that was very crowded when I went on this hike. If you have already had enough, you can take the train from here back to Wengen and Lauterbrunnen. For others, the real hike just begins. On a mountain hiking trail (red), you will slowly descend through a wonderful landscape over the Bigla and Mettla to the edge of the Hidden Valley of the Elves, and finally, on an easy hiking trail, back to Wengen.

Alternatively, I can recommend the detour via the Eigergletscher station, but the hike is long enough without this detour for a start. Another option is to descend to the Trümmelbach Falls and from there take the bus back to Lauterbrunnen.

99 (left) The Mönch, the Jungfrau, and the Silberhorn (from left), from the path to Kleine Scheidegg. The photo viewpoint is marked on the map.

245

Hike 2:   Rivendell—Wengen-Lauterbrunen-Mürren

Hike 2 is all about Rivendell, the Hidden Valley of the Elves. Again, we took the train towards Wengen, but this time, we got off in Wengwald. The village offers one of the best views of the Lauterbrunnen Valley, with the glittering Jungfrau towering above it on the left (Figure 101). A little to the right of it above the Hunnenfluh, one can well imagine the Hun threat in William Morris' *The Roots of the Mountains* and the Orkish-Hun threat in Middle-earth. Rivendell and Burgdale (in Morris' work) are in danger.

The path from Wengwald down to Lauterbrunnen is the perfect path into the Hidden Valley of the Elves. In about an hour, we reached Lauterbrunnen and from there followed Tolkien's path to Mürren. In Lauterbrunnen, you have several options. Either you choose the hard tour and hike steep and exposed up to Winteregg and then on to Mürren, or you take the cable car to Grütschalp and hike from there to the hiking destination via one of the various trails. For lunch, a picnic or the Winteregg restaurant are good options.

The village of Mürren is spectacularly perched on a rock throne. It has already been suggested, Mürren may have inspired Tolkien for the Rohirrish refuge of Dunharrow. From the picture, this would fit, but from the location and name, I suspect a stronger inspiration from Belalp (Hikes 4 and 5). For

00 Route, source: Swiss Federal Office of Topography; tour/profile drawn with schweizmobilplus.ch.

the way back to Lauterbrunnen, I recommend the cable car via Gimmelwald to Stechelberg, and, from there, the bus back to Lauterbrunnen.

Stechelberg, the Tolkien researcher John Garth suggests, may have inspired Tolkien for the Elven realm of Hollin (Eregion), which is located at the feet of the Mountains of Moria in the Second Age (Garth 2020, 129). He bases this primarily on the name *Stechelberg*, for it can be translated into English as "Holly Mountain." It would also fit location-wise since the village lies just below the Silberhorn, which inspired Tolkien for the Silvertine, and only a few miles from the mines in Trachsellauenen. In any case, the panoramic view is magnificent here also—but you might see a crazy base jumper, for they jump down the rock face from Mürren in wingsuits and not infrequently have fatal accidents.

If you have enough time—and if you did not already do this the day before—I can recommend a stop at the Trümmelbach Falls on the way back, where a path carved into the rock leads up an underground cascade of ten waterfalls fed by glacier water. There is an entrance fee to visit, but it is a truly unique and inspiring place where you can really feel the power of water.

101 (left) View into the Lauterbrunnen Valley, the Hidden Valley of the Elves, behind it the Jungfrau (left) and the Breithorn (right, further back). The photo viewpoint is marked on the map.

Hike 3:   The Mountains of Moria and the Last Homely House—Stechelberg-Obersteinberg-Stechelberg

Hike 3 leads to the Obersteinberg mountain inn and into the dreamlike mountain landscape of the rear Lauterbrunnen Valley. There are three paths; we chose the middle one from the parking lot in Stechelberg—you are not allowed to drive any further. Alternatively, you can get to Berghotel Obersteinberg from Gimmelwald (cable car from Stechelberg) via Busenbrand, which must be incredibly beautiful. We did not do it for two reasons: first, a colleague with a fear of heights accompanied us, and the upper path under the Tanzbedeli is very exposed; and second, according to historical maps, there was only the lower path when Tolkien was in Switzerland. Presumably, Tolkien himself thus took this path from Mürren via Gimmelwald to the Obersteinberg mountain inn, where he signed the guest book on August 5, 1911.

From Stechelberg to the Obersteinberg mountain inn, there are more than 800 meters of altitude to be climbed, and even this middle path contains a few exposed spots in the Schwendi forest, where streams have to be crossed. Hiking boots, surefootedness, and freedom from snow are therefore necessary. But when you get above the timberline, you are rewarded with a fantastic view. On the left, you can see up to the Silberhorn, the Jungfrau, and the Rottalhorn, the Mountains of Moria (at least the Silberhorn for sure). It is an excellent place to read about the legend of the Lords of the Red Valley (p. 42

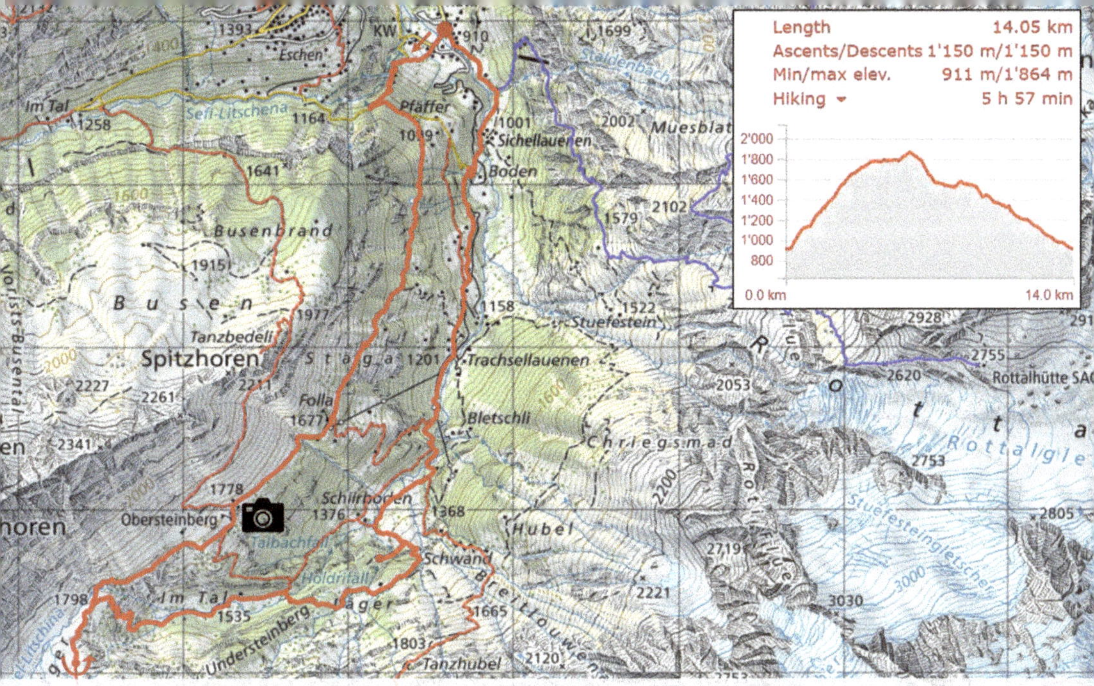

2 Route, source: Swiss Federal Office of Topography; tour/profile drawn with schweizmobilplus.ch.

ff.). Just speechlessly beautiful are the landscape and view then at the Obersteinberg mountain inn, with the mountains and the Schmadribach Falls on the other side of the valley. If it were easier to get here, there would be a lot more people, but as it is, the place is simply fantastic. It is also the perfect place for a rest and lunch, and I would love to spend a night there someday. Seeing the mountains from here in the evening glow must be magical.

From the mountain inn, you can either hike right back down into the valley or, like us, continue a little further to Schafläger. I suspect that it was there where the moraine wilderness that Tolkien described in his letter was located. Today, with the retreat of the glaciers, it is certainly more overgrown than it was in 1911; a wild tundra-like plateau has emerged here. There, we turned back and descended into the valley, where we made the small detour (right path) to the waterfalls (Schmadribach Falls and Holdri Falls), which I can also highly recommend. The area below the Schmadribach Falls is definitely a must-see for any game designer and also known as a place of power: *may the Force be with you*. Finally, we headed down the valley past the old mining village of Trachsellauenen, likely one of the sources of inspiration for the realm of Moria, and walked back to our starting point in Stechelberg.

103 (left) The Obersteinberg mountain inn and the Schmadribach Falls; here, Tolkien signed the guest book on August 5, 1911. It is the Last Homely House in the valley. The photo viewpoint is marked on the map.

Road Trip to Rohan—Lauterbrunnen-Grimsel-Brig

Should you wake up the next day without sore muscles—respect! For everyone else who needs a more relaxing day, the road trip to Rohan is just the thing. On this day, we took it a bit easy and did not do any actual hiking. Tolkien himself hiked from Lauterbrunnen via Grindelwald to Meiringen, but we went by car via Interlaken to the Hasli Valley. The first stop was at the Aare Gorge (Aareschlucht West). Other possible stops are at the Giessbach Falls, the Ballenberg Open Air Museum, and the Reichenbach Falls, made famous by the Sherlock Holmes finale. Admission to the Aare Gorge costs, but it is worth seeing. Through it, Tolkien probably hiked toward the Grimsel Pass; and it has already been suggested that it may have inspired him for the path through Moria, the Argonath Gorge, and Cirith Ninniach in Beleriand (Lewis and Currie 2019, 86). Apart from this, one can also imagine oneself on the hidden path to Gondolin, but you may judge for yourself.

Continue past the Arkenstone—uh, I mean the Achistone—at Innertkirchen and then up through a landscape of stones and reservoirs to the Grimsel Pass. At the very top is the Totensee, which was mentioned in connection with the Dead Marches (p. 96 ff.). The lake is originally natural but today somewhat dammed and enlarged. After that, the path leads down into the Goms region, where I had cholera for lunch—yes, you read right, that is what a local pie with leek, potatoes, cheese, and apples is called. More importantly, here in the green plain of the upper Rhône Valley on the other side of the

104 Route; map source: Swiss Federal Office of Topographie, map.geo.admin.ch.

Misty Mountains, I could well imagine myself in Rohan when I drove towards Brig and the Weisshorn. Also, the view is reminiscent of Tolkien's sketch of Roverandom, as Denis Bridoux has pointed out, and the side hills of Tolkien's drawing of the palace in the Woodland Realm. I would like to spend some more time in this area sometime—though not necessarily on a 50-kilometer march like Tolkien.

If you have time, you can continue after Brig to the Gestelnburg ruin and back, but there is also the option to do this later; we were already late and only made it as far as Brig. We chose Brig mainly because of its location as a starting point for the next hikes, but (unlike Tolkien) we liked the town—even if it is not really reminiscent of Edoras. It can be warm there in the evenings in summer, and the restaurants in the historic center are cozy. That was really nice after the strenuous hikes.

105 (left) View down the Rhône Valley to the Weisshorn, probable sources of inspiration for Rohan and the White Mountains. In this direction, Tolkien hiked to Brig. Photo: User Flöschen at wikivoyage shared, *The village of Ulrichen in Goms*, detail, slightly edited, CC-BY-SA 3.0.

251

Hike 4:   The Mountain Path—Belalp-Oberaletsch Glacier

From Brig, you can go by car (18 min) or bus (23 min) to Blatten (bei Naters) and then by cable car to Belalp. We chose the car because it was the only way to reach the first cable car in the morning. We went so early to link the Hikes 4 and 5, but I can only recommend this to athletes. Before you set off, you should consult the cable car timetable online (www.belalp.ch).

Once at the top, you can already enjoy a magnificent view. Theoretically, for we were in the middle of a dense cloud of fog and could barely see 10 meters, but we (or at least a part of us) were optimistic—rightly so, as it would turn out. From the Belalp mountain station, we reached the Hotel Belalp in about 25 minutes. At this place, there is an even more fantastic panoramic view—especially for us as the fog just lifted when we reached the hotel. On the left, you can see the Great Aletsch Glacier (Figure 37, page 102). It is still a beautiful view, but the glacier was much larger and closer in 1911. The town down in the valley is Brig; behind it rises the Glishorn, which Tolkien may have seen burning from here. The highest mountains are on the right edge of the panorama with the Dom (4545 meters) and the Weisshorn (4505 meters). These are likely the White Mountains, for behind this southern alpine ridge lies Italy, Gondor. And between the two mountains, the Matterhorn (4478 meters), Mount Doom, towers somewhat obscured.

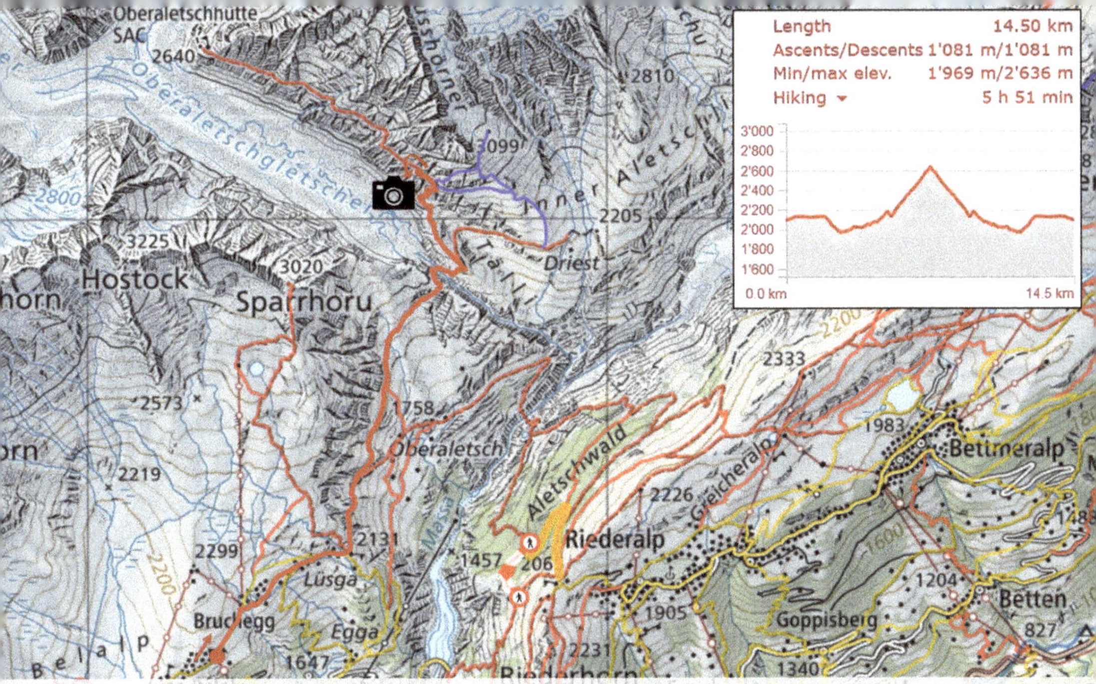

06 Route, source: Swiss Federal Office of Topography; tour/profile drawn with schweizmobilplus.ch.

After the Hotel Belalp, the path leads left over the fascinating "Steigglen," an old path construction, down and then over through a marmot area up to a ridge. Behind it, there is a gorge to cross, but the path and the bridge over the stream were in good condition. After that, it is a steep climb, but better and better views of the Oberaletsch Glacier open up with the sharp Nesthorn on the left. I suspect that the perspective in this direction may have inspired Tolkien for his drawing *The Mountain Path*. From the lookout and turnaround point, an exposed mountain trail leads to the Oberaletsch Hut; however, we turned around ahead of time and switched over to Hike 5. If you continue to the hut, you should turn around no later than about 1:00 p.m. to get back to Belalp in time.

By the way, this panoramic trail to the hut did not exist in Tolkien's time. The path led over the glacier there, which at that time was thicker, and the path was shorter. To me, it seems most likely that the rockfall mentioned by Tolkien happened near the hut.

107 (left) View of the Oberaletsch Glacier with the Nesthorn (left); the view recalls Tolkien's drawing *The Mountain Path* from *The Hobbit*. The photo viewpoint is marked on the map.

Hike 5:   To the Ents—Belalp-Riederalp

The start of Hike 5 is the same as for Hike 4. Again, you start at the Belalp mountain station and hike past the Hotel Belalp to the left down the Steigglen. If you do not want to walk this path twice, you have several options: (1) you can hike the first day via the exposed path to the Oberaletsch Hut, spend the night there, and from there take the path suggested here the next day; (2) you link the two hikes together like we did, but we only recommend this to athletes; (3) you stay in the beautifully located Hotel Belalp so that the overlap is much shorter; or (4) you do an easy circular hike through the Aletschwald from Riederalp. But the hike suggested here is visually very diverse, and I found it most inspiring.

After the Steigglen, you choose the right path towards Riederalp this time—which, I just notice, sounds a bit like a rider alp in English, but I probably just see phantoms. Anyway, through an idyllic alpine landscape, you gradually descend into a region where a hundred years ago, the glacier was still rolling over the rocks. The vegetation has a hard time in this lunar landscape. For me, the area with its rock formations and sparse vegetation was strange and unique. A friend who was hiking with us said at one point that it was as if we were walking over a whale, and he was right. It really felt like that on an elongated piece of rock carved by the glacier.

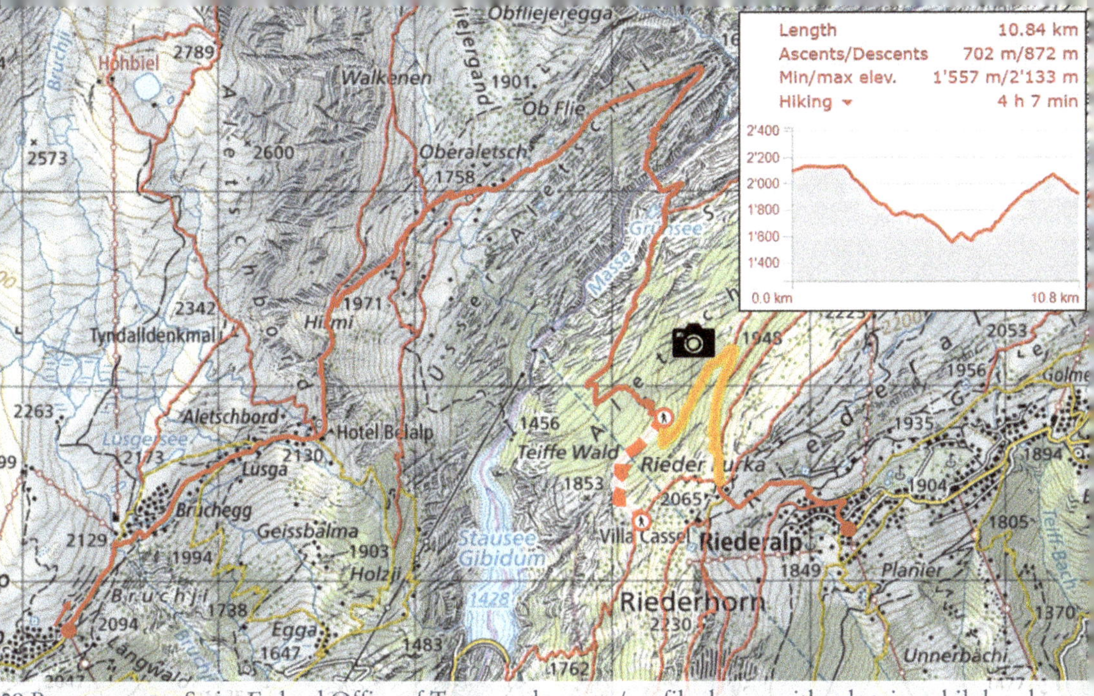

08 Route, source: Swiss Federal Office of Topography; tour/profile drawn with schweizmobilplus.ch.

Once down in the Massa Gorge, a spectacular suspension bridge crosses the stream. The crossing is definitely not something for people with a fear of heights: the bridge is 407 feet (124 meters) long and 262 feet (80 meters) high, and you can see through the grids below your feet down into the gorge while you sway in the wind. Some enjoy the view; others are glad when they arrive safely on the other side.

On mainly solid ground again, the path then leads up to the Grünsee (Green Lake)—also a magical site: with the lake, the round rocks, and the nature that tries to conquer the place; slowly, a moor is emerging here. This is now part of the nature reserve; so pay attention to the information boards and warning signs. After a short break, we continued through the Aletsch Forest up to the Rieder Furka (Pass) and then behind it down to Riederalp. The direct path was closed due to rockfall danger, and so we hiked up the left trail, where we found many beautiful tree specimens. These were all in the higher part of the forest; I marked the area on the map with a camera symbol, but you might find better places.

From Riederalp, you can take the gondola and then the train back to Brig—or, of course, you can spend the night there. We treated ourselves to a late dinner in the old town of Brig.

109 (left) Swiss stone pines (*Arven*) in the Aletsch forest. The photo viewpoint is marked on the map.

Hike 6:   The Ice Dragon — the Great Aletsch Glacier

The next day we drove from Brig to the Betten Valley Station (parking lot on the left) and then took the cable car to Bettmeralp. From there, it was a 15-minute walk over to the Bettmerhorn gondola valley station. Once at the top of the Bettmergrat, some 6,500 feet (2,000 meters) above Brig, a magnificent view opens up again on all sides: on one side towards Monte Rosa, Dom, Matterhorn, and Weisshorn, and on the other down to the Great Aletsch Glacier. Alternatively, you can also start the hike from the Moosfluh, which you reach via Riederalp. In this case, you will forgo some altitude, but you will get a beautiful view from the end of the Aletsch Glacier and a flatter circular hike; from the Bettmerhorn, you first have to descend relatively steeply to the Panorama Trail.

While the glacier looked relatively small from Belalp, its still majestic size becomes quickly apparent on the Bettmerhorn; photos do a poor job showing this. But it is a fleeting natural wonder that is unlikely to exist for much longer; so go there while you still can. In any case, pay your respects to the ice giant when you are in the area, even though it may not be so easy to place in Middle-earth.

Yet, with Middle-earth in mind, you may note that the glacier looks quite flat from up here, but, much like in the case of the Mordor plain, this is deceptive. And you can look at the medial moraines (brown stripes in the ice)

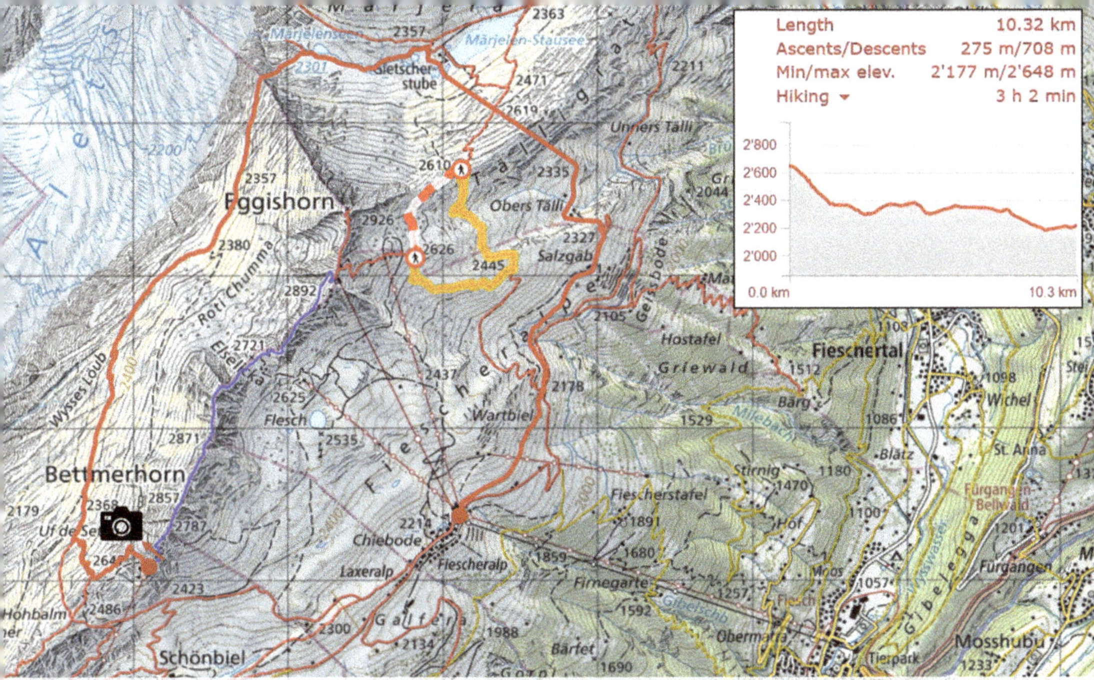

Route, source: Swiss Federal Office of Topography; tour/profile drawn with schweizmobilplus.ch.

since these can be seen in Tolkien's sketch Shelob's Lair. Please only step on the glacier with a mountain guide; you do not want to be caught by this icy spider.

From the Bettmerhorn, the trail thus leads steeply down to the Panorama Trail and then right, along the glacier, to the Märjelensee. This was a tourist hotspot in the nineteenth century when the lake was much larger and icebergs piled up on it, reminiscent of the Arctic; but those days are gone. We stopped at the restaurant Gletscherstube and then made our way back to the other side through the Tälligrat Tunnel, which is about a kilometer (0.6 miles) long. Already in Tolkien's time, there was a tunnel here; its purpose was to drain the lake when the ice of the glacier dammed it too much, but it was hardly used and soon unnecessary since the glacier melted quickly. Walking through the new tunnel, almost something of a Moria or Shelob's Lair feeling comes up.

On the other side, a beautiful view of the Fiescher Glacier, the third-largest Alpine glacier, opens up on the left before you hike to the right and on to the Fiescheralp, accompanied by a splendor of pink blossoms in August. From there, the gondola quickly takes you down the 3,753 feet (1,144 meters) in altitude to Fiesch from where you reach Betten-Talstation or Brig by train.

111 (left) The Great Aletsch Glacier from the Bettmerhorn, a melting giant. The photo viewpoint is marked on the map.

257

Hike 7:   Mount Doom I—the Matterhorn

After Hike 6, we drove to Zermatt the same day, arriving just in time for check-in. We then went heretically for once not to a Valais restaurant, but to the Papperla Pub, which we can highly recommend for its excellent atmosphere and good pub food. Please open a branch in Zurich!

The next morning, we took the Matterhorn Express up to Schwarzsee. The lake is just behind the station, and Mummery's Dead Marshes are probably a little to the right below it (Figure 55, page 149). The path up to the Hörnli Hut was marked on the maps as a mountain hiking trail (red), but when we got there, it was freshly marked as a blue-white-blue alpine hiking trail. Perhaps the people in charge concluded that some tourists were hiking up there who should not. There are a couple of steep stairs and one passage where the trail is carved into the rock and seemed slightly damaged. But other than that, the trail was good. However, the hut is at an altitude of 10,696 feet (3,260 meters), so there is a quite high risk of snow even in August, and I would not recommend the trail when there is snow. To check the snow situation before a hike to such high places, I always consult local webcams. In this case, the Hohtälli webcam is comparable in altitude.

Whether Tolkien climbed to the Hörnli Hut is not known. But as seen, he was in Zermatt according to his account, and the Matterhorn probably co-inspired Mount Doom. And while climbing this path up to the Matterhorn,

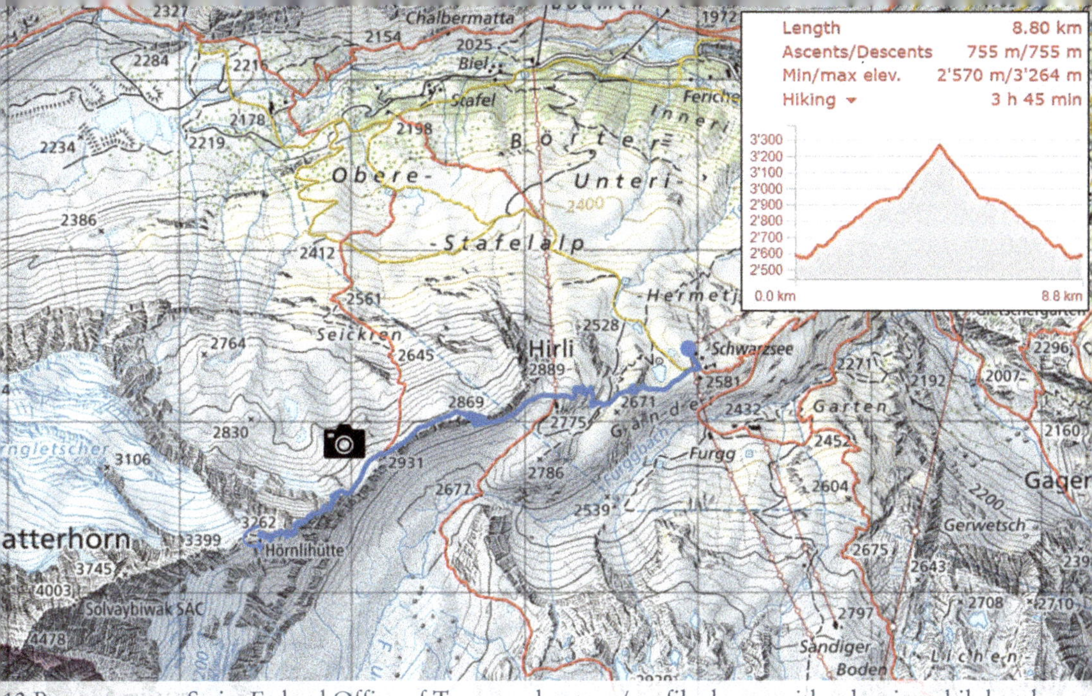

12 Route, source: Swiss Federal Office of Topography; tour/profile drawn with schweizmobilplus.ch.

I could well feel with Frodo and Sam as they struggle up Mount Doom; it would certainly be an obvious source of inspiration. Moreover, in 1911 the path was certainly not as well built as it is today, and the climb was thus more arduous.

At the hut at the top, I enjoyed what was probably the most expensive iced tea of my life, as there was not much room for a picnic. But the view of the surrounding mountains was magnificent. Especially the Monte Rosa massif shines wonderfully in eternal white when seen from here. Back we went on the same way since we wanted to drive to Arolla the same day, for which you need more than 2 hours from Zermatt, but of course, you can also choose one of the other hikes down and stay longer in Zermatt.

High on my personal to-do list is a hike to the Monte Rosa Hut, from where the Matterhorn rises majestically above the Gorner Glacier (see Figure 53, page 139). But for this tour, an ordinary experienced hiker needs a mountain guide because the path to the hut leads over the glacier.

113 (left) The Matterhorn from the path to the Hörnli Hut (small white dot on the ridge in the center of the picture). The photo viewpoint is marked on the map.

Hike 8:   The Pass to Mordor—Arolla-Bertol Hut

Arolla forms a nice contrast to Zermatt. The ruins of the Hotel Mont Collon at the village entrance indicate that the village has experienced more glorious times from a tourist development point of view. The lack of such a development is certainly not due to the wild romantic mountain landscape; for nature lovers, Arolla is a paradise.

We treated ourselves to the Grand Hôtel et Kurhaus, which was still quite reasonably priced for Switzerland and gave us a bit of an idea of how the English used to stay in Switzerland a hundred years ago. The rooms and bathrooms are no longer quite so "grand," but the main rooms offer a beautiful atmosphere, the garden is gorgeous, and the food was excellent. However, Tolkien did not stay there—the hotel staff has clarified this from their archives; so he probably slept in the now-closed Hotel Mont Collon.

The hike itself I have already described (p. 150 ff.). As mentioned, it is a true crescendo. From the parking lot at the end of the valley road, the trail first leads comfortably along the valley on a gravel road before it branches off to the left onto the mountain trail and leads steeply up to the Plans de Bertol; the path is a probable source of inspiration for the stairs of Cirith Ungol. Before the ascent, a mountain on the right has crenelated structures that may be interpreted as Minas Morgul. At the top of the Plans de Bertol, the valley opens up, and one can see the Bertol Hut sitting on a rocky peak above the scree slopes and the glacier residue at an altitude of 10,863 feet (3,311 meters)—*all paths to Mordor are guarded.*

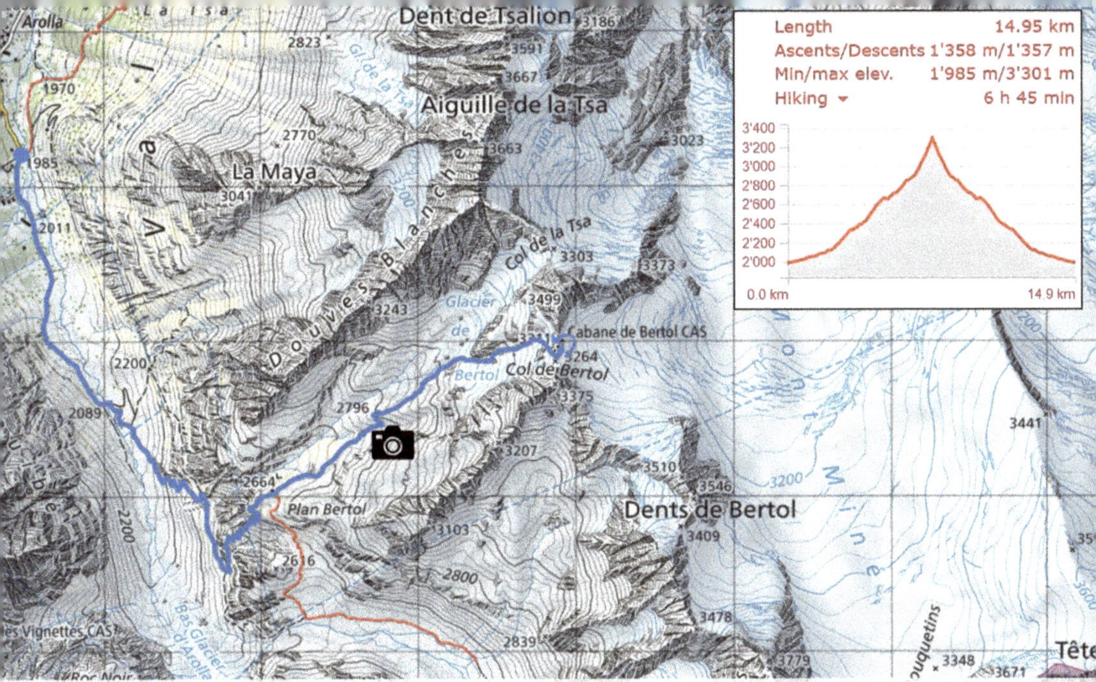

4 Route, source: Swiss Federal Office of Topography; tour/profile drawn with schweizmobilplus.ch.

The view up to the hut resembles a sketch that Tolkien made of the pass, whereby the then much larger Bertol Glacier with its crevasses likely inspired the caves of the giant spider Shelob (Shelob's Lair).

From the Glacier de Bertol waypoint, the trail leads up to the hut as a blue alpine route over scree, snowfields, and finally vertiginous ladders. On the SAC scale, this path is classified as a demanding alpine hike (T5). The requirements for such a trail can be found here on page 274; crampons and poles are definitely recommended on the steep snowfields. But once you reach the top, the view opens up to a glacier landscape like that from another planet. And behind it, a few miles away, the black cone of the Matterhorn rises over the white snow-desert—a likely inspiration for the Plain of Gorgoroth and Mount Doom.

Turn back any time if you feel uncomfortable. I myself did not climb the ladders—which I now regret—and my fellow hikers turned around earlier. The good thing is that as a hiker, you have to go back the same way anyway. But Tolkien climbed up here in 1911, for in the Bertol Hut, he signed the guest book. Actually, they were literally pulled (with ropes if I understand right) the last 100 feet by the stalwart Swiss guides according to Colin Brookes-Smith (1982). It was quite an adventure.

115 (left) The view up to the Bertol Hut, *all paths to Mordor are guarded*. The photo viewpoint is marked on the map.

Hike 9:   Mount Doom II—Mont Miné

After the exertions of the previous day, we chose a short hike for the following day and combined it with a road trip via Sion (Minas Tirith) to Saint-Maurice (Gap of Rohan) and back to Sion. First, we drove via Les Haudères to the end of the passable road in Ferpècle. Although it is only about 11 miles (18 kilometers), we needed about half an hour since the crossing with oncoming vehicles is difficult after Forclaz.

From the small parking lot in Ferpècle, you have two options: either you hike through the plain towards Mont Miné, or you climb up left to the alp Bricola. We chose the first option to approach this Mount Doom in the plain, similar to Frodo and Sam's route.

Here at the tree line, it is a special, barren landscape, which plants have been slowly reclaiming since the glaciers melted back. In 1911, the glaciers still enclosed Mont Miné, so the plain below was certainly more barren and thus more like the Plain of Gorgoroth. A positive aspect of the glacier recession is the beautiful waterfalls that now appear, especially to the right of Mont Miné.

Approaching Mont Miné, you can well imagine that you are walking towards Mount Doom. The form and texture of the mountain are exactly how Tolkien drew and described it. And in shape and color, the mountain is even somewhat reminiscent of a volcanic cone. It appears like a foreign body in the Alps, the unreal counterpart of the white, sparkling Silberhorn.

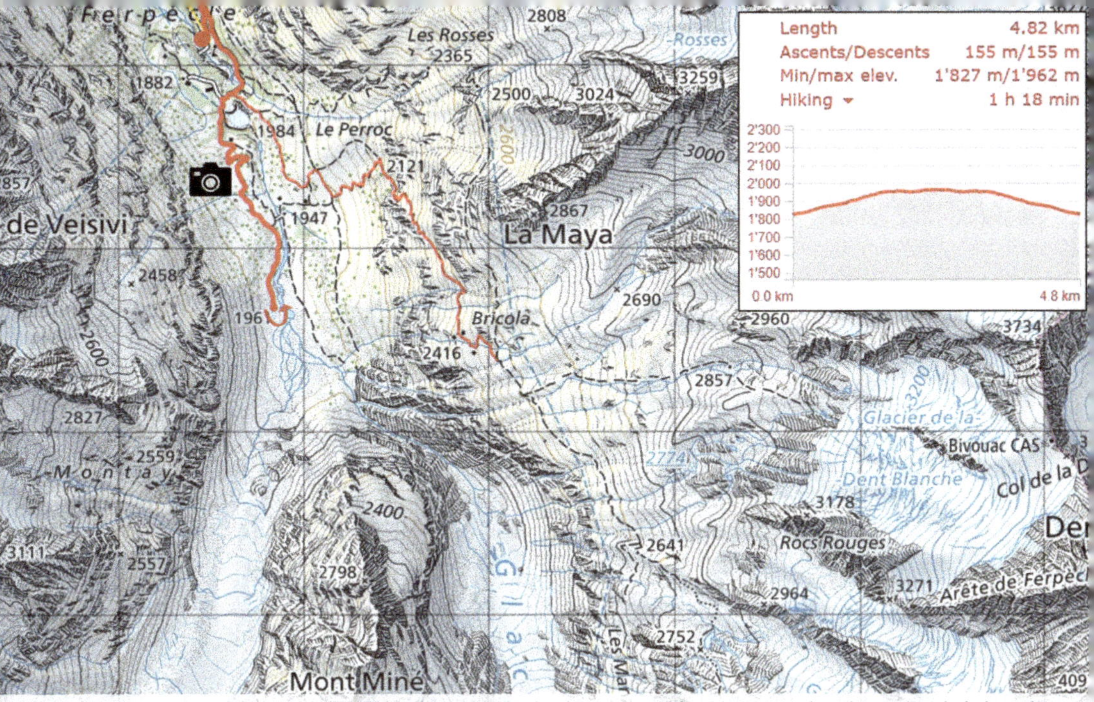

16 Route, source: Swiss Federal Office of Topography; tour/profile drawn with schweizmobilplus.ch.

The majestic mountain rising into the sky on the left is Dent Blanche, and closer, to the left of Dent Blanche, towers a peak called La Maya. This is remarkable insofar as Sauron is a so-called Maia (from Elvish *maya*), as is the mountain spirit Gandalf. In Tolkien's legendarium, the Maiar are powerful spirits that can take on a physical form. So, it seems at least somewhat indicative that a Maya is standing here right next to Mont Miné.

After the hike, we had a snack with wild mushrooms in the cozy restaurant Le Petit Paradis just above the parking lot. And then, we continued towards Sion, that is, from Mount Doom directly to Minas Tirith—like at the end of *The Lord of the Rings*.

117 (left) Mont Miné, its shape recalls Tolkien's sketch of Mount Doom. The photo viewpoint is marked on the map.

263

Road Trip via Minas Tirith—Arolla-Sion-Kandersteg

From Ferpècle, it takes less than an hour to reach Sion, but we made a short stop at the Pyramids of Euseigne, a remarkable natural monument. Then, instead of going directly into the city of Sion, we continued to the Gate of the Valais at Saint-Maurice and Bex. However, I did not suggest Bex in this road trip since the Tower of Bex is not open to the public and the Grotte aux Fées not that impressive. I would probably not include it in a one-week tour. The old town of Saint-Maurice with the abbey is nice and cozy, but there is only a limited connection to *The Lord of the Rings*, perhaps through the Saracen plundering or the legend about Saint-Maurice. Visiting the salt mines of Bex seems to be an exciting and informative experience, but you need a reservation, which we did not have.

In Sion, the climb up the castle hills of Valère and Tourbillon is essential to any Middle-earth trip in Switzerland. On the terrace, in front of the Valère basilica, you can still feel a bit like you are in Minas Tirith. But you need to imagine the urban sprawl is gone (see the cover image). So, I hope you are not too disappointed if it does not quite match your image of Minas Tirith. Still, I suspect it was Tolkien's strongest autobiographical source of inspiration for the city. Down in the old town, there is another Witcher's Tower (Tour des Sorcier), where you can stop by and think a bit about Saruman and the Witch-King of Angmar. After all, the latter was defeated by Éowyn in the Battle of the Pelennor Fields outside the gates of Minas Tirith.

From Sion, we made a detour to the Hermitage of Longeborgne the next day, primarily because I was considering it as a source of inspiration for the Henneth Annûn hideout in Ithilien. This is the place where Frodo and Sam are taken by Faramir and his men. We reached the hiding place from above

118 Route; map source: Swiss Federal Office of Topographie, map.geo.admin.ch.

as Frodo and Sam do, but the access from below is easier. If you do the road trip in one day, I would probably skip it. We then drove up the Rhone Valley back to Niedergesteln, where we finally visited the Gestelnburg Castle ruin, a likely source of inspiration for Helm's Deep. On the way, there is also the underground lake of St-Léonard, but this was not a site in Tolkien's time.

From Niedergesteln, we reached the south portal of the Lötschberg Tunnel in Goppenstein in about 15 minutes. If you have enough time, you can make a detour to the Lötschental Museum in Kippel with its orcish masks. Unfortunately, we did not have the time and went directly by car train transport through the Lötschberg Tunnel, Moria, to Kandersteg.

119 (left) View from the Tourbillon castle hill down over Sion with the Valère Basilica on the left and Mont d'Orge on the right; Sion is a likely source of inspiration for Minas Tirith. The photo viewpoint is marked on the map.

265

Hike 10: The Mountain Path II and Mirrormere — Leukerbad-Gemmi Pass-Kandersteg

This hike leads from the Valais over the Misty Mountains back to the Bernese Oberland. It is the only hike here that I have not done myself yet, but it is very high up on my to-do list. It is especially suitable for travelers who carry all their luggage with them. To include the hike in our round trip, we would have had to drive first to Kandersteg and from there travel by train and bus to Leukerbad early the next morning (about 2h30). Alternatively, we could have spent the night in Spiez to get to Leukerbad in about 1h30; but at the end of the hike, we would, in that case, have needed to travel from Kandersteg back to Spiez (30 min. by train, one connection per hour). It would have been a bit inconvenient, and time-wise, it did not fit well into the one-week tour, so I plan a weekend trip.

Leukerbad, the starting point of the hike, is known for its thermal springs. If you spend a day in Leukerbad, you can, for example, visit the spectacular Albinen ladders (*Albinenleitern*) as well as the village of Albinen and later take a hot bath in Leukerbad. The ladders are an especially fascinating place for writers and game designers in search of inspiration.

The actual hike from Leukerbad to Kandersteg leads first spectacularly up the 600-meter-high Gemmi Wall (*Gemmiwand*), which is divided into several almost vertical rock layers. The path seems good, but it is nothing for hobbits

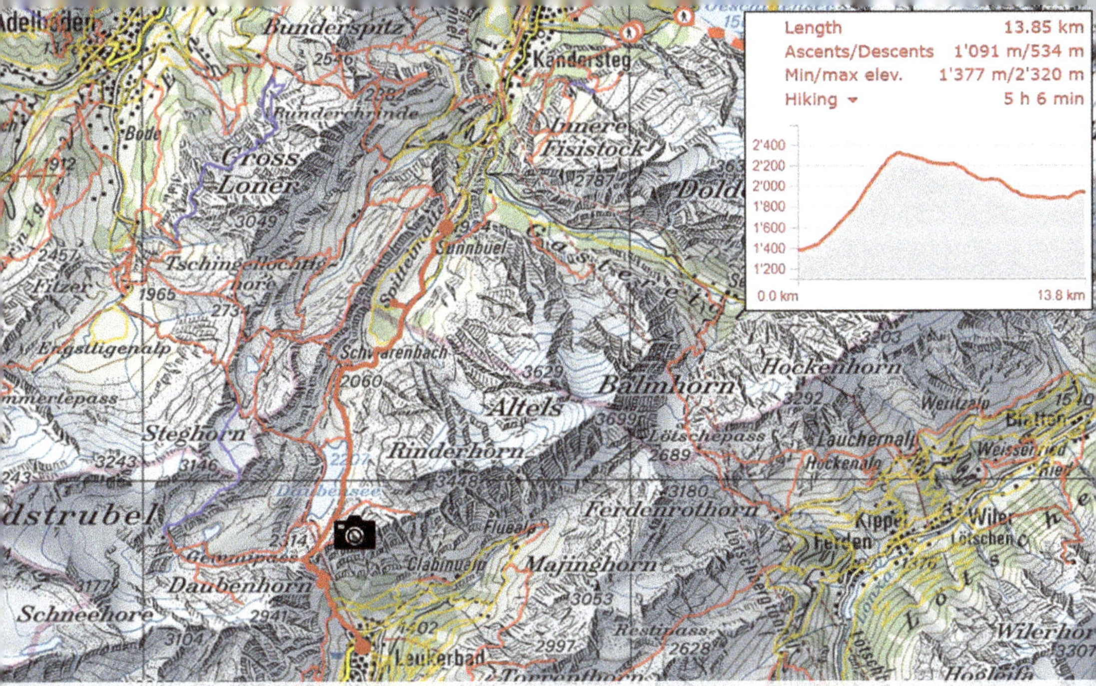

20 Route, source: Swiss Federal Office of Topography; tour/profile drawn with schweizmobilplus.ch.

with a fear of heights. From the Gemmi Pass, the way is fairly flat for long stretches on an easy path toward Kandersteg. Alternatively, there are red mountain trails, which I usually prefer, but they do lengthen the hike.

After the pass, the yellow trail first passes Lake Dauben, a possible source of inspiration for Mirrormere, and then continues through a rocky landscape to the historic Schwarenbach mountain inn. The power lines are a bit of a shame, but the tundra-like landscape is still picturesque. Continue to the beautiful Arveseeli, perhaps the source of the Silverlode, and then along the Schwarzbach Valley or Dimrill Dale to the Sunnbüel mountain restaurant, from where you have the option of taking the cable car down to Kandersteg. However, I would probably choose the red mountain trail into the Gastern Valley, which is considered one of the most natural and beautiful alpine valleys. It is perhaps the best way to recreate the hike from Mirrormere to Lothlórien and the slide down into the pine woods in *The Hobbit* (cf. Letters of Tolkien, no. 306).

121 (left) The drainless Lake Dauben resembles Mirrormere; photo: Adrian Michael, *Daubensee1*, slightly edited, CC-BY-SA 3.0. The photo viewpoint is marked on the map.

Hike 11: Moria's Watcher in the Water—Lake Oeschinen

After a night in Kandersteg, we undertook a half-day hike to Lake Oeschinen the next morning. With the gondola Kandersteg–Oeschinen, we reached the starting point. From there, we chose the easy tour, which you can see red-marked on the right. Next time, however, I will probably choose the longer circular hike to Oberbärgli (approx. 3h30 according to Schweizmobil Plus). The demanding and very exposed alpine trail (SAC T4) around the lake is currently (2021) closed due to the danger of rockfall. And even once it is open again, it requires you to be surefooted, free from vertigo, and with alpine trail experience (see also p. 274); I, for one, would have great respect for this hike.

At the restaurant *zur Sennhütte*, the wonderful view opens over the lake with its turquoise water to the rugged rock faces on the other side. Not far from the northern portal of the Lötschberg Tunnel, it is a possible source of inspiration for the lake at the West-gate of Moria. That is how I would have imagined it, and I would not be surprised if there were a monster lurking in the water—but I did not find a corresponding legend, nor the monster. We enjoyed the fantastic view for a while, then ate something in the Berghaus, and finally hiked back to Kandersteg. The place lends itself to lingering, though.

The lake has become a bit of an Instagram hype, so we were not the only ones. Therefore, if you can make it, I recommend doing the hike during the

2 Route, source: Swiss Federal Office of Topography; tour/profile drawn with schweizmobilplus.ch.

week. Besides, in Kandersteg you should book your accommodation early enough. We started booking quite late and had difficulties finding an affordable room. But we also were reserving there from Saturday to Sunday; the weekend nights especially should always be booked early.

By the way, from Mürren or Gimmelwald you can also hike to Kandersteg in two or three days, thus linking the different probable sources of inspiration for Moria.

123 (left) Lake Oeschinen as a possible source of inspiration for the lake at the West-gate of Moria. The photo viewpoint is marked on the map.

Road Trip to the Long Lake — Kandersteg-Spiez-Thun

At the end of your Middle-earth journey, there is a little road trip that will make you feel like you are in *The Hobbit*. If you drive from Kandersteg in the direction of Lake Thun, you will reach the Blausee (Blue Lake) after about 10 minutes. This pearl, too, is very crowded in summer, especially on weekends, but it is certainly worth seeing. For a short visit, the entrance fee is a bit high, but we got a discount because of our overnight stay in Kandersteg. The surprising highlight for me was the various forest trails between the parking lot and the lake. On a good day with few visitors, you might feel a bit like in the Woodland Realm of the Elvenking.

For a next stop, I recommend Spiez. The peninsula with the castle, the park, and the thousand-year-old castle church is really pretty, and with the view over the lake and of the Niesen, I could well imagine myself there on the Long Lake in Middle-earth. We ate very well at the Riviera by Elio.

It is a good endpoint for the trip, but if you still have time, I recommend driving around the lake to the right. At the exit Interlaken West, you can leave the highway and drive past the small nature reserve Weissenau to the St. Beatus Caves, where you should definitely stop. It is the place with the dragon legend, and so the *The Hobbit* experience immediately becomes a little more real. Be sure to climb up to the cave entrance and have a coffee or snack there, as the layout and view are picturesque. And you can also visit the

caves if you have time. There are no very large chambers, but the visit gives a bit of a Moria feeling. And there is also a stone in the caves that looks like the heart of the mountain, the Arkenstone.

Once you are on the road again, I recommend another quick stop in Gunten or further up in Sigriswil. From there, you have the best view of the Niesen pyramid (Figure 125). It is a worthy finale to a Middle-earth journey. Maybe you will have the opportunity to eat something or sleep and relax in the area. But at the very end of the trip, I also highly recommend a stop in Thun, for its old town is very charming and cozy.

That is it from me. I hope you enjoyed the trip and will return home with many magical impressions you will never forget. From now on, you have two options: either you let yourself be enchanted by this landscape again and again like me (see msmonsch.com), or you do it like Tolkien and Bilbo and turn to the mountain spirit Gandalf now and then to tell him, "I want to see mountains again, Gandalf—*mountains*." But secretly, you will know that it would never be the same. And perhaps that is why Tolkien never repeated the journey, but instead processed it in his imagination, in his work—in Middle-earth.

125 (left) The Niesen, a truly worthy candidate for the Lonely Mountain. The photo viewpoint is marked on the map.

271

IV. Reading List

Hike	This Book	*The Hobbit*	*The Lord of the Rings*
before	Preface, 51–96	I	B1
H1	17–21, 26–31, 36–42, 48–49	II	B2.I
H2	21–26	III	B2.II
H3	26–36, 42–48	IV–V	B2.III(–VI)
Rt1	96–114	VI–VII	(B2.VI–X), B3.I–III
H4	114–129	(VI)&VIII	(B2.III, B5.II–III, VIII)
H5	(114–129)	–	B3.IV–VI
H6	(129–138)	–	(B3.VII-XI)
H7	138–150	–	B4.I–III, (B6.III)
H8	150–153	–	B4.(IV–VII), VIII–X, B6.I
H9	153–156	–	B6.II–IV
Rt2	156–197	–	B5, B6.V(–VI)
H10	197–206	–	(B2.VI–VIII)
H11	(30–36)	–	(B2.IV)
Rt3	206–232	IX–XVII	–
after	Concl. Rem.	XVIII–XIX	B6.VII–IX

The reading program, as you can see, is a bit sporty in parts. But of course, you can gear your trip even more to *The Hobbit*, *The Lord of the Rings*, or this book. In the case of *The Lord of the Rings* (and also my book), a longer stay in the main valley of the Rhone is suitable; in the case of *The Hobbit*, a longer stay at Lake Thun is best.

V. Requirements of the Different Trail Categories

Categ.	Definition acc. to Swiss Standard 640 829a (transl.)
Yellow H9 H11	Hiking trails are generally accessible and usually intended for people on foot. They run, if possible, away from roads for motorized traffic and have as little asphalt or concrete as possible. Steep passages are overcome with steps, and fall-off points are secured with railings. Watercourses are crossed on (foot)bridges. Hiking trails do not require any special skills from the users. The signalization of the hiking trails is yellow.
Red H1 H2 H3 H4 H5 H6 H10	Mountain hiking trails are hiking trails that partly open up impassable terrain. They are mostly steep and narrow and partly exposed. Particularly difficult passages are secured with ropes or chains. Streams may have to be crossed via fords. Users of mountain trails must be sure-footed, free from vertigo, and in good physical condition, and must be aware of the dangers in the mountains—falling rocks, danger of slipping and falling, weather conditions. It is necessary to wear sturdy shoes with a good grip, have the equipment appropriate to the weather, and carry topographic maps. The signposts are yellow with a white-red-white tip, confirmations and markings are white-red-white.
Blue H7 H8	Alpine hiking trails are demanding mountain trails. They lead partly through pathless terrain, over snowfields and glaciers, over scree slopes, through rockfall gullies, or across rock with short climbing sections. Structural precautions cannot be expected and are limited, at most, to securing particularly exposed places with danger of falling. Users of alpine hiking trails must be sure-footed, free from vertigo, and in very good physical condition, and they must be able to handle rope and ice ax and to negotiate climbing sections with the aid of their hands. They must know the dangers in the mountains. In addition to the equipment for mountain hiking trails, an altimeter and compass are required, and rope and ice axe for glacier crossings. Trail markers are blue with a white-blue-white tip, confirmations and markings are white-blue-white. The information board „Alpinwanderweg" points out the special requirements at the beginning of the trail.

The Swiss Alpine Club (SAC) further divides the alpine hiking trails into two subcategories. These are of importance for hike 7 (to the Hörnli Hut) and for hike 8 (to the Bertol Hut).

SAC-Category	Path/Terrain	Requirements
T4 Alpine Hiking H7	Trail not necessarily available. In certain places, you need your hands to move forward. Terrain already quite exposed, tricky grassy slopes, crags, easy firn fields, and snow-free glacier passages. If marked according to SWW standards: white-blue-white.	Familiarity with exposed terrain. Sturdy trekking shoes. Some terrain judgment and good orientation skills. Alpine experience. Retreat may be difficult in the event of a sudden change in the weather.
T5 Demanding Alpine Hiking H8	Often pathless. Some easy climbs. Exposed, demanding terrain, steep scree. Snow-free glaciers and firn fields with danger of slipping.	Mountain boots. Secure terrain assessment and very good orientation skills. Good alpine experience and in high alpine terrain. Elementary knowledge of the use of ice ax and rope.

The path up to the Hörnli Hut is only newly officially categorized as an alpine hiking trail; on the online map of the SAC, it was (at the last editing of this book) still classified as T3 (demanding mountain hiking). But probably too many tourists went up there who should not, and the trail was a bit damaged in parts when I was there.

Appendix 2: Key Dates in Tolkien's Life

1892 *January 3:* John Ronald Reuel Tolkien is born in Bloemfontein, South Africa, the son of the English Mabel Suffield and Arthur Reuel Tolkien.

1894 *February 17:* Birth of Tolkien's brother Hilary.

1895 *Spring:* Tolkien's mother moves back to England with her two sons. His father remains in South Africa.

1896 *February 15:* Tolkien's father dies unexpectedly of rheumatic fever; news reaches Tolkien's mother in England. She moves with her sons to Sarehole (now Hall Green), then a rural suburb of Birmingham, where they will live for four years; the place and region will shape Tolkien's Shire.

1900 Tolkien enters King Edward's School, which he attends until 1911, except for a brief interruption. Tolkien's mother joins the Catholic Church. She moves with her sons first to Moseley (1900), then to Kings Heath (1901), both suburbs of Birmingham, and, finally, more centrally, to Oliver Road (1902).

1904 Tolkien's mother is diagnosed with diabetes; she dies on November 14 at age thirty-four (pre-insulin era). Tolkien is twelve years old and now an orphan. He is placed in the care of his aunt Beatrice (Stirling Road). The Catholic priest Francis Xavier Morgan becomes his guardian.

1908 Tolkien (now sixteen) and his brother are placed in the care of Mrs. Faulkner (on Duchess Road). Tolkien meets Edith Mary Bratt, who is three years older; they declare their love the following year. When father Morgan learns of this, he forbids him to have any contact with the Protestant Edith until he is twenty-one.

1911 Tolkien and three of his friends, Rob Gilson, Geoffrey Bache Smith, and Christopher Wiseman, found the academic-recreational Tea Club and Barrovian Society (T.C.B.S.). The members are regarded as probable sources of inspiration for the four hobbits in *The Lord of the Rings*. In the summer, Tolkien graduates, and his aunt Jane Neave takes him and Hilary on the trip to Switzerland that is the subject of this book. In the fall, Tolkien begins his studies at the University of Oxford. Sarehole, his Shire, is incorporated into Birmingham.

1913   *January:* On the evening of his twenty-first birthday, Tolkien writes to Edith and declares his love for her. Edith is already engaged at this point, but she returns her ring, a minor scandal, to become engaged to Tolkien.

1914   *Summer:* World War I breaks out. *September 24:* Tolkien writes the first identifiable Middle-earth fragment: "The Voyage of Éarendel the Evening Star."

1915   *Summer:* Tolkien graduates from the University of Oxford and begins his military training.

1916   *March 22:* Tolkien and Edith marry. *Summer:* Tolkien is transferred to France. He fights in the Battle of the Somme, one of the bloodiest battles in world history with over a million dead. Two of his T.C.B.S. friends fall. In October, Tolkien falls ill with trench fever, which probably saves his life. He is brought back to England.

1917   After recovering somewhat, Tolkien works for the military in England. He writes his first longer stories, beginning with *The Fall of Gondolin.* *November:* birth of his eldest son, John. Three more children will follow: Michael (1920), Christopher (1924), and Priscilla Anne (1929).

1920   Tolkien first works on the Oxford English Dictionary and then becomes Lecturer in English at the University of Leeds.

1925   Tolkien becomes Professor of Anglo-Saxon (Old English) at Pembroke College, University of Oxford. Tolkien publishes with E. V. Gordon their English translation of *Sir Gawain and the Green Knight* (from Middle English).

1930   *Approximately:* Tolkien writes *The Hobbit* (until 1932), reads it to his children, and gives it to various colleagues for review, including C.S. Lewis.

1931   The Inklings literary group, which included Tolkien and C.S. Lewis, among others, is founded by Edward Tangye Lean at the University College, University of Oxford.

1936   Tolkien delivers and publishes his famous lecture "*Beowulf*: The Monsters and the Critics."

1937   *The Hobbit* is finally published; Tolkien is forty-five years old. He starts writing *The Lord of the Rings*, initially as a sequel to *The Hobbit.* He will give a first manuscript to his publisher for review in 1947.

1939   *September:* World War II breaks out. Already in January, Tolkien is asked if he would be willing to work in the cryptographic department of the Foreign Office. Tolkien agrees and attends a course, but a collaboration with Alan Turing was not to come, for his services were not called upon. Tolkien gives his famous lecture "On Fairy-Stories."

1945 The war ends. Tolkien becomes Professor of English Language and Literature at Merton College, University of Oxford.

1954 *The Lord of the Rings* is published that year and the following year (that is, not until five years after the manuscript had been completed due to a back-and-forth with publishers); Tolkien is sixty-three years old when *The Return of the King* is published.

1955 Tolkien travels in the footsteps of Frodo on the Simplon Express to Italy, from the Shire through (what I believe to have inspired) the Gap of Rohan and the White Mountains to Gondor.

1959 Tolkien retires and in the following years becomes increasingly famous for his literary work. In 1961, C. S. Lewis nominates him for the Nobel Prize for Literature, but he does not receive it. After his retirement, the Tolkiens move to Bournemouth in southern England.

1967 Tolkien writes a letter to his son Michael in which he tells him about his trip to Switzerland. Tolkien is seventy-five years old.

1971 *November 29:* Edith dies at the age of eighty-two. Tolkien has "Lúthien" engraved on her tombstone, in reference to his tragic love story *Beren and Lúthien*. He moves back to Oxford.

1972 Tolkien is appointed Commander of the Order of the British Empire (CBE) by the Queen.

1973 *September 2:* Tolkien dies at the age of eighty-one after a short illness in a hospital in Bournemouth, southern England. Beren's name is engraved below Tolkien's name on he and his wife's joint tombstone.

Since then, many of Tolkien's manuscripts have been published by his son Christopher Tolkien (1924–2020), including *The Silmarillion* (1977), *Unfinished Tales of Númenor and Middle-earth* (1980), *The Children of Húrin* (2007), *Beren and Lúthien* (2017), and *The Fall of Gondolin* (2018).

List of Figures

1. Data: © OpenStreetMap.org-Contributors, CC-BY-SA; the design is based on that of user datendelphin [www.openstreetmap.org/user/datendelphin]; Topography: ASTER GDEM. The map is available under: https://umap.osm.ch.

ASTER GDEM: NASA/METI/AIST/Japan Spacesystems and U.S./Japan ASTER Science Team. *ASTER Global Digital Elevation Model V003*. 2019, distributed by NASA EOSDIS Land Processes DAAC, https://doi.org/10.5067/ASTER/ASTGTM .003.

2. Bergfex-Maps: Created by the bergfex GmbH based on © OpenStreet-Map.org-Contributors, CC-BY-SA. The map is available under: www.bergfex.ch.

3. The use of the route maps used in the appendix was kindly granted to me by the Stiftung Schweizmobil (SwitzerlandMobility Foundation; www.schweizmobilplus .ch). The map data was made available to the public by the Federal Office of Topography on March 1, 2021 (see www.swisstopo.admin.ch/de/swisstopo/kostenlose-geo basisdaten.html).

Bibliography

Aeby, Christoph, Edmund von Fellenberg, and Rudolf Gerwer. 1865. *Das Hochgebirge von Grindelwald*. Coblenz: Karl Baedeker.

Artist & Illustrator: see Hammond, Wayne G. and Christina Scull. 1995.

Becher, Matthias. 2012. *Otto der Große, Kaiser und Reich: Eine Biographie*. Munich: C.H. Beck.

Bechtel, Dale. 2004. "Frozen ghosts haunt Gemmi Pass." *Swissinfo*, January 12, 2004. www.swissinfo.ch/eng/frozen-ghosts-haunt-gemmi-pass/14676.

Berno of Reichenau. ca. 1001. *Vita Sancti Uodalrici confessoris atque pontificis (The Life of the holy confessor and bishop Ulrich)*. Quoted from: D. Blume. *Bern von Reichenau (1008-1048): Abt, Gelehrter, Biograph: Ein Lebensbild mit Werkverzeichnis sowie Edition und Übersetzung von Berns Vita S. Uodalrici*. Ostfildern: Thorbecke. 2008.

Bernward of Hildesheim. ca. 1019. *Vita Bernwardi episcopi Hildesheimensis*. Quoted from: H. Hüffer and W. Wattenbach. *Die Lebensbeschreibung der Bischöfe Bernward und Godehard von Hildesheim. 2. Aufl.* Leipzig: Verlag der Dytschen Buchhandlung. 1892.

Billwiller, R. 1911. "Übersicht über den Witterungsverlauf in der Schweiz im Jahre 1911." *Annalen der schweizerischen meteorologischen Zentral-Anstalt* 48. www.meteoschweiz.admin.ch/product/input/documents/annals/annalen-1911.pdf.

Bleicher, Niels. 2015. "Auf verlorenem Pfosten: Ein polemischer methodologischer Nachruf auf den Pfahlbaustreit." *as. (archäologie schweiz)* 38, no. 4: 24–31.

Bourrit, Marc-Théodore. 1781. *Description des Alpes Pennines et Rhetiennes*. Geneva: J. P. Bonnant.

Bowers, John M. 2019. *Tolkien's Lost Chaucer*. Oxford: Oxford University Press.

Bridel, Philippe-Sirice. 1820. *Essai statistique sur le Canton de Vallais*. Zurich: Orell Fussli et Comp.

Bridoux, Denis. 2016. Presentation at Oxonmoot 2016. https://www.youtube.com/watch?v=A--NE6B3UBM.

Brookes-Smith, Colin. 1982. *Some Reminiscences of J.R.R. Tolkien*. Bloxham: unpublished memoir.

Bunting, Nancy, and Elizabeth Currie. 2021. "The 1911 Swiss Walking Tour: A Sentimental Education and Some of Its Fruits." *Beyond Bree*, May 2021 issue.

Businger, Joseph. 1811. *Die Stadt Luzern und ihre Umgebungen*. Lucerne: Xaver Meyer.

Bütschi, Dominic. 2008. "Die Kander als historisch gewachsene Flusslandschaft." Thesis at the Historical Institute of the University of Bern. http://kanderwasser.ch/fileadmin/user_upload/Downloads/GEKa_Dossier_Gesamtprojekt/c_Modul_Gesellschaft_Wirtschaft/Fachbericht_HistoKa/Fachbericht_HistoKa.pdf.

Byron, George G. 1816. *Alpine Journal, September 18th–29th*. Edited by Peter Cochran, with that of John Cam Hobhouse for the same expedition. https://petercochran.files.wordpress.com/2009/03/alpine_journal.pdf.

Caesar, Julius. ca. 50 v. Chr. *De Bello Gallico*.

Carpenter, Humphrey. 1977. *J.R.R. Tolkien, A Biography*. Boston: Houghton Mifflin.

Carpenter, Humphrey, and Christopher Tolkien. 1981. *The Letters of J.R.R. Tolkien*. London: George Allen & Unwin (quoted as: *Letters of Tolkien*).

Cilli, Oronzo. 2019. *Tolkien's Library: An Annotated Checklist*. Edinburgh: Luna Press Publishing.

Cohn, Willy. 1926. "Capristano, ein Breslauer Judenfeind in der Mönchskutte." *Menorah* 4, no. 5: 262–265.

Dal Farra, Dino. 2011. "Als die Simmenfluh lichterloh brannte." *Thuner Tagblatt,* September 21, 2011. www.bernerzeitung.ch/region/thun/Als-die-Simmenfluh-lichterloh-brannte/story/213125 82.

Dübi, Heinrich. 1931. "Zwei Walliser Volkslieder über die Schlacht auf der Planta." *Archiv des Historischen Vereins des Kantons Bern* 31: 59–71.

Dubler, Anne-Marie. 2009. "Flösserei." *Historisches Lexikon der Schweiz HLS,* entry of November 5. https://hls-dhs-dss.ch/de/articles/014055/2009-11-05.

Dubler, Anne-Marie. 2012. "Thunersee." *Historisches Lexikon der Schweiz HLS.* https://hls-dhs-dss.ch/de/articles/008647/2012-10-05.

Dummermuth, Gottfried. 1889. *Der Schweizerapostel St. Beatus, Sage und Geschichte.* Basel: Max Birkhäuser & Carl Huber.

Ehrismann, Otfrid. 2002. *Nibelungenlied: Epoche – Werk – Wirkung.* 2. Aufl. Munich: C.H.Beck.

Ekkehard IV. ca. 1035. *Casus Sancti Galli.* St. Gallen. Quoted from: G. Meyer von Knonau. *Ekkeharts IV. Casus Sancti Galli nebst Proben aus den übrigen lateinisch geschriebenen Abtheilungen der St. Galler Klosterchronik.* In *Geschschr. dt. Vorz.* vol. 38, 2. Aufl. Leipzig: Dycksche Buchhandlung. 1925. www.sanktgallus.net/ekkehards-casus-sancti-galli.

Elmer Wood, Edith. 1910. *An Oberland Châlet.* New York: Wessels & Bissell.

Engelhardt, Christian M. 1840. *Naturschilderungen, Sittenzüge und wissenschaftliche Bemerkungen aus den höchsten Schweizer-Alpen, besonders in Sud-Wallis und Graubünden.* Paris: Schweighauser'sche Buchhandlung.

Ezard, John. 1991. "Tolkien's shire." *The Guardian,* December 28, 1991. www.theguardian.com /books/1991/dec/28/jrrtolkien.classics.

Fahy, Jo. 2015. "The Lord of the Illustrations: How John Howe turns Tolkien's words into film." *Swissinfo,* February 5, 2015. www.swissinfo.ch/eng/the-lord-of-the-illustrations_how-john-howe-turns-tolkien-s-words-into-film/41253038.

Fisher, Jason. 2006. "Reluctantly Inspired: George MacDonald and J.R.R. Tolkien." *North Wind: A Journal of George MacDonald Studies* 25: 113–120.

Fisher, Jason. 2012. "Dwarves, Spiders, and Murky Woods: J. R. R. Tolkien's Wonderful Web of Words." In *C. S. Lewis and the Inklings: Discovering Hidden Truth,* edited by Salwa Khoddam and Mark R. Hall, 104–115. Newcastle upon Tyne: Cambridge Scholars.

Flodoard of Reims. ca. 966. *Annals.* Quoted from: C. Bandeville. *Chronique de Flodoard de l'an 919 à l'an 976.* Reims: P. Regnier. 1855.

Frías Sánchez, Fernando. 2009. "Suiza en la obra de J.R.R. Tolkien: La experiencia de 1911." Primer puesto, premios Ælfwine.

Furrer, Sigismund. 1850. *Geschichte von Wallis.* Sion: Calpini-Albertazzi (Geschichte, Statistik und Urkundensammlung über Wallis, vol. 1).

Furrer, Sigismund. 1852. *Statistik von Wallis.* Sion: Calpini-Albertazzi (Geschichte, Statistik und Urkundensammlung über Wallis, vol. 2).

Garth, John. 2003. *Tolkien and the Great War.* London: HarperCollins.

Garth, John. 2020. *The Worlds of J. R. R. Tolkien: The Worlds That Inspired Middle-Earth.* London: Frances Lincoln.

Gattlen, Anton. 1948. *Die Totensagen des Alemannischen Wallis,* PhD thesis Fribourg. Naters-Brig: Buchdruckerei Oberwallis.

Gelpke, Ernst F. 1862. *Die christliche Sagengeschichte der Schweiz.* Bern: Verlag der J. Dalpschen Buchhandlung.

Gempeler-Schletti, David. 1904. *Heimatkunde des Simmentals.* Bern: A. Francke.

Germann, Pascal. 2017. "Wie kam das Jod ins Salz?" *Schweizer Zeitschrift für Ernährungsmedizin,* no. 5: 14–17.

Gibbon, Edward. 1776/89. *The History of the Decline and Fall of the Roman Empire.* London.

Goethe, Johann W. 1779. *Gesang der Geister über den Wassern (Gedicht).*

Goethe, Johann W. 1830. *Goethes Werke*. Band 16 (vol. 16). Stuttgart: J. G. Cotta'schen Buchhandlung.

Gottet, Mathias. 2017. "Auf den Spuren von J.R.R. Tolkien." Blog article, October 9, 2017. http://mathiasgottet.ch/2017/10/09/auf-den-spuren-von-j-r-r-tolkien.

Gotthelf, Jeremias. 1941. *Die Rotentaler Herren*. Published from the estate by Hans Bloesch. Erlenbach: Eugen Rentsch.

Grand, Alfred. 1913. *Der Anteil des Wallis an den Burgunderkriegen*, PhD thesis Fribourg. Brig: Buchdr. Tscherrig und Tröndle.

Grimm, Wilhelm. 1867. *Die deutsche Heldensage*. 2. Aufl. Berlin: F. Dümmler.

Grün, Karl. 1844. *Friedrich Schiller als Mensch, Geschichtsschreiber, Denker und Dichter, Ein gedrängter Kommentar zu Schillers sämmtlichen Werken*. Leipzig: F. A. Brockhaus.

Hammond, N. G. L. 1988. "Which Ptolemy Gave Troops and Stood as Protector of Pyrrhus' Kingdom?" *Historia: Zeitschrift für Alte Geschichte* 37, no. 4 (4th Qtr.): 405–413.

Hammond, Wayne G., and Christina Scull. 1995. *J.R.R. Tolkien, Artist & Illustrator*. Boston: Houghton Mifflin (quoted as: *Artist & Illustrator*).

Hamon, Albert. 1996. "Sion et les Sédunes." *Annales valaisannes*: 153–157.

Harb, Christian; Hafner, Albert; Harb, Pierre. 2010. "Die UNESCO-Welterbe-Kandidatur 'Prähistorische Pfahlbauten um die Alpen.'" *Jahrbuch des Oberaargaus* 53: 123–148.

Hartmann, Hermann. 1910. *Berner Oberland in Sage und Geschichte, Band I: Sagen*. Bümpliz: Benteli.

Hassler, Donald M. 1988. "Some Asimov Resonances from the Enlightenment." *Science Fiction Studies* 15, no. 1: 36–47.

Hein, Rolland. 1993. *George MacDonald, Victorian Mythmaker*. Eugene OR: Star Song Pub Co.

Heinzle, Joachim. 1999. *Einführung in die mittelhochdeutsche Dietrichepik*. Berlin: De Gruyter.

Hermann of Reichenau. ca. 1054. *Chronicon de sex aetatibus mundi (Chronicle of the Six Ages of the World)*. Quoted from: K. Nobbe. *Die Chronik Herimanns von Reichenau*. Berlin: Besser. 1851.

Holl, Hanns P. 1985. *Gotthelf im Zeitgeflecht*. Tübingen: De Gruyter.

Howe, John. 2018. *A Middle-Earth Traveller*. London: HarperCollins.

Howe, John. 2019. *Artbook*. 2nd ed. Aix-en-Provence: Nestiveqnen.

Hutton, Edward. 1913. *Ravenna: A Study*. London: J. M. Dent & sons. www.gutenberg.org/cache/epub/12542/pg12542-images.html.

Imseng, Raoul. 2017. *Halbmond über der Rhone*. Saas-Fee: St. Joder Verlag.

Ischer, Theophil. 1911. "Die Erforschungsgeschichte der Pfahlbauten des Bielersees." *Anzeiger für schweizerische Altertumskunde: Neue Folge* 13.

Jablonka, Eva; Lamb, Marion J.; Avital, Eytan. 1998. "'Lamarckian' mechanisms in darwinian evolution." *TREE* 13, no. 5: 206–210.

Jaccard, Henri. 1906. *Essai de Toponymie: Origine des noms de lieux habités et des lieux dits de la Suiss romande*. Lausanne: Georges Bridel.

Jackson, Peter. 2018. *The Mongols and the West: 1221-1410*. 2nd ed. Oxon: Routledge.

Jarnut, Jörg. 2009. "Thüringer und Langobarden im 6. und beginnenden 7. Jahrhundert." In *Die Frühzeit der Thüringer*, edited by Helmut Castritius, Dieter Geuenich, and Matthias Werner, 279–290. Berlin: De Gruyter.

Jordanes. ca. 550. *De origine actibusque Getarum (= Getica)*. Quoted from: C. C. Mierow. 1997. https://people.ucalgary.ca/~vandersp/Courses/texts/jordgeti.html.

Keller, Ferdinand. 1856. "Der Einfall der Sarazenen in der Schweiz um die Mitte des X. Jahrhunderts." *Mittheilungen der antiquarischen Gesellschaft in Zürich* XI, no. 1.

Kohler, Beat. 2012. "Die Geister sind erfolgreich vertrieben." *Jungfrau Zeitung*, January 3, 2012. www.jungfrauzeitung.ch/artikel/116028.

Kohlrusch, Clemens. 1854. *Schweizerisches Sagenbuch: Nach mündlichen Überlieferungen, Chroniken und andren gedruckten und handschriftlichen Quellen*. Leipzig: R. Hoffmann.

Kormos Buchwald, Diana, József Illy, Ze'ev Rosenkranz, Tilman Sauer, and Osik Moses. 2015. *The Collected Papers of Albert Einstein, Volume 14: The Berlin Years: Writings & Correspondence, April 1923-May 1925*. Princeton: Princeton University Press.

Kovach, Tom R. 1996. "Ottoman-Hungarian Wars: Siege of Belgrade in 1456." *Military History.* www.historynet.com.

Kuonen, Theodor. 2003. "Die Holzausbeutungen im 19. Jahrhundert im Drittel Mörel, insbesondere in der Aletschregion." *Blätter aus der Walliser Geschichte* 35: 143–169.

Lee, Stuart, and Elizabeth Solopova. 2015. *The Keys of Middle-earth: Discovering Medieval Literature Through the Fiction of J. R. R. Tolkien*. 2nd ed. Basingstoke UK: Palgrave Macmillan.

Letters of Tolkien. See Carpenter, Humphrey and Christopher Tolkien. 1981.

Levy, Richard S. 2005. *Antisemitism: A Historical Encyclopedia of Prejudice and Persecution*. Volume 1: A-K. Santa Barbara: ABC-CLIO.

Lewis, Alex. 2013. "The Road to the Misty Mountains and beyond – Alpenwild tour 'In the footsetps of Tolkien,' October 12th–20th 2013." Blog article, November 4, 2013. www.tolkienlibrary.com /press/1120-alpenwild-tour-in-the-footsteps-of-tolkien.php.

Lewis, Alex, and Elizabeth Currie. 2019. *Tolkien's Switzerland: A Biography of One Special Summer*: Elansea.

Liechti, Erich. 2006. *Die Mauern von Wimmis*. www.wimmis.ch/documents/Mauern_von_Wimmis .pdf.

Lienert, Meinrad. 2006. *Schweizer Sagen und Heldengeschichten*. 2. Aufl. (1. Aufl. von 1915). Wiesbaden: Marix.

Liutprand of Cremona. ca. 962. *Antapodosis (Retribution)*. Quoted from: K. von der Osten-Sacken. *Aus Liudprands Werken*. Berlin: Duncker. 1853.

Lohbauer, Rudolf. 1838. *Der Kampf auf der Grimsel am vierzehnten August 1799: Eine militärische Studie*. Bern: L. R. Walthard'sche Buchhandlung.

Lütolf, Alois. 1871. *Glaubensboten der Schweiz vor St. Gallus*. Lucerne: Gebrüder Räber.

MacDonald, George. 1872. *Wilfried Cumbermeade*. London: Hurst and Blackett.

Mackenzie, Donald A. 1912. *Teutonic Myth and Legend*. London: Gresham.

Maenchen-Helfen, Otto J. 1973. *The World of the Huns*. Berkeley: University of California Press.

Magnusson, Eiríkir, and William Morris. 1888. *Völsunga Saga: The Story of the Volsungs and Niblungs, with certain Songs from the Elder Edda*. Walter Scott Press.

Masterson, Andrew. 2018. "Identifying the beasts in Caesars forest." *COSMOS*, November 2, 2018. https://cosmosmagazine.com/biology/identifying-the-beasts-in-caesar-s-forest.

McGann, Jerome. 2002. *Byron and Romanticism*. Cambridge UK: Cambridge University Press.

Meyer, Adrian. 2014. "Herr der Bilder, John Howe, künstlerischer Leiter von 'Der Hobbit', lässt sich in der Schweiz inspirieren." *Blick*, December 10, 2014 (last mod. on October 9, 2018). www.blick .ch/people-tv/kino/john-howe-kuenstlerischer-leiter-von-der-hobbit-laesst-sich-in-der-schweiz -inspirieren-herr-der-bilder-id3337408.html.

Meyer, Johann Rudolf. 1831. "Der Geist des Gebirges." *Alpenrosen*. Quoted from: Rémy Charbon (ed.). *Fundstücke der Schweizer Erzählkunst*. Erster Band (vol. 1): 1800-1840, pp. 170-199. Basel: Birkhäuser Verlag. 1990.

Meyer, Patricia. 2015. "Brig, Brigerberg und Burgspitze: Bronzezeit und keltisches Erbe." In *Archäologie im Oberwallis: Vom Mesolithikum bis zur Römerzeit*, edited by Philippe Curdy and Patricia Meyer, 98 f. Sion: Amt für Archäologie.

Modestin, Georg. 2005. "'Von den hexen, so in Wallis verbrant wurdent,' Eine wieder entdeckte Handschrift mit dem Bericht des Chronisten Hans Fründ über eine Hexenverfolgung im Wallis (1428)." *Vallesia* 60: 399–409.

Moore, Thomas. 1830. *Letters and Journals of Lord Byron with Notices of his Life*. Paris: A. and W. Galignani.

Morris, William. 1889. *The House of the Wolfings*. ed. 1904. London: Longmans, Green, and Co.

Morris, William. 1893. *The Roots of the Mountains*. ed. 1896. London: Longmans, Green, and Co.

Morton, Andrew H. and John Hayes. 2008. *Tolkien's Gedling*. Studley (Warwickshire): Brewin Books.

Moulton, William G. 1941. "Swiss German Dialect and Romance Patois." *Language* 17, no. 4: 8–75.

Mühlbauer, Peter. 2009. "Ein Judenverbrenner als Schutzpatron der Anwälte." *Telepolis*, September 7, 2009. www.heise.de/tp/features/Ein-Judenverbrenner-als-Schutzpatron-der-Anwaelte-345 5165.html.

Mummery, Albert F. 1895. *My Climbs in the Alps and the Caucasus*. London: T. Fisher Unwin.

Murray, John. 1886. *A Handbook for Travellers in Switzerland, the Alps of Savoy and Piedmont*. 17th ed. London: John Murray.

Murray, John. 1904. *Handbook for Switzerland and the adjacent regions of the Alps*. 19th ed. London: John Murray.

Norako, Leila K. 2014. "Merlin, Odin, and Mountain Spirits: The Story of Gandalf's Origins." In *The Hobbit and History*, edited by Janice Liedl and Nancy R. Reagin, 153–170. Nashville TN: John Wiley & Sons Inc.

Partridge, Eric. 1966. *Origins, A Short Etymological Dictionary of Modern English*. 4th ed. Abingdon (Oxon): Routledge.

Pfaff, Karl. 1977. *Die Inschriften des Kantons Wallis bis 1300*. Fribourg: Universitätsverlag.

Pliny the Elder. ca. 77 AD. *Natural History*.

Plutarch. ca. 100. *Bíoi parálleloi (Parallelbiographien)*. Quoted from: B. Perrin. *The Parallel Lives by Plutarch*. Loeb Classical Library edition. Vol. IX. Cambridge MA: Harvard University Press. 1920.

Pope Gregory I. ca. 590. *Dialogorum libri IV*. Quoted from: E. Gardner. *The Dialogues of Saint Gregory the Great*. London: Philip Lee Warner. 1911.

Rampton, James. 2019. "10 breathtaking Swiss alpine areas in the Bernese Oberland region that inspired literary greats." *the travel magazine*, June 15, 2019. www.thetravelmagazine.net/10-breath-taking-swiss-alpine-areas-in-the-bernese-oberland-region-that-inspired-literary-greats.html.

Rateliff, John D. 2015. "A New Idea About Madlener." Blog article, February 2, 2015. http://sac noths.blogspot.com/2015/02/a-new-idea-about-madlener.html.

Ruppen, Peter J. 1851. *Die Chronik des Thales Saas*. Sion: Calpini-Albertazzi.

Schärer, Lukas; Ramstein, Marianne. 2017. "Pfahlbauer am Thunersee – Neue Fundstellen im unteren Seebecken." *as. (archäologie schweiz)* 40, no. 1: 16–23.

Scull, Christina, and Wayne G. Hammond. 2017a. *The J.R.R. Tolkien Companion & Guide: Chronology*. revised and expanded ed. London: HarperCollins.

Scull, Christina, and Wayne G. Hammond. 2017b. *The J.R.R. Tolkien Companion & Guide: Reader's Guide*. revised and expanded ed. London: HarperCollins.

Sears, Jeanette. 2014. "In Tolkien's Footsteps in Switzerland." Blog article, June 29. https://jeanet-tesears.com/wp/?p=403.

Shippey, Tom. 2003. *The Road to Middle-Earth*. Revised and expanded edition. Boston: HarperCollins.

Slavet, Eliza. 2008. "Freud's 'Lamarckism' and the Politics of Racial Science." *Journal of the History of Biologogy* 41: 37–80.

Snyder, Christopher. 2013. *The Making of Middle-Earth: A New Look Inside the World of J.R.R. Tolkien*. New York: Sterling.

Sommer, Hans. 1957. "Der Wald in Orts- und Flurnamen." *Sprachspiegel* 13, no. 4.

Speidel, Michael A. 2003. *Die Thebäische Legion und das spätrömische Heer, Vortrag am Mavors-Institut für antike Militärgeschichte*. Basel. https://web.archive.org/web/20130108041134/http://www.mavors.org/PDFs/ThebaeischeLegion.pdf.

Sprecher, Fortunat. 1672. *Rhetische Cronica*. Chur: J. G. Barbisch.

Streich, Albert. 1978. *Brienzer Sagen, Tschuri, Gedichte*. Bern (Albert Streich, *Gesammelte Werke*, vol. 3).

Tamassy, Zoltan. 2018. "Das Tal der Hunnen." *der arbeitsmarkt*, January. https://derarbeitsmarkt.ch /de/reportage/das-tal-der-hunnen.

Thomas Cook & Son. 1908. *Cook's Tourist's Handbook for Switzerland*. London: Thomas Cook & Son.

Tolkien, J. R. R. (1937): *The Hobbit or There and Back Again*. London: George Allen & Unwin (quoted as: *The Hobbit*).

Tolkien, J. R. R. (1954/55): *The Lord of the Rings*. London: George Allen & Unwin (quoted as: title of the book).

Tolkien, Christopher. 1953. "The Battle of the Goths and the Huns." *Viking Society for Northern Research, Saga Book Vol. XIV 1953-1957*: 141–163.

Tolkien, J. R. R. 1977. *The Silmarillion*. London: George Allen & Unwin (quoted as: *The Silmarillion*).

Tolkien, J. R. R. 1980. *Unfinished Tales of Númenor and Middle-earth, hrsg. von Christopher Tolkien*. London: George Allen & Unwin.

Tolkien, J. R. R., and Christopher Tolkien. 1975. "Guide to the Names in *The Lord of the Rings*." http://tolkien.ro.

Tolley, Clive. 2007. "Old English Influences on the Lord of the Rings." In *Beowulf & Other Stories*, edited by Richard North and Joe Allard, 23–62. Edinburgh Gate: Routledge.

Vetter, Ferdinand. 1908. "Und noch einmal: 'Bern' ist Deutsch-Verona." *Blätter für Bernische Geschichte, Kunst und Altertumskunde* IV: 1–35.

von Moor, Conradin. 1865. *Codex Diplomaticus, Sammlung der Urkunden zur Geschichte Cur-Rätiens und der Republik Graubünden*. Chur: Hitz.

von Tillier, Anton. 1838. *Geschichte des eidgenössischen Freistaates Bern*. II. Band (vol. II). Bern: C. Fischer.

Wacker, Romedius. 1912. "Zur Anthropologie der Walser des grossen Walsertales in Vorarlberg." *Zeitschrift für Ethnologie* 44: 437–524.

Walther, Christoph. 1997. "Zur Entwicklung von forstlichen Nutzungs- und Transportkonzepten im Gebirge seit 1850." *Blätter aus Walliser Geschichte* 29: 107–196.

Wang, Yan; Liu, Huijie; Sun, Zhongsheng. 2017. "Lamarck rises from his grave: parental environment-induced epigenetic inheritance in model organisms and humans." *Biological Reviews* 92, no. 4: 2084–2111.

Weiß, Karl. 1872. *Geschichte der Stadt Wien: 2. Abteilung: Die neue Zeit und die Gegenwart*. Wien: Lechner.

Wellig, André. 2017. "Eiger, Mönch und Jungfrau: Mythos: Das Rätsel um die Namen der Eisriesen." *Jungfrau Region Stories*.

Welten, Max. 1976. "Eis, Wasser und Mensch haben das Aaretal verändert: Ergebnisse von 50 Jahren Pollenanalyse in Bern." *Mitteilungen der Naturforschenden Gesellschaft in Bern* 36.

Werlé, Christine. 2019. "John Howe et sa terre du bas." *Migros Magazine (fr)* MM43 October 21.

Whymper, Edward. 1880. *The Ascent of the Matterhorn*. London: Murray.

Widukind of Corvey. ca. 973. *Rerum gestarum Saxonicarum libri tres (The Deeds of the Saxons in Three Books)*. Quoted from: R. Schottin. *Widukinds Sächsische Geschichte*. Berlin: F. Duncker. 1852.

Wisniewski, Roswitha. 1986. *Mittelalterliche Dietrichdichtung*. Stuttgart: Metzler.

Woodburn Hyde, Walter. 1918. "The Curious Animals of the Hercynian Forest." *The Classical Journal* 13, no. 4: 231–245.

Wyss, Johann R. 1817. *Reise in das Berner Oberland*. Bd. II. Bern: J. J. Burgdorfer.

Zimmerman, Manfred. 1983. "The Origins of Gandalf and Josef Madlener." *Mythlore* 34, Article 7.

Zschokke, Heinrich. 1836. *Ausgewählte Novellen und Dichtungen*. Band 2. Aarau: Sauerländer.

Acknowledgements

I would like to express my gratitude to everyone who supported me in one way or another over the past few years as I drifted between different worlds and times. Thank you all so much! In particular, I am deeply grateful to John Howe for his profound and beautifully written foreword; I am delighted that you were willing and found the time to write these words. And I would also like to express my special thanks to Jennifer Paxman, Victoria Paxman, and John Garth for giving me access to and allowing me to quote from Colin Brookes-Smith's most relevant unpublished memoir. It was a really special moment for me to read this first-hand account after having studied this subject for so long.

Special thanks also to my parents, Yvonne and Martin Monsch, for reading the first manuscript, for your great inputs, and for your emotional support in whatever I do. For reading parts of my book, I would like to send my thanks also to Camilla, Nathalie Caballero, and Nathan Atkinson. Thank you, too, so much for all your great inputs. And I would like to send my gratitude to my editor, Kathie Weaver, for her great work, and to my cover designer, Elisa Pinizzotto, for creating the beautiful cover. It was a pleasure working with both of you. Also, I would like to thank Marco Bomio, Markus Bhend, Willy Tanner, Christine Grandjean, and Carlo Albisetti for their research and Axel Langer, Andreas Rüfenacht, and Erich Liechti for their permissions to reproduce images in this book.

To Camilla I am infinitely grateful for all her love and patience, for keeping up with me all this time, and for forgiving me all the moments when my mind was somewhere far far away—attending a council in Rivendell, riding with the Riders of Rohan, or scaling a mountain pass into Mordor. You are truly the best person imaginable in this world or any other, Middle-earth included.

Last but certainly not least, I would like to thank Cathleen Blackburn and the Tolkien Estate for having no objection to the title or cover of the book; and I would like to send my gratitude to John Ronald Reuel Tolkien himself for all the wonderful literary masterpieces and visual works he left us and the creative power with which he inspires us to dream, imagine, and be creative. Perhaps most of all, he inspires us to create something new, and he was clearly an inspiration for me, for one thing I can say for sure: without J. R. R. Tolkien, this book would not have been possible.

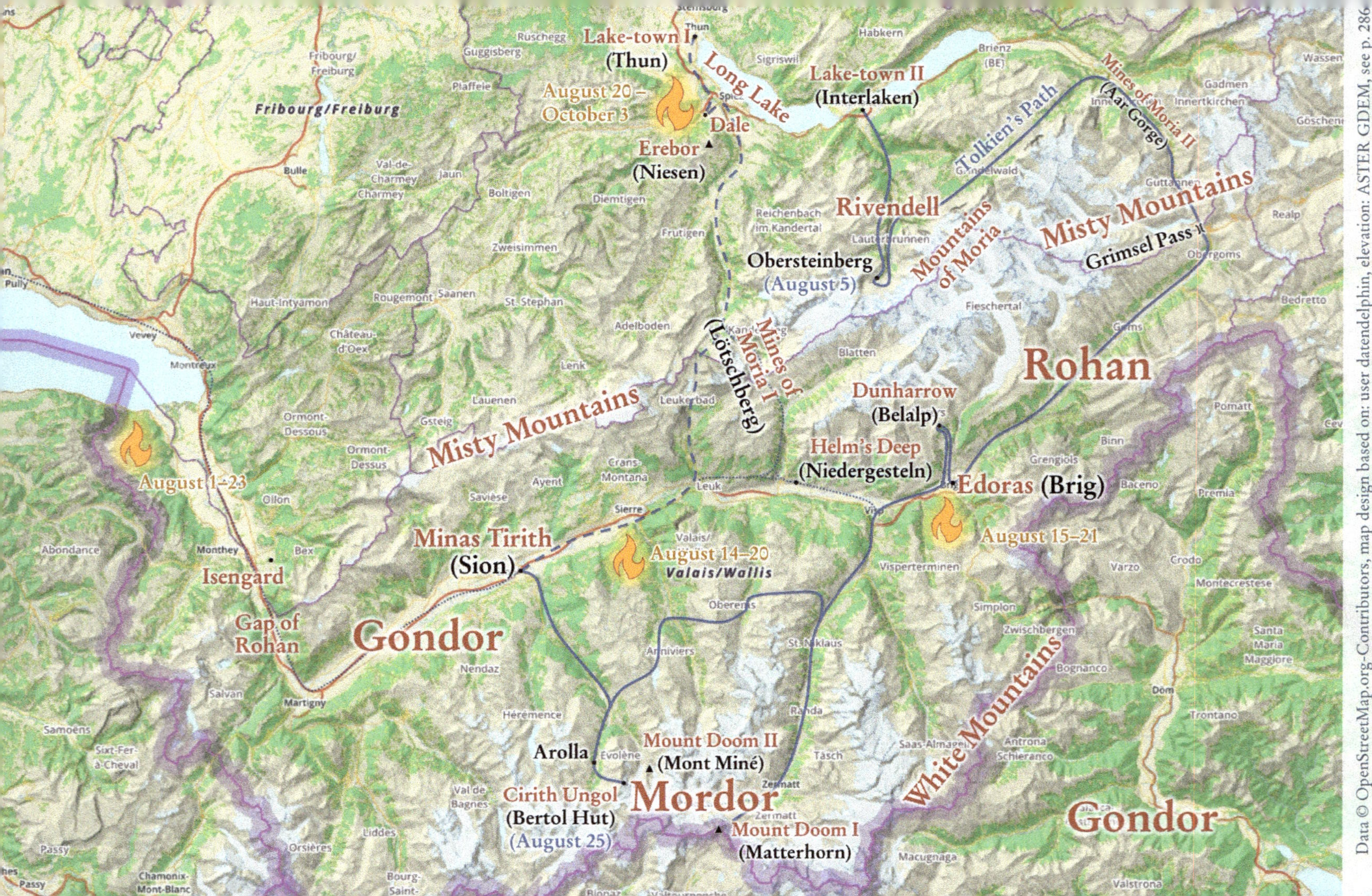

Gap of Rohan
Isengard
Gondor
Minas Tirith (Sion)
August 1–23
Fribourg/Freiburg
Lake-town I (Thun)
August 20 – October 3
Erebor (Niesen)
Dale
Long Lake
Lake-town II (Interlaken)
Rivendell
Obersteinberg (August 5)
Mines of Moria I (Lötschberg)
Mountains of Moria
Misty Mountains
Tolkien's Path
Mines of Moria II (Aare Gorge)
Grimsel Pass
Arolla
Cirith Ungol (Bertol Hut) (August 25)
Mount Doom II (Mont Miné)
Mount Doom I (Matterhorn)
Mordor
Valais/Wallis
August 14–20
Helm's Deep (Niedergesteln)
Dunharrow (Belalp)
Edoras (Brig)
August 15–21
Rohan
White Mountains
Gondor

www.ingramcontent.com/pod-product-compliance
Lightning Source LLC
LaVergne TN
LVHW071440190726
843512LV00025B/851